presence occupied every compartment of my mind, filling me up, spilling over, and pouring out like some giant sprinkler onto everyone around me. No hanky could wipe away my tears, no comfort was enough, no words, and there was nothing that could reach me. I was utterly alone in my grief.

We had plans, she and I. She was getting better, or so I thought. She was sitting up and chatting about going on holiday. The build up to recovery, the hope, the dreams; and then the empty bed, the deathly silence, the sad looks, followed by the crushing news; and the shattering bitter blow leaving me, open, raw, bereft of emotions, as if the warmth that Joyce brought to me was in an instant drained away.

We shared everything together, our clothes, our worries, just about everything girlfriends shared. Yes, she could be unreliable at times. But I accepted that in her; that was Joyce.

Joyce, I keep imagining I see you lying there, sleeping in the coffin, and I want to wake you. There are so many questions you have not answered. You have to throw me into this world of chaos! If I tell you now, will you listen from wherever you are? I look upward and ask why you had to die. I never thought your life would end this way. It should have been me, good God! I had reason enough. But *you*, Joyce, you didn't have a good enough reason to do it! How can you do this to me? You told me I did everything perfect.

Joyce, if only you knew!

2

Losing Les

TO UNDERSTAND THE EVENTS that led up to the shooting, and why I was so lucky to have a friend like Joyce, I need to go back to when my story began.

My father James stumbled into the poverty stricken world of East End London, in April 1923, the second youngest of ten children with all the prospects of fighting World War Two as a young shaver in the Catering Corp. But slicing spuds wasn't his strong point, and after he was demobbed his prospects never amounted to anything; he was a natural born loser. He was a tall dashing man in uniform, dark hair, with spectacles like panda eyes. Perhaps that was the appealing feature that attracted Nellie, a small mousy women born in 1916 to a well off family of bakers who lived in Chiswick. But later I realised it was more to do with funding the child she already had by a married man. That child was my half brother, Les.

I was born in 1948, in Gracie Fields Nursing Home, 136 Bishops Avenue, Hampstead, London. My legacy was my bright green eyes and full lips. Now, nine years later, my shoulder-length fair hair and slim build made me what my teachers kept on telling me—an exceptionally pretty girl; perhaps I would have preferred it if they told me I was good at Maths, or English, or *something*—but they didn't.

I was just nine years old in 1957 when we moved, with my Mum, Dad and older brother Les, now aged fourteen, to a new Council Maisonette in Edmonton, North London. Of the four blocks ours was a ground floor unit in the centre nearest to the railway. It was okay as long as I held my cup firmly when the train went by. A single bare electric light bulb sucked its power through a thin cable from the outside lamp of the house above. It competed for light against the musty curtains that imprisoned me with a faint glow. It was like living in a vomit-stained refuge of a mangrove swamp.

In winter, the bone-chilling cold would draw the black damp from the air as I laid the open fire. Mum could use the gas pipe that ran into the side of the grate. But it was too frightening for me to use; instead, I would lay the fire with rolled up newspaper, and then make squares of toilet paper from the fragments that remained.

My home was a minefield littered with constant fights, latent arguments and simmering rows that festered between my parents, James and Nellie, and my fifteen-year-old brother Les. I guess the upside was it blocked out the sound of the trains. But I lost count of how many times I heard them going at it hammer and tongs, screaming and shouting at each other. Not surprisingly, I suppose, the neighbours listened into our lives.

"Well Lill, did you hear that last night?" they would say.

It was better than listening to the Archers for them because the characters were real; they had genuine black eyes, no make-up to cover it up. No, not for us: real blood and pain!

Reality for me consisted of scampering off upstairs, hiding out of the way in case they suddenly turned on me. But, of course, I couldn't stop it and the fighting continued, day after day. Eventually it got to me—the expectation, waiting for it to happen, trying to pretend it wasn't happening when it was, and then banging my head into the pillow trying to make it stop.

I was trapped. There was nothing I could have done, except pray that somehow they would see sense and resolve their differences; but it never seemed to happen, and every day was just like Groundhog Day, grinding me down until it was a relief to go to school.

At school I appeared to be happy, popular and carefree. I never spoke about my life at home and to everyone around me, I appeared a joyful little child without a care in the world. I enjoyed nothing better than listening to the other children telling me about their problems, trying to think up different ways in which they might adapt themselves, and to pass on some of the solutions that had worked for me.

What was so frightening for me was the constant threat of the family torn apart, promising to catapult me into what Mum called 'Care'. It was all right for Dad as he disappeared into a bottle most nights away from it all, down the pub or betting shop or both, but I had no such escape; I had to stay there in the thick of it.

'Care'? I didn't really understand what she meant when she said 'taken into Care'. But it seemed to scare her. One day she told me if I were taken into 'Care', then all the family would be punished and split up. Apparently it was a cross between a holiday camp and a prison, and I would be sent away never to see my Mum again. I didn't know what a holiday camp was, but the prison bit scared me. I simply wanted the fighting to stop!

Then one day I came home from school, and everything was to change. After months of fighting with Les all the time, I discovered Mum sitting in the kitchen by the old Formica table. It stood on an old off-cut of Linoleum that attempted to cover the floor like some discarded rag. Our fridge was a cold stone slab sat at the bottom of the larder. It was designed to keep food fresh, although my Mum never used it either because she didn't understand its purpose, or because we never had food long enough for it to go off.

Puffing away on one of her fags, muttering to herself, she was drawing so deeply on the cigarette, I thought she was going to swallow the bloody thing. She continued to puff out great smelly clouds of blue smoke, one after another, until the kitchen stank of it all. I hadn't seen her like this before.

"Fucking sod!" She spat venom and hate with her spiteful words. "Les slapped me, he did!" She coughed and continued: "Stormed off out of the house! Don't know where he is."

She shook her head from side to side, and rocked back and forth in the chair.

I didn't think she really cared; she seemed preoccupied about how she was going to punish him.

"Serves him right, that'll show him. Yeah, that's it," she muttered under her breath. "Fucking sod!"

The door swung open, and before Dad could get in the kitchen, she was ranting.

"Les, the little sod, he's hit me! Slapped me round the face he did, little fucker." She pointed to the side of her face trying to justify her anger.

"What yer on about?" Dad lurched to one side. "Yer face always looks like that."

"Yeah, see, look at it! Les, the little bastard, belted me one." Turning her face to one side, she pulled her hair back as if to expose some marks, but there was nothing there I could see.

Dad snatched a glance at her through his misty thick-rimmed glasses, leaned a little and tried to steady himself on the handle of the kitchen door. But it swung away from him and smacked him in the face. As he lurched forward trying to regain his balance, he flung me a puzzled gaze before slumping down onto the nearby kitchen chair in a drunken stupor.

She knew she wouldn't get any sense out of him until he had sobered up a bit. She snatched his dinner from the oven, spat in it and thumped it down in front of him, slopping the gravy onto his shirt.

"Oh, shit," he squirmed as hot liquid burned his flesh.

I made myself scarce and escaped up to my room. I knew better than to get too close when they were going to have a row. My room had a bed and an old wooden chair that served to stop what clothes I had from falling on the bare floorboards. By means of a single candle stuck to the windowsill, I was able to keep my hands warm from time to time.

Mum started first. "I'm not having it! No, I'm not going to put up with it any more. You mark my words, and as for Les— well, he'll have to go, and that's it!"

The next thing I heard was someone knocking on the door. *Bang, bang, bang!* I didn't know if Les had lost his key, but it was enough to make me jump.

It was Dad who first broke the silence and started whispering again, arguing with Mum in the kitchen until finally I heard Mum's voice booming out: "I'm not having 'im here and that's final!"

I heard heavy footsteps on the stairs. It must have been Dad rummaging around in Les' room. He was gathering all his stuff, wrapping it up.

Bang! The letterbox snapped back. Les was clearly getting impatient at the door.

By this time Mum had disappeared into the living room, hiding behind the door. It gave her a clear view down the hall. Not that she appeared to be frightened, as I might have imagined, but to ensure Dad did as he was told.

"Go on then—tell him!"

She was standing back like a referee at a wrestling match, and no doubt she figured that if someone was going to get hurt, it wasn't going to be her.

I watched as Dad picked up a brown paper parcel all wrapped up with string. He stood there like a refugee in some sort of paralysed indecision. Like a fox in the headlights, he turned round and round, until, eventually he turned away, as if to make a run for it into the living room.

She reached out and grabbed his arm. "Go on then, tell him!" Mother shouted again, attempting to drag his arm back along the hall.

Stepping back from her, he broke free, hesitated, and I sensed he didn't want to do it. His whole character was like the drink: pathetic. He flung his arm round to hit her, missed and almost fell over, then, recovering his composure, lurched in the direction of the front door, muttering. It was as if he were rehearsing what to say in his mind.

I tottered downstairs, my head between the balustrades as though I were in the front row of the cinema waiting for the start. I was ready for the entertainment for the night, and although I fully expected Dad to give Les a good belting, I wasn't really ready for what happened next.

All Les' things, bundled and tied with string, lay behind the front door.

"I've had enough of your arguments," Dad said. "Mum has had enough of yer, and she doesn't want you here anymore! So you're not coming in!" He calmly turned and picked up the parcel.

I didn't hear what Les said to him, and maybe Les didn't say anything at all; perhaps he had already anticipated this, I didn't know.

"I've got all yer stuff wrapped up: now you'd better go and live with your Aunt Glad and Grandma in Chiswick." He shoved the parcel at Les and pushed him away.

Les shrugged his shoulders and accepted it, and I wondered later if he was as happy to go as they were to get rid of him. They used him to claim overcrowding with the impending arrival of a new baby, and now they had their new house, it seems they didn't need him anymore.

The door quietly shut and I heard the sound of someone walking back up the path that I assumed was Les. Rushing up into the bedroom at the front of the house, I pinned my nose to the window trying to catch a glimpse of Les as he left. I tried to wave but he never saw me. I banged on the window trying to get his attention. But he didn't look up. I strained to catch sight of him as he reached the end of the block, and I remember desperately trying to open the window, and then falling back onto the bed shocked and saddened that he had left. I sat at the window for ages looking for him, searching as I sobbed into the night. But as the hours ticked by, my heart sank as the disappointment took hold.

I remember thinking, what did I care? After all, he was the source of all the shouting and arguing and stuff. But then I *did* care, of course I cared; he was my only contact in this hellhole to share the misery. How could I find myself thinking that I didn't care? No longer was there anyone to stand up for me, to protect me from the horror of it all.

Unwittingly I found myself expecting him to walk into the room. But he never did.

No one prepared me for it, the searching, and the daydreaming trying to remember his voice in my mind, but gradually I found myself struggling to build him into my dreams. It was as if he had died and I remember feeling strange and crying quietly to myself at night. Unconsciously I would wander into his room to talk, and realising he was no longer there I would unexpectedly wake up in the darkness, stare at the menacing shadows flickering on the wall, and bolt back to my room in terror.

Emptiness and those nighttime anxieties replaced the little irritations Les brought to my life. The impish pranks he would spring, making funny faces, farting and other noises to scare the wits out of me; 'nankering' I think they called it.

After slinging Les out, Dad ambled back into the living room. Mum glanced up but didn't say anything.

Turning to pick up his newspaper and packet of fags, he slumped into his fireside chair. Mum looked down at the floor.

She always did that when she was afraid to say anything and for a moment I wondered if she later regretted complaining so much. But if she did she never said anything about it after that, and I was just left to get on with my life without him.

Dad started doing his usual 'lost child routine'. He looked at Mum and moped about. Finally, irritated, she slung him half a crown, and he sloped off down to the pub. I didn't see him return, but I noticed another vomit-stained burn mark in the arm of his chair.

Some time later Les went to live with the Rolling Stones at 102 Edith Grove and wrote a book about the experiences of living with Keith Richards and Brian Jones, called *Phelge's Stones*.[1] They called him 'Nanker Phelge' on their record labels because of his nankering ways. Why he called himself James Phelge I never knew. But he described his early life saying that he escaped his unhappy childhood, begging and beaten, at the age of fifteen.

After Les left it was just my Mum and Dad—apart from me, of course. I was really grateful at first and the house was strangely quiet. But I was puzzled when I began to realise there was only baby food in the house—there was nothing for me. And I worried I would be slung out next.

---

[1] *Phelge's Stones.* ISBN 0-9664338-0-7

3

My Wooden Leg

I **REALLY WANTED A LITTLE SISTER** to play with, and I thought it would be great, as all young girls did. What I didn't realise was how the family dynamics would place the burden on me.

Born in February 1957, my sister Jane tripped helplessly into my world, to share with me the pain of screaming, glue-trap-poverty. I could see no other advantage. Except, perhaps now the fighting between my parents was punctuated by the tormented hunger of a baby. The little crumbs of comfort afforded by an increase in state benefit hardly compensated for the misery that came with her.

Most days Mum would sit in her apron, puffing a fag, her slippered feet resting on the old black enamel oven door, the distinctive smell of burning town gas wafting up her open skirt.

This day was different.

As I came in from school the stench of tobacco smoke choked the air. I found her upstairs muttering to herself, staring out through the old yellow stained net curtains that clung to the back bedroom window.

"What's for dinner, Mum?"

Silence

I thought it a little strange, although as a child, I did not take too much notice. I was more preoccupied with my hunger because I hadn't eaten anything, apart from the free school milk at morning break. If I qualified for free school dinners (as I did from time to time), I would be called up to the desk at the front of the class and the teacher would shout out: "Those for free school dinners!" I would have to traipse out to the front, the only one, singled out, and the teacher would tick off my name in the register. Sometimes I would rather go hungry. I know I should have suffered the humiliation of it all, but I thought I would get a hot meal at home, even though it might only have been potato and cheese mash.

"Him again, all his fault—fucking sod."

"What is, Mummy?"

Silence,

"Are you coming down to do dinner?" I tried again.

"I don't know—there isn't any food to eat!" she shouted back. "It's your father's fault—we haven't got any fucking money—I don't know."

Her voice trailed off in a series of mutterings I didn't hear. I wandered downstairs, keeping my coat on.

"Why isn't the fire lit?"

"There's no fucking coal."

"Why isn't there any coal, Mummy?"

"It's all yer father's fault—now stop asking fucking stupid questions."

"Can I have something to eat?"

"There isn't anything, all right? Now fucking shut up about it—you'll have to wait until yer father gets home."

I skulked off into the kitchen, opened the tall larder cupboard and peered into the musty darkness. I waited impatiently for my eyes to adjust in the vain hope there would be something.

A few currants lay scattered on the middle shelf. I dragged the nearby kitchen chair across to the cupboard, and careful not to wake the baby, I stepped up.

High up by the window, I spotted a tall round packet of Farleys Rusks, some malt, and powdered baby milk. The rusks were free from the baby clinic, but for some reason Mum still didn't like me taking them. Perhaps that was why they were high up!

I didn't like malt, but what else could I do? I was hungry.

My little hands struggled to open the big jar of malt, and despite several attempts, it proved a puzzle. In the end I found if I wrapped the top in a tea towel, and wedged it close against my body, one determined effort would see it open.

Listening out for Mum all the time, I sat down at the table, and scraped out a spoonful of malt, spread it thinly on the rusk, and scoffed it before mother had a chance to find out. Afterwards, I sat silently cleaning the spoon by the old butler sink, before clambering back up on the chair to return the jar.

Scampering back to my room I snuggled, cocooned on my bed, losing myself in an old copy of the *Beano* I had scrounged from a kid at school.

Slam!

The house rocked. Dad didn't usually slam the door so hard. He burst in and disappeared straight into the kitchen. Mum raced down the stairs. I heard loud voices.

I rushed to the landing and, straining to listen, I wondered if it signalled the start of another row. I heard only the last part of their conversation.

"Yeah okay, all right then, I'll go and get her."

"Get down here now, come on, get yer bloody shoes an yer coat, we're going out!" Mum snapped.

I wondered what was going on. I hastily clambered down the stairs, grabbing my shoes and grubby little coat on the way.

"Where we going?"

Turning away from me, she looked at the floor, said nothing, then took my shoes.

"You'll see—now don't ask questions, and get yer shoes on."

"Awe," I groaned.

"Come on, lift yer bloody feet." She dug her nails into my flesh.

Tugging my foot roughly, she caught my toe, sending a spike of pain up my leg. I didn't dare say anything, and for once, I just did as I was told. I lifted my foot up, shoved my other shoe on, and left her to tie the laces.

"You've done 'em too tight."

"Don't fuss—they'll be all right once you get moving—now shut up—get on the step!"

My coat had come from a mail order catalogue and it wasn't too warm; the sleeves were too short, leaving my hands frozen in the cold night air. As the door slammed behind me I was jostled down the short path.

Mum wore a dark woollen coat that rendered her almost invisible, and I remember thinking how funny it looked, as if the pram was pushing itself. She grabbed my hand tightly, dragging me down Langhedge Lane, and along to the High Road.

It was cold, dark, and I could feel myself panic.

"Where we going? My feet are hurting. I don't want to go— I don't want to go! I want to go home." I stamped my feet on the pavement and pulled my hand away.

"Be quiet, it's not far now." She dragged me back, squeezing my hands so tightly I couldn't break free. Dad snatched the pram and left Mum to keep hold of me. Frightened and confused, I clenched my little fists in my pocket as my mind started to worry. Were they going to dump me like Les? They had got rid of Les. Were they going to get rid of me? Dump me at the hospital or something?

"Mummy, I want to go home—I'm hungry," I wailed, kicking the pram with my shoe so hard it almost tipped over.

Whack!

I fell back, my face stinging. I suddenly realised I had been given a message.

Between streams of warm tears, I desperately tugged at her hand, but it was no use—she was too strong for me and she wrenched me back time and time again.

"I want my dinner! Mummy, I'm hungry—I wanna go home!"

Thwack!

I could no longer feel my face; instead, it was replaced by an intense, numb tingling, as the full force of her rings bit into my flesh. For the first time I felt the taste of fresh blood. It trickled down the back of my throat, leaving a bitter raw taste.

I understood the message.

My lip, torn open, was now zipped shut. I backed off. This was new. Was it my turn now Les had left? But I was only a little girl—I hadn't expected this.

As we approached Bruce Grove, Dad stopped by a high street shop, its bright lights glowing through the plethora of advertising posters pasted to the windows. I stood there, watching at the shop door as each customer came and went, flashing, like a lighthouse beacon in the mist.

Dad grabbed both my arms and raised his hand as if to hit me. I flinched. He knelt down to me and I could smell the drink on his breath. He wiped away my tears and, lifting my chin, he used his hanky to clean the blood from my lip. For a moment I felt his gentle touch, his caring side as if he was feeling guilty, although I couldn't be sure.

He spoke softly.

"We need you to go into the shop and give the man a note for us." He crooked round to Mum. "'Ave yer got the note?"

She left the pram and sidled up.

"Yeah." She retrieved a crumpled note from her coat pocket and quietly shoved Dad out of the way.

Held like a prisoner before the gallows, I gazed up at them as they both plotted and schemed. It was like they were on a secret mission, planning each move like some spy spoof movie, with one exception: I was the only one who wasn't in on it. I wanted to escape, but Mum's steely grip dissolved any thoughts of making a run for it.

"Here," she muttered, thrusting the paper into my hand.

"Now look here." She bent down to my face, holding my arms tightly. "I need you to go into the shop now and hand the man this note. Now you must make sure that yer give him this note, do yer understand?" She shook me as she spoke. "Have yer got it?"

"Yes!" I glanced back at her, sniffing through my tears.

"Are yer sure you know what to do?"

"Yes," I said, still snivelling and trying to nod at the same time.

"Now don't forget to wait for him to read it, yeah—that's very important, have you got that?"

"Yes"

"And then—you've got to say that you haven't had anything to eat—yeah—and please can you have it on tick? Now that's important you *say that right*!" She lifted my head roughly, forcing me to look at her.

"Yes." I lowered my head in nervous silence, and then, shuffling my feet from side to side, I attempted to kick a stone across the pavement, pretending to make out I wasn't really with them.

"Now don't forget to say you haven't had anything to eat." She shook me violently and I braced myself for another smack, but it didn't come. Perhaps they didn't want my face marked anymore.

Shivering from cold or fear, I don't recall which, I stood on the pavement outside the shop door. I glanced back with a mixture of outright trepidation and sheer fear.

Spinning round, I faced the door. The shopkeeper stood in his white overalls, a big man, ruddy face, and it might have been fancy, but I swear he was angry as soon as he clapped eyes on me. It was like he knew what I was about to say.

Mum came up behind me and held me by the shoulders, then pointed me at the entrance to the shop once more.

THUMP.

I felt the blow of a hammer thrust me forward, as the light from the shop exploded full in my face like a stun grenade. Blinded and confused, I found myself half in and half out, in some sort of no man's land.

Mother recoiled like a chameleon's tongue, shooting back like some horrible vampire, gobbled up by the night.

Frantically I glanced back, but she had abandoned me. I was alone in the bright lights.

I wiped away my tears with the back of my cuff and took a deep breath. But it was no use—I could feel the panic rising in my tummy. I refused to enter.

THUMP.

I felt another hammer blow between my shoulder blades, and suddenly I was staring into the abyss.

Spinning round, the shopkeeper spotted me clinging to the counter, a rather grubby note clutched tightly in my right hand. I sheepishly spat it across and stood back.

His sharp tongue cut the silence, bellowing so loudly the windows rattled.

"Can't yer read?"

The customers turned to see his fat fingers pointing at the sign on the wall.

I swallowed hard. I shrivelled down. I hadn't noticed the sign, and I didn't think Mum had either, but it said, "No credit."

"I don't want the likes of you here, so get out of my shop and don't come back. Do yer see that, there on the wall?" His fat finger wagged at the notice once more. "Now what does it say?"

"Ner…n…no credit," I stuttered.

"So bloody get out and stay out!" He grabbed the nearby broom as if to chase me out of the shop, although I thought it was more for effect than anything else.

I bolted out of the shop like a wounded whippet, anywhere, nowhere, blindly into the darkness of the High Street; fighting my way through the gathered crowd until I felt the cover of the darkness envelop me like a huge sheet of smog.

Finally I came to rest in a crumpled heap, surrounded by the familiar smell of beer, wafting like smoke signals, out onto the steps of the Red Lion pub. If beer were as volatile as petrol I wouldn't have lit a match.

I looked back through my tears searching for Mum, but she wasn't there, or the pram for that matter. I so wanted to run away and be like Les—to disappear silently into the night; yet I was too hungry. Instead, I sat there watching people come and go. I just didn't know what to do.

A bunch of lads stumbled out through the pub door. I noticed that the tall skinny one, with his greasy hair and long sideburns, carried a packet of Smiths Crisps. I could taste them in the air from where I stood, just a few feet away. At first, the lads didn't seem to take much notice of me as they wandered over and lounged by the corner of the road. They were all laughing and joking with each other, and I could see they were in a boisterous mood. Then, without warning, the tall one turned round and clocked me as I sat, on the step of the pub, all alone.

My scruffy hair prickled as I shrunk back into the shadows, sliding slowly over against the side wall, its rough surface, like the night, cold and damp. I ruffled the collar of my coat, straightened my dress and tried to make myself invisible, although it didn't seem to be working.

The tall one walked over to me, his knuckles clustered with rings, a chunky gold bracelet dangling from his wrist. Looking directly into his face was like staring into the dark eyes of a

Panther. The friendly banter was now choked into silence, as I felt a pervading sense of menace. Were they going to play some trick on me?

For the first time I wished Mum and Dad were close.

"Oh, no," I muttered under my breath.

I got up and backed off, now terrified they were going to do something nasty. I half shuffled, half clawed myself away awkwardly, keeping my back against the wall, and trying to stay close to the pub door in case I needed to get help. Luck didn't appear to be on my side and I was praying he would go away.

He didn't. He crept towards me, holding out a bag of crisps, as if trying to entice me closer.

I wasn't convinced. After losing Les I didn't trust anyone, not even my own Mum and Dad, let alone him.

I jumped back, my heart bursting in my chest, trapped up against the wall of the alley!

They all herded round like towering cattle ready to trample me, fencing me in with their intimidating wisecracks. I didn't understand exactly what they were saying to me, but I began to realise from the tone of their voices, it didn't sound good.

One of them suggested taking me back to their place and 'giving me one'. I didn't know what that was. I thought they were talking about a packet of crisps, until another said he wanted his turn, and apparently he was going to give me one as well. Either they were very kind, or I was about to be in grave danger. I couldn't work out which way it was going to go.

"Here love, want a crisp?" the tall one lunged at me with an open packet.

I flinched and shot backwards, cracking my elbow against the wall. But despite the searing pain, I was determined not to let it distract me from my gaze. I started to shake uncontrollably. I tried to stop it. I couldn't. I looked up at his face, now scared, alone, cold, and hungry.

"Please mister, leave me alone."

The fat one reached over to claw at me.

"Don't yer want it?" the others all jeered, egging him on.

I closed my eyes and then, collapsing to the floor like a rag doll, I put my hands over my face to make it all go away. It didn't!

As I peered out from between my fingers, the tall one came so close I could read the tattoo on his wrist: 'I Love Polly'.

"Here!" He flung the bag at my feet.

Turning quickly to his mates who were now all laughing, he grabbed the fat one by his jacket, and tried to drag him off and pull him away, but it didn't work. The fat one snatched back, and grasping me by my coat, he lifted me up and swept me down the side of the pub, his big rough hands muffling my screams.

"Come on!" the tall one shouted, pulling at him once more. "Leave her alone. I've got some more beer at the flat."

"Sounds good to me," his fat friend grunted.

Dropped like a bundle of elephant dung, bruised and clinging to the floor, I was left there. They staggered off down the side of the pub, their rowdy banter echoing into the night.

I was still licking the salt from my lips when Mum arrived. I quickly stuffed the empty packet into my pocket and tried to look pleased to see her. She didn't say anything. Instead, she grabbed my hand tightly. Dragging me along the High Street, we shot back down Joyce Avenue, across the ramp and over the railway line, until we came to a little corner shop off Somerset Road.

It was full of light spilling onto the pavement like a sheet of golden custard; an oasis in the urban desert, it stood proudly silent.

Without a word, she launched me into the shop and up to the empty counter.

The shopkeeper stopped what he was doing. It wasn't difficult to spot me because I was the only person there.

He wandered over to me.

"Hello," he smiled. "What's this then?" He pointed to the little piece of crumpled paper tucked in my hand.

I looked up at him for what seemed like ages, struggling to contain my fear, and then, without taking my eyes off his face, I hesitatingly pushed the note halfway across the counter, and sprang back.

"Right," he drew a deep breath, "let's see what it says, shall we?" His voice was loud, and his face towered above me as he glanced down. "It's a note from Mum, is it?"

I didn't answer, but stood frozen with my mouth open, eyes wide. Somehow I managed a nod whilst he fiddled in his top pocket for his reading glasses.

Everything seemed to be in slow motion as I watched him unfold his round spectacles, bending them over his ears. Picking up the note in his right hand, he began reading the first line.

He stopped, glanced down at me, shook his head, and then looked back at the note.

I just stared, frozen. I didn't know why, but I guess I was watching for him to tell me off, or worse, chase me out of the shop and—I didn't know, but I thought if I kept watching him perhaps I could tell what he was going to do.

He strolled over to me and peered down. His glasses slid down like the barrel of a gun, and the beads of his eyes shot me a glance for the first time.

Startled, I cowered down, my heart pounding as his apparently kind eyes turned frosty and cold.

I was ready to spring at the first sign of danger. But it was my turn to say it—to say my bit!

My throat dried. Perhaps it was the salt crisps, I didn't know. I was struck dumb, as if suffering some frightening seizure. For a moment I thought I heard my mother prompt me, although it could have been the wind.

"Well come on—I haven't got all night, you know," his voice echoed around my head.

I sprang back—I looked up at him expectantly and then...

"I haven't got anything to eat and...er...er... can I have it on tick, please?"

His eyes shot at me and I felt his stare, questioning, knowing, and telling. It was like being in the headmaster's study, his eyes boring into my very soul. Could he see the truth inside me?

My resolve withered. I shrank back. He looked up.

His face changed, and then I noticed the hardness spreading like some awful rash across his face until he looked positively evil. I avoided his glance. I bowed my head, like my dad did when he went for a pee in the street.

Then he shone his gaze outside like some sort of super searchlight, peering out into the blackness. I watched him, my eyes now fixed on his gaze. Where he looked, I looked. I followed his every move, his every gesture, and I noticed his every breath.

Would he, or wouldn't he? I couldn't tell—I didn't know.

Looking up and down, I started to notice the stiffness in his back, and a slight change of the shape of the muscles on his shoulders. They were barely detectable as the hunch changed; yet I noticed a subtle shifting.

His eyes flicked down at the note once more. I followed his gaze as he stared out through the door. He shook his head, drew a deep breath and sighed like a dying man.

My tummy was gnawing inside. I asked myself why I chose to miss my dinner.

His shoulders dropped as he turned away from me. I watched the tension slowly disappear, almost as fast as it had begun, and then, his back straightened as he swung round to face me once more. I detected a softening, but I couldn't be sure.

It was like watching someone blow up a balloon, puffing into it and then, with each additional breath, wondering if it would burst. What would he do? I couldn't stand it anymore—the not knowing. Something inside of me snapped. I knew I had to get out.

I could feel a sickening knot in my tummy, writhing and twisting like some awful snake. Trapped between the shopkeeper and Mother, I retched with bile. I was going to throw up. I turned my head and was just about to run out. I froze. An intense fear ripped into me.

I felt the warm comforting wet trickling down the inside of my leg.

Finally he picked up the note in his left hand! No one else knew what it meant, but it told me a great deal. It signalled the preparation to fetch things with his right hand. I had watched him through the window when I first arrived and I knew he was right handed. Was he, I wondered, about to select items from the list?

He glanced down at me and his mood appeared to change, as if I was not the first little girl he had seen. In silence he turned back toward the shelves. I watched. I held my breath.

"Okay, now let's see what we can do for you then, shall we, young lady?" He started to run through the list.

The air was tense as he began to lift cans from the shelf. Then, walking past me, he fetched the potatoes from a big Hessian sack by the door. Carefully, he weighed them on the old scales before tipping them into a paper bag. He continued gathering things until, finally, he took a small packet of chocolate biscuits from the shelf beneath the counter and popped them into the bag. He left them on top for me to see.

"That's about all I can manage for you today, love. Now tell your Mum she needs to settle up at the end of the week—Friday." He pushed the bag across the counter.

"Thanks mister."

I grabbed the bag and carried it outside into the darkness.

"Okay, I'll take that." Mum snatched the bag out of my hands.

Then, dragging me away as fast as she could, we slipped out into the blackness of the night.

Once over the ramp of the railway tracks, she bundled the shopping onto the bottom shelf of the pram. Dad came over and lifted me up on his back and gave me a piggyback home.

I was so pleased with myself—I felt the Hero! I had managed to get all the food for the family. I felt elated and happy, happier than I can remember. There I was with Dad giving me a piggyback. He was so proud of me and it felt so good. I really loved my Dad that day.

Begging for food from the shopkeepers became a way of life for me. Scouring the streets for a new shop further away in the hope that I wouldn't be recognised became a challenge and a battle of wits. It didn't get any easier and each time I was just as terrified.

There was always a sense of luck attached and when it didn't turn out well, the trauma was horrendous. If I didn't get it right, then we didn't eat, or we didn't have any coal to heat the house; either way, we all suffered.

I found I had to develop an intuitive understanding of body language to improve my chances of success. I learned to watch from the shop window, pick my time and choose my words carefully. It was a good strategy to wait for the wife to be out of the way. Women were the least compassionate, the more spiteful and hurtful. They would send me packing as soon as they saw me enter the shop, and then, turning to their husbands, scold them for not kicking me out sooner.

♣

It upsets me when people say, "Doesn't time heal and, besides, surely you must have got over your childhood by now?" Except, perhaps, they hadn't considered that as a result of my childhood I am forever changed.

A man might lose his leg and people might say "Are you getting over it?" in the sense that, "Have you recovered and the wounded stump healed?" A man might have 'got over it'—but he will always be a one-legged man.

They don't understand. It never really goes away. I can't change it or forget it. It is always there. Perhaps I shall be given a wooden leg one day. But for me it still feels like I am on crutches.

It was as though I had experienced some frightful brain transplant, and suddenly I had the full responsibility of the family. I was now financing my mother's fags, my father's drink and bringing up a baby. I was a mule in harness.

My spirit broken, my childhood in tatters—and this was just the beginning.

My childhood stopped the day Les left home. My innocence was lost because of what happened on that day. I told myself I must carry on because I knew nothing else, and what else could a little girl do?

I lived for hope—hope that it would get better. It got worse.

I died of shame—oh, so many times I could not tell. I let the tears fall in silence—I wanted it to stop. It didn't.

Unlike Peter Pan, I didn't lose my shadow—I lost my childhood.

And I will never get it back.

4

Hospital

I WAS TEN YEARS OLD when I came home from school with a sore throat and a fever. I ended up in North Middlesex Hospital to have an operation to remove my tonsils. I had been off school with throat infections for some time, and I suppose the doctors thought it best in the long term. The hospital was only half a mile from our house and so I expected Mum and Dad would visit.

I remember the hospital and its long tiled corridors, the high ceilings with lamps hanging down on thin cables and chains, like some underground prison. I did not recognise the strange smells.

I arrived in the Children's Ward, and once settled in I was enjoying a brief moment of new-found freedom, talking to the other kids there. Hopelessly lively, I started running around until I went a step too far and the nurse told the other children to sit on my bed to stop me getting up. Then I was given this drink and I spent the rest of the morning on the toilet. I had a healthy disrespect for the nurse after that!

Surrounded by two nurses and a man in a white coat, I was told I was being taken away to another room, under the guise of making me better: I was not to worry. I was shaking with fear when they lifted my small frame onto a trolley and whisked me away. The trolley squeaked and banged against the first wall, and then we had to squeeze past the laundry basket and other obstacles I did not recognise. We turned right, then left, and then right again down this long corridor. In the end I had no idea where I was. If it was their aim to make me mess myself; that would have been a miracle, because I didn't have anything left in me to mess.

As I arrived in this little room, they lifted me off the trolley and onto a raised bed, all padded with a pillow in place ready for me. Hanging on the wall was a large glass cupboard, a display case with all its shiny instruments. If I wasn't scared before, I was sure scared now! When a doctor approached with a big rubber facemask, I was in sheer panic. I shrank back into the pillow.

"Don't worry," he said, "I'm just going to put this over your face—like this."

Raising the mask up to his face to reassure me that it was safe, and then turning the mask toward me, he spoke softly.

"I want you to count down from ten, slowly—ten, nine, eight—and then you will feel drowsy and fall asleep. Now tell me—what is your favourite dream?"

I didn't know—I always forgot my dreams and woke up with the harsh realities of life. Dreams were having hot water, heating, and clean sheets on my bed. I didn't know what he expected me to do.

Recoiling back into the pillow, I turned my face away as he brought this big black rubber gas mask closer to me. I retched as the smell of gas wafted up into my face, and then I struggled, pushing him away with my hand with such force that it sent a bowl crashing to the floor. I screamed out my terror.

"Nurse!" He beckoned sideways with his hand.

The nurse stood by my side for a moment, but I couldn't make out her words. Perhaps I had suddenly gone deaf with my upset, although somehow I sensed her voice was soft and comforting, reassuring without me realising it. Even her eyes were calming, as she stroked my hair, her gentle face so close to mine that I could smell the freshness of her smooth warm skin;

such was the alluring scent of soap, I was sure she was an Angel sent from heaven.

"Now breathe deeply and count down from ten slowly." She talked me through it together like a duet.

"Ten, nine, eight, seven..." I didn't remember anything after that.

When I woke up I found myself in the Children's Ward. Gone was the lively young girl who had come into hospital a few hours earlier.

Painfully swollen, my throat so tender I could neither swallow nor speak, I often felt sick. Mealtimes came and went, and soon I lost what little weight I had gained. Finally I coughed up a huge clot of blood. I cried frantically for the nurse. She brought me a bowl, and comforted me until I felt better.

The doctor arrived at about 10 o'clock. I didn't know if he was on his rounds anyway, but if he seemed to be concerned, he didn't show it. He had a little shiny torch, and I remember thinking how lovely it was, and dreaming that I wanted one for myself, although I knew it was out of the question. He peered down my throat.

"Doctor, can we…" the nurse interrupted.

He screwed up his eyes, and continued to push my mouth ever wider.

"Doctor—she doesn't like Jelly"

"What do you like then, young lady?"

"Peaches," I said.

"Well, let's see if we can get this young lady some peaches to eat for lunch today?" Turning first to the nurse and then glancing back down at me, he winked. "I think that if we give her a few peaches then she might eat something, and we can get her weight up." He looked at me. "Perhaps you could get your parents to bring you some when they visit, okay?"

I laughed and nodded both at the same time. But my heart sank—I knew inside that Mum would never bring peaches. Mum never bought fruit of any description.

Flicking down at the clipboard, the nurse snapped away, scribbling as she went. "Yes Doctor," she said, glancing up, smiling and writing frantically. She dropped the clipboard back at the end of the bed before rushing ahead to keep up with the chase, the doctor, and on to the child in the next bed.

I was lying back in my bed when the visiting time bell chirped into action. Looking back, I recall watching the mothers, herded like cattle in a stampede. Some were clutching bunches of grapes, others smiling and waving. They appeared so desperate to see their children that I could see the love on their faces. One I saw was carrying a large packet of chocolate biscuits, although I was sure that matron would not have been best pleased—I thought of all those crumbs in the bed.

I was sitting there surrounded by it all, people watching, and observing what was going on, when I felt a sadness inside; in part because of my own situation at home—although more frequently because I saw the pain and disappointment on the faces of some of the other children on the ward. Some had bragged during the day that they were going home tomorrow, and then I watched their parents, and particularly I noticed those breaking disappointing news.

Some mothers did better than others, but more often than not, Mum would have wiped away the tears. I watched it all unfold as it followed a familiar pattern. The shaking of the head; the look up at Mum; the "I'm sorry love"; the disbelief; and then, the glance round to see if anyone had noticed, the muffled tears, the blotchy eyes and finally the red face.

When the ward fell silent and the visitors had gone, the children fell into a different world.

I knew about the secret tears, the quiet sobs deep into the night, the night nurse in her attempts to console, to comfort and to coax. The worry, anxiety, torture, grief, misery and the wretchedness of their plight; it wasn't their fault, but somehow it upset me so much that I found myself crying for them. Although I could have been crying for myself.

Nurses, young and old, got upset at the sight of it all; they would disappear from the ward, and I would listen, and hear a nurse sobbing quietly in the kitchen. Some got used to it, but others never did, and they would be moved on.

On more than one occasion I noticed a pretty, tall and well-dressed lady in a beautiful red coat. She had been a frequent visitor to a little boy in the bed opposite—Michael, I think his name was. Always there right from the start, until the Staff Nurse would ask her to leave, she brought little books, and sitting by his bedside, she would read him stories. He seemed such a nice little boy, and I remember thinking, as I looked at her, that I wished I could have been born out of her tummy. She would often glance back at me and smile; perhaps she felt sorry for me, or perhaps she wondered why she never saw my visitors. On one occasion I noticed her talking to the nurse. I didn't hear much of what they said, although I suspected she was asking about my Mum and Dad.

Watching anxiously as the visiting time ticked by, I put on a brave face and read a comic.

The large clock on the wall ticked again and again as the minutes went by. With each tick of the clock I became more and more embarrassed that I had no visitors.

Chatter, chatter, tick, tock. It felt like an unexploded bomb.

The first twenty minutes was not so bad. I could suffer that; after all, they could be held up, missed their bus or something. But as the half hour turned to forty-minutes I found the clock ticked even louder. I watched the beds around me to see who would be first.

Tick, tock, forty-one minutes, *chatter, chatter,* and then one Mum noticed.

My shame exploded in my face for the first time—Mum had not come.

The lady turned, then pointed, then whispered, "No visitors, poor girl—no, don't look—not now!"

The child looked. Glancing down, I died inside. Now the child knew! I had to live there—oh, I felt so ashamed and desperately alone and it hurt me so.

The Staff Nurse looked. She sighed and looked at her watch, and then at me.

Tick, tock, forty-two minutes, *chatter, chatter.*

I didn't want her to come over! The kid next door dropped a spoon. The chatter stopped. They looked.

No! Not now—I felt it would draw attention to me, and I was beside myself with upset. I didn't want it!

She reached out for a book she had on the desk and turned to come over to my bed. I screamed silently for her not to come, but it was too late and another tick of the clock exposed my dignity.

One mum looked round.

Tick, tock, forty-three minutes, *chatter, whisper, whisper.*

She tossed her head in my direction. She hoped I wouldn't notice, but I saw. I saw it all.

Tick, tock, forty-four minutes, *chatter, whisper.*

They didn't realise I could anticipate their moves. They looked at the child that was me, and to them I was just that—a child. But inside I was thinking like an adult, and I knew what they thought.

How dreadful, all alone, shame, *chatter, chatter,* poor thing. I shrank down and dived under the covers to hide the humiliation of it all.

Staff Nurse gave me another book to read. Another mum turned and looked. I was mortified. Then another and each in turn, like targets on the firing range. I felt the pain as each target was hit, each layer of self-respect peeled away, exposing the raw hurt. I felt the awful shame as I was singled out again and again.

Silence.

Then the hubbub of conversation started again.

Tick, tock, forty-five minutes, and suddenly it was clear to everyone that I had been abandoned and was unloved.

I noticed the lady with the red coat snatch a glance.

Perhaps it was the sudden rush of warmth that came over me, but I swear I felt from her an overwhelming love, a compassion that seemed to stretch, seamlessly, tumbling out across the ward.

I watched her twitch with an anxious hesitation. Was she going to come over to me? I could see her glancing across at me like a lookout on a heist, nervously flicking her head. She paused, then glanced first at the nurse, then back at me, and finally glanced back to her little boy. She appeared to whisper in his ear.

The scraping of the chair, loud and piercing, announced her intention to act.

I felt both naked and frightened all at once, and with my heart pounding I shot down into the bed. I did not want her to do this. I felt so humiliated, so ashamed, and burrowing my face awkwardly into my pillow until the feathers pricked my face, I pretended I wasn't looking, although of course I was.

I prayed she would go away.

Family secrets; I couldn't tell her that my life was like a delicate pack of cards, balanced on a knife-edge. My imperfect world was the only world I had, and the threat of losing even that, was my biggest fear.

She carried on walking. I wanted the floor to open up and swallow me.

Bang, bang. The ward doors clattered as Dad stumbled in, all dressed up with his collar and tie. Mum followed in her old green coat, a thin georgette scarf, her handbag slung over her arm.

It was just three minutes before the end of visiting.

The lady with the red coat froze, glanced at my Mum and Dad, and then, realising the situation, slowly and sheepishly retreated back to her little boy. I didn't know if I was disappointed; at the very least it might have shown my parents that someone cared for me. But I quickly dismissed the idea because in my heart I knew they wouldn't have taken much notice.

Struggling to contain my feelings of upset, I forced myself to welcome my parents, managing a short smile; I was so angry at them for coming late. Oh! I wanted to cry so much. At that moment I wanted to shame them. To scream to the world and tell how they were destroying me—destroying my love and walking over all my feelings. I didn't matter.

I stifled my upset. I knew that everyone on the ward would see me. I couldn't have that. The lady in red probably thought I was a quiet good girl and here is mummy and daddy after all and now I am loved; isn't that nice?

If only she knew! I hurt inside, but I cannot say. I cannot tell that they always do this and yet—I never get used to it. I feel the upset and anger each and every time. The wound is just as painful, just as deep and yet I notice that the last cut seems to be more painful than the first.

Do they not realise I was wounded the first time? I didn't understand why they needed to wound me again. Are they stupid or didn't they love me? Do they think I didn't need them? My mind was dizzy with thoughts.

"How are you then?" Mum dropped herself into the chair. "Yer looking a bit thin—are you eating anything?" She turned to look at all the others.

Struggling to say something nice, I nodded and indicated that I couldn't talk too much.

They sat there in silence.

Dad brought me some Orange Squash and made me up a drink. Putting it down on my tray, he sat on the end of the bed, gazing uncomfortably around the ward.

Silence.

I took a few sips, but the acid sharpness burned my throat and I choked and spluttered.

"I'll put it on the side so you can have it later, shall I?" Dad shoved the bottle into my cabinet at the side of the bed, and as he did so, I caught the familiar smell of drink on his breath. He looked around nervously.

"Are you eating anything?" Mum tried to make some sort of small talk, before glancing round at the other mothers.

"I can't eat much," I whispered. "My throat hurts too much."

They sat there like condemned killers in the courtroom dock, their heads held in shame. Mum shuffled uncomfortably, then lent forward. "Nice ward then?"

Leaning back to look at the passing nurse, Dad snatched a glance at the clock, then at his watch, then up at the Staff Nurse.

The bell was first to break the awkward silence. Its stuttered rattle was right on cue.

"Well, er...eh... we had better go," Mum glanced at her watch with a sigh of relief, and they both slinked off down the corridor out of sight. I wondered why they had come.

The nurse brought me some peaches the following day. She must have known I couldn't rely on my parents to bring them in. It was just what I needed to boost my confidence and gradually I started to eat again, putting back some of the weight I had lost until I was looking almost normal.

Then something happened that I couldn't explain. Dr John came into the ward unexpectedly. He was much younger than the other doctors and seemed to take an interest in me; perhaps he was still in training. He came straight to my bed with a twinkle in his eye, pushing an old wheelchair and for a moment I was worried about what was going to happen.

"Come on," he said excitedly, lifting me into the wheelchair. "We're going for a ride."

We rattled off down the corridor, grabbing some blankets from a trolley on the way. He stopped to wrap them tightly around me, tucking them into the chair. We raced down the ramp, burst through the exit doors and then emerged into the brilliant warm summer sunshine.

"Are you ready?" he asked. "Hold tight, we're going to race down the hill!"

Suddenly he pushed me down the hill with all the sound effects.

"*Whoosh, broom-broom!*" He turned the chair at breakneck speed ready for the next run. "*Whoosh*! Come on!" he shouted as we raced down the pavement and then back up the other side, and then back down again!

I laughed and laughed.

"*Broom, broom!*" He scooted off again at great speed, crashing all around the grounds of the hospital, up the ramps and then plunging down again.

Two nurses watched from the window; I can't imagine what they thought.

I screamed with such joy and laughter as we turned first left, then right, then left again. The chair rocked off the ground once more, flying through the narrow paths like Stirling Moss. Finally we came crashing back through the double doors and into the warmth of the corridor once more.

I laughed and chuckled and, in those few brief moments, I was able to forget the pain and discomfort, and the world once again seemed happy and full of laughter.

Somehow I found a renewed hope, lifting me up from the curtain of despair that had dogged my every waking moment, and in those few precious minutes, I felt a sudden overwhelming sense of happiness rise inside me. It lifted my spirits and gave me a lesson for life. I often thought about the kindness and thoughtfulness of that one person, Dr John, who will never be forgotten and will always have a place locked in my heart.

A few days later I was sent home, and then shortly after that I returned to the hospital doctor for a check up.

There was an examination of my throat and then they weighed me on the big scales.

Noticing I was still underweight and painfully thin, they started to ask me awkward questions about what I had for breakfast and dinner. I didn't get to answer any questions myself, as Mum jumped in every time, making sure the truth would remain hidden from the outside world.

Dad reverted to his hangdog look as if he were about to be shot, and Mum sat there staring down at the floor.

If only I had known how painful the recovery was to be.

5

Convalescence

AS SILVER STREET STATION was only a mile from our home we didn't need to catch the bus. Arriving on the platform, I stood there with Mum and Dad, and it wasn't long before the train to Liverpool Street arrived. Mum gave me a ticket, my little bundle of clothes, and took me onto the carriage to settle me down.

"Now don't forget you're going to Hastings," she said. "It's all arranged, so don't forget now."

I thought Mum was just closing the door, but it slammed behind her and the next thing I remember was the stationmaster's whistle, coupled with the smell of smoke and soot.

Chug, chug, chug!

I watched helplessly as the platform was swallowed up in a huge cloud of white steam, and then in the next glimpse, they were both standing on the platform; my little compartment was consumed by the steam and thunder of the train.

I had thought they were coming with me. How could they do that to me? How could they?

Suddenly there was the bittersweet taste of life at home. They knew I wouldn't go if they told me, so they tricked me!

I slumped down in my seat, looking around the little cramped carriage. It was just big enough for eight people, a bench on either side, a netted luggage rack above.

The lady sitting opposite looked directly at me.

"Hello," she said. "My name is Miss Maria Allen." She held out her hand. "I'm the lady your mummy would have told you about."

I shook my head, and looked up at her. I was upset and could not speak.

She lent forward and as her bosom unfolded she held out her hand once more.

"I am to take you to the convalescence home with Roger and Joe here." She cautiously gave a half smile before turning back and glancing at the other two children. "So I need you to follow us when we get to the station and not get lost."

I glanced up at her once more, flicking the hair from my eyes. I refused to take her hand and clenched my fists in the pocket of my coat.

Rejected again by my parents! Why do they not trust me?

"I hate her," I muttered quietly to myself.

The worst of it was the betrayal. I started to realise I trusted my family the least and I found that strangers would do more for me. Tortured by my thoughts and unable to hold back the jerking sobs, I cried for what seemed to be most of the journey.

I looked up and tried to dry my tears on my cuff. Miss Maria tried to distract me with games of 'I Spy' but I found it too difficult to swallow my pride. I could not be bothered with 'I spy' games, and all that. I seemed to be far more interested in watching the people getting on and off. That was my game.

The train clattered and rattled, and then I heard the sound of squealing brakes as it slowed at White Hart Lane.

I played my game—I watched to see what the people on the platform were really saying to each other. Not by the language, lip-reading or anything like that—no, purely by observation alone. Besides, I found myself too far away to hear. Sometimes I was unable even to make out their faces. I rarely needed facial expression—just the slight gestures, the flick of the wrist, or the wave of the hand. A man might greet a woman, he might hug her, and she might be young. Was he father or brother? Did she kiss him back, and if she did, would it be on the cheek or on the lips?

I found watching people fascinating because I was able to shut out the world of hurt. Their stories were betrayed by the briefest of movements, and the faintest of gestures. Were they angry, happy or gay?

"Bruce Grove—Bruce Grove!" The stationmaster's whistle blew. I looked up and then the stations arrived in quick succession, Seven Sisters and so on until we got to Bethnal Green.

"We're changing at Liverpool Street," Miss Maria said. "We have to get out with all our things and go onto the Tube."

"What's the Tube?" My question went unanswered.

"Don't forget your things—now bundle up children, bundle up," she called.

Miss Maria pulled the big leather strap that opened the window, and then putting her hand outside, she opened the door just as the train was pulling into the station.

We jumped off at Liverpool Street. As I glanced back at the train I noticed the doors all swung open like a swarm of butterflies drying their wings in the sun. But in my distraction I became overwhelmed by it all. Porters in their black waistcoats, pushing large carts of luggage and goods, their iron wheels banging and clattering on the hard station surface, all seemingly at once; crammed into one gigantic station dwarfed by the deafening roar of engines and whistles, echoing behind the billowing smoke. All of it drowning out the voices of Miss Maria and the boys.

I scurried off down the platform dragging my belongings as best I could. I struggled to keep up with the boys, now racing into the maze of tunnels, first left, then right as we headed for the underground train that would take us across London. Plunged into a writhing snake pit of a carriage, I tried to grab hold of a pole by the door. It slipped from my grasp. Unexpectedly, Miss Maria grabbed me and shoved me into the corridor. The train lurched forward, and I almost fell over struggling with my belongings between my legs. As the familiar whine of the train snaked through the tunnels, I glanced up at the faces: all different. Black, white, yellow, none of the umbrellas were the same. No one spoke. Instead, they stared blankly at the floor, or at the ceiling, but never at me. I caught a lady's eye. She looked away in silence like an inmate in a prison.

The train stopped at the station, the doors opened, and bodies drifted in and out like seaweed on the tide. I noticed a smart businessman, his newspaper firmly tucked in his jacket pocket and his umbrella outstretched like a Zulu spear. He looked determined not to miss his train. He pierced the sliding doors with the tip of his umbrella, and having forced them to open, he leaped the gap with the agility of a gazelle, only to be swallowed up in the stuffy compartment like half melted butter: his luggage too big and the space too small.

The train unexpectedly stopped then started, then stopped again, and we were stuck in the darkness of the tunnel. Fear gripped me as the lights flickered off, then on. There was silence. I heard a baby's cry and then the clunking of a motor that churned beneath my feet.

Everyone turned and looked. The familiar rattle of newspapers, magazines and books, and then—all faces down as if in prayer. The train started again and finally we pulled into the station. Someone snatched my collar. I looked up and found Miss Maria pulling me through the crowd, and then she dropped me down into the sudden stampede. I was thrown to the floor, trampled. I picked myself up and jumped off the train onto the hard paved surface of the platform.

I looked up. London Bridge was written on the wall in big bright letters, set against the background of white tiles that lined the large curved surface of the tunnel. It was as though I had been shrunk down real small and standing inside the top half of a big Smartie tube.

The train doors closed, a whistle blew as the familiar whine and clattering carriages faded, and I was left with the warm oily breeze, sucked in by the vanishing train.

Charging left along the platform, we turned right into another tunnel, and then up a long flight of stairs. Learning fast, I realised that falling over wasn't an option now, such was the force of the charging crowd. It flowed quickly through the turnstiles. It was as if time itself was as precious as blood: none was to be spilled.

Bursting up onto the overhead platform like a surfacing bubble in the fizzy pop, I breathed in the fresh air. Blinded by the sunlight, I strained my eyes at the notice board and waited for the Charing Cross train to Hastings. Meanwhile the two boys dived into the waiting room and sat huddled around the flames of a coal fire burning in the old Victorian tiled black open grate. I stayed outside on my own with Miss Maria, as we both gazed down the railway track, lost in our own thoughts.

It could only have been about fifteen minutes before our train pulled in. Miss Maria gathered us together, and quickly she ushered us through the clouds of sooty steam and into an empty carriage for the last part of our epic journey. It was like the one from Silver Street Station, about eight feet wide with two soft cotton long benches, one on either side with enough seating for eight people. I sat on the first seat on the right-hand side nearest the door. Miss Maria sat opposite and the boys curled up on the other side away from us both.

We must have been travelling for hours, and by now I was starting to get hungry and tired. Perhaps I slept the rest of the way as I remembered nothing of that part of the journey, until finally we arrived at the convalescence home. Miss Maria promised that if we were good boys and girls, we would be in for a special treat, and we could all join someone's birthday party.

As I recall, the garden was decorated like a scene from the Mad Hatter's Tea Party. One side of the garden was decked with long white trestle tables, laid out with cakes, sandwiches and jelly-trifles. One might have been forgiven for thinking this was some sort of magical treat. But I didn't remember it that way. I was lifted up and sat down amongst strangers. I refused to eat with them. I just felt so overwhelmed by the journey, and so very angry with my Mum. I just would not be cajoled and they appeared completely baffled as to why I would not join in. They simply did not understand what I had just gone through or how fragile it had made me feel.

I stared up at this seemingly large boarding house. I was shown into my bedroom where I was introduced to the other three girls who would be sharing with me. I was shocked to find they were all so much older, talking about all the boys and swimming. Unpacking my things onto my bed, I started to look around, peering in cupboards and drawers. Without warning the other girls started fingering and pulling at all my things, like a pack of wolves at a kill. One girl who seemed to be the leader of the pack picked up my swimming costume. She paraded it around like she was on a fashion shoot, posing for the other girls to see, showing off and stuff.

"Can I borrow it?" She swept it up from my bed. She pulled at it and pranced around the room, wiggling and holding it against her. Then she looked in the mirror to see if it might fit.

"What do yer think, girls?" she mocked, flicking her eyes around the room. "Do yer think it suits me then? New girl eh? Eh, new girl?"

"Well," I said sheepishly, feeling myself going red with embarrassment.

"Want it back then?" Suddenly she snatched it away behind her once more, taunting me with it all the time, and then making funny faces, pulling her mouth sideways and flicking her eyes up.

"Hey!" I reached out and made a grab for it. But my response was drowned by the noise and heckling of the baying mob, and suddenly the girls all started screaming, jumping up and down, caught in a wave of excitement.

"Can I borrow it then?" she asked once more. Then she turned. "I'll take that as yes then," she swiped it away and danced out of the room.

I didn't like the idea of someone else using it, especially as she was much older than me. But she took no notice and the girls quickly followed her as they all disappeared out of the room together, all laughing and joking to each other.

I avoided the older girls after that and tried to be a bit streetwise, hiding anything I valued and keeping my head down. Sometimes it didn't always save me, and it was clear they seemed to pick on anyone who was different. I tried to be hard and spiteful like them, but it wasn't really me. In the end, I just avoided them whenever possible. Eventually they lost interest in me and went on to bully someone else.

It was my first experience of real bullying. Name calling and the normal rough and tumble that girls do to each other I had learned to cope with; although, I was never picked on by older girls before. It was a new experience that made me realise I was moving into a different phase of my life. Although I didn't have much in life, and anything I did have I had to fight for, it didn't harden me like these girls.

When I managed to talk to one of this group, a girl called Jill, I found out that she had quite a privileged background. On the surface at least, she seemed to have everything so I didn't understand why she had to behave in the way she did. After a while I got to know her quite well, but that was only when she was on her own, and I think she must have realised I simply didn't possess anything of value she might want to nick.

Experience became a hard lesson, and by God I learned not to approach her when the other girls were around. She would turn on me, tearing into me, leading the others like a pack of wolves. I found it quite interesting that she was quite a nice girl underneath, and the bullying was a behaviour she only switched on when she was in sight of the other girls. Even at that age I realised she felt weak and probably thought the other girls would bully her unless she took on the role. It started to dawn on me that I was the stronger of the two of us because I had to struggle in silence.

Bullying wouldn't work for me, in the main part because I just did not have the build for it, and then, I just did not see the need to hurt other people. What was the point? They would only hit back at me! But for other girls it seemed to be a way of surviving their inner weakness. Were they jealous of me in some way? I couldn't imagine why—I had nothing. However, in the days that followed, my weakness would be fully exposed.

Thunder rocked the house. The walls shuddered, and as night fell, the lightening scorched eerie shadows upon the wall. The other girls were probably gathered together and having a good laugh somewhere, but I huddled under the covers of my bed, my face firmly buried in my pillow, hiding all alone, frightened. Sobbing quietly, I worried that the other girls might have heard me crying, and I didn't want to attract another dose of bullying.

The door flung open. My heart stopped. I burrowed under the covers like a dog on a bone. I felt a hand pull back the thick woollen blanket. A cold chill hit my face. I did not want to look. I shut my eyes even tighter than before.

Recognising the scent of fresh soap, I knew it was Miss Maria. My quiet whimpers had summoned her; she just cuddled me up in my blanket, and then in complete silence, she took me the short distance to her own room. It was sparsely furnished with a simple wardrobe, a small dressing table with a table lamp and a large double bed pushed into the corner of the room. As I recall, I seemed to be more concerned with trying to hide the hole in my pyjamas as she gently laid me on her bed. Her arms wrapped around me, as she pulled me into the pillow of her tender bosom; she cradled me like a baby and whispered reassuringly throughout the night, until eventually I remembered no more.

I never forgot this first sign of comfort and warmth. Most people would probably expect it from their mother as part of the natural nurturing act. But not from my Mum. I cannot remember any sign of affection or comfort from her, for she was always stern and distant. I think she was frightened to show love. I didn't know why.

Waking up in fine sunshine the following morning, I felt I was in a new calm day, and I remember feeling much brighter and fresher, as if the storm had somehow cleansed my mind. Perhaps this was because of the comfort I received from Miss Maria the previous night, although it did occur to me that it might have been more fundamental than that. Was it the realisation that I was loveable in the sense that someone could pick me up and comfort me and feel pity for me, love me and accept me as a child? That someone could see the innocent honesty of my plight and that I wasn't the ugly duckling after all?

I ran downstairs for breakfast, playing with the other children, running around the room and screaming and shouting with joy. It seemed to be great fun, and everyone was talking excitedly about the thunder and lightening the night before. In the rush of excitement, I hadn't noticed the hole in my pyjamas had grown bigger, and suddenly my bottom was starting to show through. I worried that the boys would see and laugh at me. Despite my best efforts to stuff a hanky down, my bare bottom continued to show, until I was forced to sit down.

Why couldn't Mummy just think of me for once and sew up my pyjamas? I felt it was like a punishment for having fun. As soon as I was enjoying something it seemed it would be snatched away from me. My parents could reach out like some invisible monster with long tentacles—no matter where I was. They had the power to spoil every moment of play, no matter how small.

Putting my upset aside, I remember one little boy who was making me laugh and scream. We were jumping up and down when Matron came in the room.

"Who's doing all the screaming down here!" She scanned the room as if to sniff out the culprit.

It was me who had been screaming. But for some reason I couldn't say anything—I was struck dumb. I remember looking at the boy who was playing with me, and then suddenly he stepped out of the line.

"I am sorry Matron—I think it was me," he said softly.

Turning, her face now red and flushed, she bellowed, almost spitting in his face, such was her annoyance.

"To your room Master Timmings!" She raised her finger, pointing as if to shoot the unfortunate boy. He bowed his head and sheepishly skulked out of the room and upstairs.

I didn't know why he took the blame for me. I felt really guilty about that and felt very sorry for the little boy who took the punishment. I returned upstairs and got ready for the day, making my bed and all that stuff.

"It's Sunday!" the other girls cried out with excitement and jubilation.

"What's special about Sunday then?"

"Oh! Don't yer know?" Jill said. "It's visiting time." She turned back to the others to see their reaction. I sensed she was about to make fun of me, her eyes flicking back and forth between me and the other girls.

"Mummy and Daddy will be visiting," she added in a voice loud enough for all to hear. "Aren't yours?" she blurted out.

She turned to look back at her mates, then, giving me a sideways glance, I noticed that she signalled something behind her back. I didn't see what it was. But standing there, I suddenly realised that all the other girls had stopped and were silent. I sensed something was about to get nasty.

"Oh thanks, I'd just forgotten what day it was," I said, trying my best to be as convincing as I could.

There wasn't the response that I expected, just silence and the other girls looked at me. I stood my ground and waited for what seemed ages. But it didn't go Jill's way. If Jill was hoping to start a bullying session, the rest of the girls didn't have the stomach to start an argument; after all, there was the hope that their parents might yet bring them something nice. One girl started to get on with clearing up her bed, and then slowly, one by one, the girls turned and carried on with what they were doing. Soon I was left on my own in the dormitory.

I wandered downstairs. I looked out the window expectantly. Other parents arrived and picked up their children for the afternoon. No one came for me.

Minutes turned into hours and I lost all hope of my Mum or Dad appearing through the door and the rejection and darkness descended upon me, so hurtfully, so publicly.

I felt so alone—never in my life had I felt so alone. I could not endure the pain; it was so crushing that I wanted to curl up inside and sleep. But people would see and I couldn't let people see.

My faith in people was bankrupt and I found myself with no room in my mind for faith. Faith implies hope and trust and yet I had no trust, and what trust I had in others was only wicked trust—in the sense that I could not let myself believe in them. It was too painful and so I had only myself to trust—then I should never be disappointed or be let down. I felt so unloved! The demon in my mind and perhaps my wooden leg was upon me. My crutch seemed constantly kicked away by the baying mob and the hounds were in for the kill.

I sat at the window, staring out into the street, looking for nothing, for nothing ever came for me.

Miss Maria quietly opened the door, picked me up and lifted me up to her shoulder, and then, sitting me gently on her lap, spoke to me softly. "I have something I need to tell you." She reached out and held my hand.

I remember looking up at her, almost mouthing the words as she spoke, like a puppet master. I knew the script. My Daddy would not be coming to visit, I whispered inside my head.

"Mummy isn't coming—is she?"

I looked up at her. I saw the look in her eyes. She was unable to hide it from me. I was too practised at it. I knew all the looks and she thought I didn't know, but I did.

I shivered with silent tears.

"Your parents won't be coming to see you, I am afraid," she said softly. "They find it too far to come." Then, as she turned and lowered her head, I saw her pity.

"I'm going home soon though, so I don't suppose it will be long," I said.

"Well, I am afraid the doctors think you should stay another three weeks so that you can get better," she said.

By this time she was stroking my hair and giving me a cuddle, sensing I was not going to take this well.

"NO! Not three weeks. NO! NO! NO!" I screamed and wriggled to be free.

I remember shaking off her arms, and jumping down so fast that I fell over, banging my elbow on the hard floor. The feelings of disappointment overwhelmed me. I thought it would be hurtful, but I didn't think I could feel like this.

Just one week, then perhaps I could handle that, but THREE weeks! Why did I not learn? Round and round, everything seemed to repeat. Was I going in circles, or perhaps better, was I in a spiral? But if a spiral, then which way was it going—up or down? If it was going down then perhaps there was no hope for me, and I was condemned in purgatory?

I could not think and the pain in my head burned excruciatingly into my mind, exploding in on itself and falling down a pit of despair. I screamed inside. My sobs were uncontrollable. I lay prostrate on the floor with my head in my arms. I didn't care that it was cold and hard. I banged myself and thrashed against it until my hands hurt, in the hope that the physical pain would mask the real pain I felt inside.

Miss Maria picked me up. But I was limp. In my sobbing she pulled me once more onto her lap, cradling me and rocking me in her arms.

"I am going home. I *am* going home," I muttered through my sobs and stuttered breath. My bottom lip started to quiver and my nose ran continuously as I looked up at her, pleading with my blotchy panda eyes and red cheeks.

She pulled me up to her face and tried to comfort me once more. I struggled to be free, trying not to accept her kindness. I fought her, but she kept a firm hold of me until I started to calm down.

"All right," she said softly, "let me see what I can do, and perhaps we might be able to let you go home early," she added. "But I can't promise, mind." And for a moment she held me. She gave me a glimmer of hope, and I found comfort in her words.

Later that week she collected me from my room and took me to the care team in charge of the home. She walked with me into this big room. It had large bay windows, which overlooked the town. Opposite the door around a long wooden table, were seated three sad-faced men in smart suits. They just asked me my name and how old I was, and then I had to wait outside the door as they discussed my case.

I didn't hear all the conversation, but I heard some as I listened at the keyhole. Miss Maria was telling them about me and the lack of visiting, and the way I was put on the train and so forth. She expressed concern for my well being at home, and that she was worried for me.

I found out later that they wanted to get social workers to go round and find out how I was living, to see if I should be taken into care. In the end they decided it wasn't in their remit to pursue the domestic situation. Instead, they decided to let me go home as soon as I was eating and putting on some weight.

I decided to try and make the best of it for the remainder of my stay. I had done all I could!

I remember vividly those times when I received love, finding it so rarely in my life, that it shone like a beacon, so brightly amongst the hard realities of the world I knew. If there was any problem, difficulty or responsibility required from my Mum, it would provoke the answer, "It's all yer father's fault!" Though I never fully understood why.

Paradoxically I would realise later in life that it was my Mum who would make do, prepare meals and keep the family going, but only up to a point—food never came before fags.

Of the two of them, it was Dad who cared. It would be Dad who showed some compassion and tucked me in at nights. He would be the one searching for me if I was out late, although it was my Dad who would be irresponsible in a financial sense. He would drink or gamble the money away, and despite the hardship we suffered, he would continue to buy his drinks, until he literally fell off his chair.

6

Drowning

THE BLUE SKY FRAMED THE HOT SUN. It bathed my body with such warmth that I swear it lit within me a little flame of joy. We were all so excited as the chattering group loudly showed off their swimming costumes. They were still busily wrapping them in their towels when the Matron, Mr Gordon, and Miss Maria came into the room and marched us out of the Convalescent Home, along the lane that led to the beach.

I had never been to the seaside before, and certainly not on a beach swimming. At first I thought it was a boating lake, and then I saw the water plunge and tumble as if it where drunk. It sort of staggered, rolled and then toppled before throwing itself down on the stony beach—shingle, Mr Gordon called it.

I wandered close, but still I didn't know what to make of it. I found myself holding back from the others as I stood gazing out at the vast expanse of it all. There was nothing but endless, restless water, foam tops spraying a fine mist, as if from a kettle, and the occasional giant wave that crashed with such thunder it blotted out the startled screams of the seagulls overhead.

Miss Maria came over to me, took my hand and as she bent down next to me, she pointed out to sea.

"Look," she said, "look at the Sea Horses."

"What Sea Horses? I can't see any." I stared out, but I couldn't see anything and I thought she was simply teasing me.

I was more interested in being shielded from the summer breeze by the generous gathers of her skirt.

"That's what the old sailors used to call them."

"Why? They're not horses."

"Well, sailors thought that sea horses were an animal, half fish and half horse, ridden by Neptune and other sea gods. So when they saw the white curved tops of the waves, they thought they looked like horses' necks, and gave them this name."

"Oh, so they're not real horses then?"

"No, my lovely, it's just what sailors call 'em."

"That's all right then, because they're not real, are they?"

"No, they're not real. Shall we join the others, eh?" She took my hand in hers. It was a gentle hand, not harsh, and it didn't lurch with impatience: it had no anger.

She walked with me, letting me totter over the stones at my own pace, and together we slowly joined the others, who were gathered in a little collection of towels that patched the shingle. Miss Maria launched me gently amongst the other children with such confidence that I felt safe with them for the first time. The children were all gathered around, all messing about fussing with their bags and stuff. Jill, the bully in my room who first stole my swimming costume, got all the others into a group, and they started to kick a large red, white and blue beach ball to each other. When they tired of that they started throwing it around in a game of catch, until one boy threw it into the water.

I watched from the sidelines; standing there on the stones, admiring the sea, all my unhappiness put behind me. I decided I would enjoy the time I had left at the Home.

We all sniggered as Mr Gordon, a tall man, who was one of the carer's at the Home, had to roll up his trouser legs and then wade into the water to retrieve the beach ball. He jumped up and down because the water was so cold. We all laughed behind his back. He struggled to get hold of the ball as it drifted beyond his grasp, and then as he reached out to it once more a large bubble of surf soaked his trousers, like he had wet himself. Jill turned round to me, her shoulder-length hair swirling around her face like a scarf. She pulled me over to her in her excitement, pointing at Mr Gordon.

"Look, look," she said, "he's wet himself!"

I didn't say anything. It wasn't funny to me. I had seen my father drunk too many times and it threatened to snatch me back into sadness. But I promised myself I wasn't going to be sad anymore. I needed the distraction.

I saw Michael, the little boy I played with, standing about five yards from the water's edge. He somehow reminded me of my brother Les with his dark hair and cheeky smile. I probably warmed to him because he stood up for me with Matron; he took the blame. I didn't ask him to do it, but he did it for me; no one had done that before.

I watched as Mr Gordon lobbed the ball high into the air, toward the beach, for little Michael to catch. But he didn't catch it; instead there was a sudden scramble, everyone diving on top of each other laughing and jostling for the ball. A gust of wind swept across the beach, picking up the ball that bounced away from their grasp.

The children got up and raced to the sea as if to chase it, but to my surprise they ran to the water. The game had changed and without warning they started jumping up and down, splashing each other amongst the waves. They were all screaming as the cold water tumbled around them. So much fun must have been infectious.

I moved forward in a surge of enthusiasm, taking my shoes off and rushing along the beach toward the salty spray. I stopped, shuddered and then hobbled as the stones dug into my tender feet. Picking my way painfully over the stones I finally stopped at the water's edge. I stood there looking at the endless movement of the sea for ages, before I found the courage. I chanced a single foot. It was numbingly cold. I looked over at the others and saw them all larking around in the sea, and for a moment, I felt stupid inside. I jumped in with a splash, and held fast for a moment letting the sea lap my feet.

I tried to look brave and stand there like the others, but the sea sucked the warmth out of my blood like a vampire, until my toes were as white as the surf in which they bathed. I hopped back onto the warm stones and stood there for a few minutes. I wanted to enjoy the tingling feeling as the colour returned to my feet, blushed pink like petals on a flowering rose.

I ventured slowly into the surf and stayed a little longer in the fine shingle at the water's edge, but the dragging surf snatched my feet, and I toppled over onto my hands. I got up quickly and shook the grit from my fingers and glanced over my shoulder to see who was laughing. I was lucky. No one had seen me.

I ventured out again and for some reason my feet didn't feel as cold this time. I moved forward and before long I found myself amongst the other children. We were all jumping up and down over the waves, all lined up, like we did in the playground skipping within a big rope.

Mr Gordon, who had now changed into his swimming trunks, started walking out into the waves. He was already up to his waist when I decided to follow him out. As I went further the water got deeper and deeper. I didn't understand why it was getting deeper for me, but not for Mr Gordon. He didn't look as if he was getting deeper. I looked up. He was waving to me.

I went out a little further until the water reached my tiny waist. A wave splattered my face. I shuddered and shook like a dog. I heard him shout something at me, but the words were swept away. I waved at him and he waved back.

Waves were to the left of me, to the right of me and in front of me. They were breaking over my chest and pushing me back. They lifted me as I struggled to keep my footing, but each time they carried me out a little further into the swell. I found myself leaning into the waves as they crashed around me, and somehow I found it thrilling, like being on a fair ground, picked up and rocked around. It was such fun and suddenly the whole world had been forgotten. I was just a little girl lost in the moment of play for the first time in my life: jumping the surf in the ocean.

I couldn't feel my feet on the bottom anymore. The waves were lifting me up all the time and despite my best efforts I couldn't get back. I thought that if I were able to reach Mr Gordon he would be able to help me. Overwhelmed by the force of the waves and the depth of the water, warm salt spray trickled down my face, and my eyes filled with tears.

I struggled to keep my head above the waves and I wondered how long it would take for someone to notice? I tried to shout out: "HE..." Water slapped into my mouth like Mother. I pierced the surface with my hands, reaching up as high as I could, but then, failing, I fell back into the foaming sea, spluttering and paddling furiously to stay upright.

Panic started to set in as I found myself lifted up, then down, and for the briefest moment my feet touched the ground once more; I was dragged out again, until one big wave crashed over me so fiercely that I was suddenly thrown backwards, my feet swept from under me, and I disappeared beneath foam, tumbling over, up and down, then sideways and finally bouncing and banging my head on the bottom. I put my hand to my head, as if to feel for a hole, although I felt no pain.

I reached up and gulped for air, and then slapped my hands on the water as I struggled to regain a footing. It was no use: the next wave picked me up, feet first, threw me backwards, and finally dashed me onto the stones, to strip the flesh from my body once more.

Occasionally I would catch a glimpse of the sky. Amongst tumbles, I would gulp desperately for air, but more often than not I swallowed water and soon it all became too much for me.

Exhausted, I quickly tired, but I was determined I wasn't going to give up – I wasn't a quitter—I had come too far. Once more I found a surge of energy from within.

Struggling to get to the surface, half choking and coughing, I gulped like a dying fish. Again, thrusting my hands in the air as far as I could, I searched desperately for help, but each time I was slapped down. Which way was up? I didn't know anymore. I caught a precious sweet breath of salt spray, before being struck down again, sucked into the foaming mass of water.

Giving up, I let go my little body. I let it drift in endless twists, tumbles and throws, and although it might be fancy, I remember in the end a sense of calmness that descended over me; and then, as if woken from a dream and finding myself frightened of the dark, I fought with everything I had, kicking hard each time until I found myself above it all.

I could see the sky clearly now and the waves nearby, but it wasn't enough. I was sinking down into it all, and suddenly I couldn't stop myself. I took a breath. It was water that filled my lungs so deep I swear I felt my chest burst open. I could still hear the noise of the stones dragging over each other, the burble of the water and suddenly nothing mattered anymore...

It was all over and the fight for survival was at an end. The torment of my life could stop, and finally I could let it all go. The lights went out, the darkness descended upon me and I drifted into a dreamlike embrace. I saw a bright light flicker in front of me and then a black, nothing…

Noises on the beach. Chattering children. Waves crashing. Screaming shingle outsung the seagulls overhead. A boy's voice: "Is she dead Miss?"

"Hush now, children."

"Yeah, I reckon."

I found myself lying on my tummy with hands pushing on my back. My throat stung with the hacking and spluttering of salty water. Shivering with the cold, just trying to breathe normally without coughing, I lay there motionless. For a moment I couldn't take it all in and I wondered if I was in heaven. Was this what it was like to be in heaven, with people cuddling and caring?

Someone started rubbing my back and I became aware of a huddle of people around me. Miss Maria was talking to me. The water in my ears drowned her words. Someone got me a towel, sat me up and wrapped it around me. For the first time I opened my eyes. My teeth chattered and somebody found a Mars Bar.

"You are a lucky girl," Mr Gordon said. "I kept waving for you to go back—didn't you see me, silly girl?"

He looked at Miss Maria, then back at me, shaking his head.

"You gave us quite a scare there for a moment," Matron said. "You have Mr Gordon to thank for saving you, you know."

"Sorry." I looked at her blankly for I could only think about the Mars Bar.

"Do you want me to unwrap that for you?"

Taking the chocolate from me, Miss Maria unwrapped it and placed it back into my hand. As she patted me on my head, she sat down next to me and held me close.

By this time Mr Gordon and the Matron had got up to supervise the rest of the group, getting them organised ready for the return to the Home.

"Come on you lot, show's over, get packed up and changed into your clothes."

"Do we have to?" they moaned, skulking and looking for their things that they had scattered on the beach.

A fight broke out at one time when one of the girls picked up the wrong towel. The Matron and Mr Gordon busily sorted out the girls, barking orders at them, whilst I sat with Miss Maria as she helped me to get ready, holding the towel up and drying me down. She didn't say much; she just took care of me, dressing me and rubbing my hands briskly, blowing her warm breath onto my little fingers.

I didn't know why I went out so far—perhaps I thought Mr Gordon was calling me to come out, I just didn't know, but I often wonder if that is why I have a fear of drowning. It did occur to me that perhaps it was a way of ending my misery, but I didn't think that was my real intention.

I learned a lot from my stay at the Home. The children, I found, were no different to the adults I had come in contact with; sometimes spiteful and hard, and at other times I found the same mixture of sulking and brooding, some soft, some capable, and some downright nasty. On the other hand the adults had learned to switch off the outside signals—perhaps hiding their true motives, to mislead and confuse without raising concerns.

Children didn't bury what they wanted to say to me amongst long words, as some of the adults did. It taught me that I had to watch their eyes, hands, and small gestures to understand adults properly and perhaps, as a person once told me, listen to the music behind the words. Now I understood what they meant.

On my return home, things started to get better for me, and life returned to what I accepted as normal. It might have been because Dad had a job for a change; I didn't know, but I found myself happier at school and things were looking up.

7

The Wedding: School Concert

THE BRIDESMAID DRESS was so lovely. Pastel pink satin, little puffed sleeves and the skirt with an overlay of sheer pale pink netting; an overskirt of tulle, Auntie called it. I stood in the shop fitting room as Auntie Hilda fussed around me, gently taking off my old clothes.

"Come on, put your arms up." She wasn't like Mum—she didn't have to ask twice.

I clasped my hands in the air as if in prayer, and then bending my knees slightly I dived upward as Auntie slid the dress over my head. She let it descend like a parachute, guiding it over me as I blindly felt my way through the mass of satin, until my head finally reached the little ruchéd neck.

I tugged at it through the rustle of gathered skirt, but it would only just go part of the way.

"I've got my ears stuck—Auntie, I've got my ears stuck."

She heard the little tone of disappointment in my voice.

"Okay darling," she said, "don't worry, we'll get another one."

Carefully bending down, she gathered up all the skirt, lifted it clear, and then turning to the wall she hung it up by the large wall mirror.

"Stay here my love," she said, before disappearing outside through the slit in the curtains that separated us from the main part of the shop.

For a few minutes I stood in front of the mirror, peeking out from behind the dress as the grown-ups chatted outside.

Oh, I am to be a bridesmaid! The Cinderella I have read about in my storybooks at school, all dressed up and going to the ball, and it was me; it was me! For a brief moment I allowed myself a precious fragile dream, and then hearing the familiar sound of footsteps, I perched myself on the small stool that stood in the corner, and pretended I hadn't moved.

The curtains parted as Auntie carried in another beautiful dress—this time with a little pink headdress.

Overflowing with emotion, being attended to, asked what I wanted, and not only that, it was as if anything I wanted was given to me. For me it was the first time I had experienced such joy, to be equal to my friends, like a Queen for a day! I tried it on as Auntie stood there.

"That's just perfect." She knelt down beside me and together we looked in the mirror.

"What do you think, Mary?" She turned and got the pretty flowered headdress, and fitted it in place.

I didn't answer. I just stood there and looked in the mirror.

"Don't you look beautiful?"

I didn't believe her. I thought she was looking at someone else. I flicked my head, first at her face, and then back at the mirror, and as I did so, I saw her smile so broad and as happy a smile as ever I had seen. She drew me towards her and gave me an affectionate cuddle and a little peck on the cheek. For a second I felt my heart flutter with love, but like a moth to a flame it didn't last.

"Oh, careful, we mustn't crush the dress." Auntie pushed me away and stood up.

The dress was packed away and suddenly the rush to take me home replaced the dreaming. It wasn't her fault the dream had to end so suddenly because I really liked my Auntie Hilda; but she had so much to do that there wasn't really time for me.

Yet she had an infectious giggle that was always bubbling up to the surface and she took others around her with it.

The wedding day had arrived, and with it the big black car. The driver got out and opened the door as Marion lifted me up and onto the plush leather seat. There were three of us there—the two bridesmaids, myself and a little girl called Carolyn, and the Maid of Honour, Marion.

"Say hello to Carolyn," Marion said.

"Hello," I said.

She turned round and tried to look down at me, but she wasn't tall enough. Instead she poked her nose in the air.

"How low," she replied with a plumb in her mouth, all snooty and toffee nosed.

My Auntie Hilda and Uncle Norman, bride and groom, looked stunning as we entered the little church. Auntie was in her white wedding dress, and as she walked up the aisle I noticed that everyone was looking at us. I followed Marion who was wearing a long dress, and like mine, it went down to the floor. As I walked behind her, she seemed to glide along the floor like a ghost. I didn't understand why I never saw her feet move.

The organ music droned the wedding song, and the choir sung their hearts out and everyone got up as we all glided down the aisle. When we reached the front I sat in a pew to the left, and Carolyn sat in a pew to the right.

We listened in silence as Uncle and Auntie chatted to the man in the white blanket and red scarf, who Dad called the vicar. Mum didn't say anything—she just kept her head down.

After their little chat, the bride and groom kissed and everyone cheered and clapped. Then we all turned back out of the church and onto the steps outside. The photographer flashed his camera as the guests showered fistfuls of rice over everyone within reach.

First the picture of the bride and groom, then the in-laws, Uncles and Aunts and finally the ladies. I waited anxiously for my turn to feature in the family album as Carolyn continued to give me funny looks.

"Stand still, smile, look up," the photographer pointed and gestured with his hand outstretched. "There's a good girl. Cheese."

Aunty came up onto the steps and stood with me, Marion and the other snooty little bridesmaid, Carolyn. Then the photographer asked us three to stand in front of the wedding car, as if to pretend we had just arrived. Marion stood in front of the open car door, with Carolyn and I nestled into the gathers of her dress on either side. We stood, clutching our posy of flowers, splendid in identical dresses, complete with little pink gloves.

The photographer snapped, then waved with his left hand, and then he snapped again.

Suddenly I felt a snatch of irritation. I didn't look up. I knew who it was. I was led away and we walked into a large community hall nearby. We opened the door into a bustle of chatter and bubbly laughter, fun and excitement as people greeted, hugged, smiled and shouted with surprise, and then buried their faces in the wealth of food spread out as far as the eye could see. I stood in wonder at the wall of endless tables and clattering plates, of clinking glasses, each segregated along different sides, like checkers on a board. Hoards of boisterous children descended, like locusts, on the ginger pop, lemonade and Tizer, the table swimming with it all.

Dad was one of ten children and soon the little procession of aunties and uncles paraded up to my parents.

"My, how little Mary has grown—and isn't she pretty then! Where's Les these days? Isn't he here today?"

I don't remember Mum saying much as she tried to avoid most of the questions.

Crashing chairs, and scraping of tables, first signalled the start of the dance. A band of musicians formed on the stage, like mobsters on a heist, and then they tuned up with some jazz and background music. I was quietly sitting on the side next to Auntie Hilda, the new bride, when my Uncle Norman first came over to me.

"May I have the pleasure of this dance with the most beautiful young lady?"

I shot a glance at Auntie Hilda, assuming he was asking her, but she turned back to me, gesturing with her hand stretched out to me.

"No," she smiled, "he means you, darling." She took my hand and coaxed me over to Uncle Norman.

I looked right up at him, such a tall handsome man, so dapper in his wedding suit. I was filled with pride. The music played as the background chatter was hushed by the clapping.

Sneaking out through my shyness I stood next to him, but I only came up to his waist. I felt a little frightened at first, and sensing this, he took my hand in his, and slowly walked me onto the dance floor. I was beaming with happiness as he twirled me around again and again, lifting my little feet above the floor. I laughed, he laughed and the crowd laughed with me, as he swept me along on a cloud: I didn't want it to end.

Out of all the little girls there, he proudly asked *me*! My little lace gloves, the matching shoes, and stiff net petticoat that made my pink lace dress hang so beautifully—all made me look angelic.

Auntie Alice came up to me and asked me to stay at her house overnight. I really liked my Auntie Alice, Dad's older sister, because her house was so spick and span, everything so fresh and clean. Dad tried to get me to stay overnight, but I wanted to go home; I didn't know why—perhaps it was just a feeling of clinging to what I knew.

The legacy of the wedding for me was the nice new dress to wear at a special occasion, although it would be some months before another occasion would arise.

School started to become much better for me as I got older because I learned very quickly. It put me one step ahead of some of my friends, and that made me popular.

One day, out of the blue, the music teacher came and asked if we would like to play an instrument. She had taught some of us to play the recorder, and I was lucky enough to be picked from the class. For me this was a frightening prospect because there was no way I could afford to buy an instrument, so at first I declined to join in. It was a bit of a relief when I found out that the school could lend us the instruments and we didn't have to buy them. In my situation I had to think of all those things before I would volunteer for anything, although I must admit I enjoyed the experience of playing.

Mrs Ritchie, the music teacher, came in one morning and explained that we were all expected to stand on the stage and perform a concert at the end of term. I couldn't contain my excitement at being chosen to be one of the players on the platform, especially as I knew I had a nice dress to wear.

She lined us up and made us recite each piece of music in turn, and then she got us to work as a group until she was satisfied we were good enough. Each week we would rehearse together until everything was perfect and we all knew our parts.

The day of the concert arrived and I rushed home at lunchtime to pick up my dress. I bounded in, rushed upstairs and got out the pretty pink dress that I had for the wedding. It was really nice with a fine netting over it, and I had cut it down the previous week to make it a little bit shorter; but now I had the chance to look at it properly I found it crumpled on the floor exactly where I left it: there was nowhere for me to hang it.

Mother knew I wanted to wear it, but she hadn't bothered to get it out and give it an iron for me. I couldn't ask her now because she had gone to work, and I desperately wanted to wear it.

I wondered if I could wear it as it was? I looked in the mirror at it from all angles—it had hideous creases! I decided there was only one thing for it—to iron it.

Pulling the chair from the table, I dragged it over to the cupboard, clambered up and got the iron out, and then, traipsing into the kitchen, I hastily plugged it in. Putting up the ironing board proved to be a bit of a challenge. Each time I opened it up and tried to lock it in position, it would jump out and fall down, and it wasn't until three attempts later that I found the locking lever underneath. The broken spring probably explained why Mother never ironed anything. Anyway, by the time I had managed to get the ironing board in position, the iron was hot.

I smoothed the dress over the board and cautiously ran the iron over the dress, but instead of flattening the creases it clung to the iron. As I tried to clean the iron with an old tea towel and some water the steam burnt my hand, the netting stuck like glue, and gave off an awful smell.

I was mortified. I looked down at the dress and racked my brains to see what I could do. I turned it round, lifted it up and tried everything I could to do to make it wearable, but very quickly I ran out of ideas. I took the dress outside and slung it in the bin—there was nothing I could do with it now.

I sat down at the kitchen table and was determined not to cry, but still I burst into tears. I had hit the rock bottom of despair. What does a little girl do in this adult world where other mums care? My Aunties and Uncles all cared. Auntie Hilda cared for me, yet she was not my mother. I sat alone in my sobs and asked myself what I had done wrong.

As I sat in my moment of despair, I suddenly remembered a cerise dress I had.

Rummaging through the cupboard I retrieved it from the pile of assorted clothes in the old box and inspected it. It looked really good—no holes or anything on the back, and then, turning it around, my little heart sank. There on the front of the dress was a big stain. But what could I do?

I tried it on and looked in the mirror, turning round to see if I could hide the stain. No, I couldn't hide it and I just had to accept that it would show.

Time was running out and if I didn't get back to the school soon, I would be late. I couldn't have that—that would be worse and I would be humiliated in front of the whole audience.

Forgetting my hunger I ran back to my school in Grove Street, arriving in the hall just in time.

"Where have you been? You're nearly late?" The teacher ushered me up to the front row. "Get up on stage in front, next to Janet," she guided me as she gently pushed me forward.

Taking my place in the front row, I tucked the stain on my skirt between my legs.

The concert started and I played my piece with the rest of the girls and, thankfully, everything went very well. The parents in the audience applauded and the teacher was very pleased with us.

I felt a great sense of pride as I played the recorder and all the notes came out loud and clear. I remember looking at the teacher as she conducted, making sure I came in on time, and paying great attention to getting it right. I was proud of my success and my small part in the band. It felt good because I belonged. I was one of them and had been accepted.

I walked down from the stage with the other girls and sat on a row down the side of the little hall whilst the head teacher said a few closing words. I noticed that other girls went to talk to their parents who had been watching from the audience.

There were lots of cuddles, patting of heads and praising from the mums and dads.

Not mine—they never came!

Still, I looked forward to a time when I would do something good enough for my Mum and Dad to come.

8

Birthday

LIFE WASN'T SO BAD. I was in the last year of junior school. I kept telling myself I was okay and each time life bit into me I would find a way to cope.

Begging for food from the shopkeepers was more or less a routine thing now, although never easy and the trauma never got any better. Occasionally Mum was working and life was okay, but for much of the time I became ashamed of my family and the way we lived; our unique ways of getting food, money and clothes; and at the same time I had an acceptance of my situation coupled with a determination to hide it from the outside world. For me, their way of doing things was not my way, and I vowed it never would be. But for now, I had to look out for myself.

I needed to fit in. Making up stories to pretend I was like everyone else, worked well for me some of the time. If my friends had holidays and birthdays, then I would make up even better holidays and birthdays. The fact that they never took place was a depressing disappointment, which I didn't want to face. I had to live in this secret world, to which I came home. To me, the nights of darkness were part of me, and who I was. Other children played. I found I had lost the ability to play silly games. My play was keeping clean, staying warm and getting food.

At school my friends told me how they all went to what we called 'The Green' after school. It was a little patch of unkempt grassland where tarmac paths crossed, nestled in between the tall buildings. I was told that it probably was the result of bomb clearance after the war and was left, either because it was such an awkward shape, or the ownership was unknown. In any event, it provided an unsupervised patch of land on which older boys would build little camps, play cowboys and Indians, and girls would gather to play catch or roller-skating on the paths.

They would all meet up. It sounded great fun, like a little club. I went and watched the girls skating once or twice, but ended up playing with the boys in their camp. When I first met them, the boys were all throwing stones from the safety of an old wooden shelter. I say shelter, but it was more like a collection of old doors propped up against each other.

"What are you doing?" I asked.

"We're shooting stones at the old bottles over there," one of them replied, pointing to a milk crate.

I followed his gaze and saw, thirty feet or so in front of the shelter, a little mound of earth, topped with an upturned milk crate. Mounted on this were four old lemonade bottles, two of which were shattered. My first reaction was horror. You could get three pence back on each bottle, and they had four. That was a shilling's worth of bottles, or in my mind a whole loaf of bread. I wondered if they were rich kids.

The leader of the group was a lippy little rabbit of a kid, buckteeth and short trousers. He turned back to me, his eyes sparkling as though he hadn't had a girl in his gang.

"Do you want to join our gang?"

"Yes please," I said cautiously. I wasn't sure about this, but I was lonely on my own.

"All right, go down behind the target, and when I shout out, you get up there and put the bottles back. Then you can have a turn."

"Okay," I said.

"Oh, and here's a white flag."

"What's that for?"

"You need to wave it before you get up."

"Okay."

I walked over the little mound and hid behind the target. Clutching the little white flag, I kept my head down as the missiles flew overhead. I heard one smash, then another, and then silence.

"Okay, stand the bottles up!" someone shouted, I didn't know who.

I stood up and waved the white flag.

Thump.

It wasn't the rabbit. Something hit my head. It felt like half a brick, although I couldn't be sure. I reached up to my head and felt a cut. When I looked, my hand was covered with blood.

I rushed home, holding my head with a hanky. I burst in, shouted out for Mum, but she wasn't there, and so I sat by the kitchen table. I washed out my blood-soaked hanky in the old sink with cold water and then dabbed it on my head to see if the bleeding had stopped. I went upstairs to my bedroom to check in the mirror.

Parting my hair and pulling it back, I struggled to see the cut. I couldn't see much. There was a little gash about half an inch long, which had quickly dried up. What I could see was a big dried clump of blood, which had stuck in my thick brown shoulder-length hair.

I decided I had to wash it out in the sink. I got a bar of soap, wet it and then rubbed it on my matted hair as if to melt the blood. Awkwardly, I dipped my hair in the bathroom sink, running the tap and trying to wash the blood away. But it wasn't as successful as I had hoped. It was some time before I managed to brush out enough of the blood to get a comb through it. I dried it as best I could on an old jumper I found in the landing cupboard, but time was against me; I had yet to light the fire.

School had just started for the September term in 1959 and soon it would be my eleventh birthday. Meeting up at school with all the other children after the summer break, brought with it a sense of belonging. The next time I went to The Green, I noticed there were a bunch of girls on roller-skates, running up and down the smooth tarmac paths which crisscrossed this little crack in the concrete urban sprawl.

I wanted to join the roller-skating, but I knew I could never afford the skates. Yet I was so desperate to belong—to belong to anything, really. It was so important for me to join the club and be accepted, instead of always being on the fringe, standing there, and just watching from the sidelines on my own.

I went home and asked my Dad for some roller-skates for my birthday. He promised, and I was full of hope. After weeks of watching the other children skating up and down, October 30th arrived: it was my birthday! I raced home from school so excited. I rushed around looking to see if Dad had got the roller-skates. But he hadn't got in yet, and so I sat at my bedroom window and waited for him to get home. I thought he must have been late because he had to go and buy my birthday present.

I dozed off on my bed, until awoken by the slamming of the front door. Dad was home!

As he came into the hallway I bounded down the stairs and was still rubbing my eyes when I reached him.

I sensed something was wrong—I didn't know what, but somehow I knew. He didn't smile. I sensed something was coming—I felt it. But he *had* a parcel.

Shivering with excitement, I stared at the parcel in his hands. Was this really it? Really roller-skates in his hand? Maybe I was wrong in my feelings. I wasn't always right. But I knew I was right an awful lot of the time. I had to be, otherwise we didn't eat.

Standing by the door, Dad hesitated, then held back as if the parcel was about to explode in his face. It was the size of a shoebox, all wrapped up with newspaper and tied with a string. He held it out for me to take. I impetuously accepted it from him and felt the weight.

Turning away, he hurried into the kitchen where Mum was cooking mashed potato. I didn't have a good feeling about that.

I expected it to be heavy. It wasn't. It was so light that I was convinced it was empty, but then I thought that he had put some money in it for me to buy the skates, a postal order or something.

The familiar smell of drink still lingered in the air. Rum and Blackcurrant, I think it was. Usually that would have been a good sign, like he had won on the dogs, but now I wasn't so sure. I opened the parcel and peered inside. There was a packet all wrapped up, and when I opened that a pair of white long bootlaces fell out.

I followed him into the kitchen. "Why have I got Laces?"

For a moment he smiled, lurched to one side bracing himself against the wall, and then—suddenly he must have seen the look on my face.

"I'm shorry love. I couldn't afford the skates, so I got the laces. I promisch I'll get yer the skates another time." He tried to steady himself.

I stared at him, and went right up to his face.

"What's this, what's this? I wanted the *skates*. Why have I got the laces? Why?"

Silence.

He just looked at me blankly, but I wasn't going to let him get away with it.

"How could you? How *could* you?" I smacked him with my little fist, but he took no notice. He just stood there and let me swing at him.

"I'm shorry love."

"Why have I got laces—come on, tell me, *why*?"

"I'm sorry."

"Don't you see," I bellowed, "I can't join in… I can't join in with just laces!" I shouted louder: "I've told everybody that I am getting skates!" I paused to draw breath, "Don't you understand?"

"Sorry."

"Don't you understand, I can't join in with laces?" I gritted my teeth with anger. "I told everyone I am getting skates."

He tried to sneak off into the living room out of the way, but I wouldn't let him.

"I can't have fun with laces, I look silly. You've shown me up and I hate you!" I lost it and kicked the table in my upset. "They will ask me where my skates are. What am I going to say now?"

He was about to say something, but I didn't give him the chance.

"Can't you see that I will have to stand there and watch them!" I banged my fist on the table until the cups clattered. "I can't be normal, I can't join in, and I will look silly."

"Sorry."

"It would have been better if you had got me nothing. Don't you understand how silly I will look? I can't go skating with laces!"

He reached out to hold and cuddle me, but I pushed him away through my frustrated tears. I was so angry.

I turned and ran up the stairs to my bedroom and slammed the door as hard as I could. I threw myself on my pillow and banged my fist into it as hard as I could until I lay exhausted in my upset.

I couldn't believe that I fell for it; trusted my Dad for a moment—when the whole of my body and mind was telling me he would let me down; and yet within me there was some part of my stupid brain still clinging to the faith in my Dad.

I was devastated, but worse still was what I had told all my friends at school, that I was getting skates for my birthday! I talked it up to boost my confidence and try to keep the friendships going.

"I told them, I told them," I cried to myself. "Why did I let myself tell them?" I tasted that familiar torrent of salt running down my face that burnt into my very soul, each drop of poison slowly killing any hope for my little life. I plunged into a spiral of despair.

"I won't make any friends now!"

I glanced up at the mirror and saw the reflection of my blotchy red face. If I could snap my fingers and end it all there I would have done. If someone had given me a pill and told me I could go to sleep for ever, I think I would have taken it.

My life fell apart, like the shattering of a mirror, and in an instant the hurt and the upset rushed into me so suddenly that it felt like I had been shot—so great was the pain I felt inside. How would I face my friends now?

During my sobbing I wondered if it was always to be this way for me, to be different from my friends at school? It was as if I had some horrible disease that seeped into every part of my life, and no matter how hard I tried to stop it spreading, it always managed to break through.

I so desperately wanted to fit in and be accepted, yet rejection was still with me and I could not shake it off no matter how hard I tried.

I had only one choice—and that is the choice I made. I kept it inside—bottled it up and swallowed hard. I kept the secrets.

I found some roller-skates later in a junkshop that I remember had a ticket for 6/- (6 shillings) and I managed to buy them myself. Of course the shame of not getting them at the time didn't go away. But at least I had them. That was the important thing I told myself.

For a brief moment I was happy to play in the street skating up and down until one day, as all the boys and girls did in those days, I wanted more. I wanted to go to Alexandra Palace where they had a roller-skating rink. There was a bunch of us who were all going there and I was so excited that I put them on during the bus ride up there. But when I got there I couldn't skate. They told me that because my skates didn't have a rubber stopper at the front, they couldn't let me use them, which perhaps goes some way to explain why they were in the junk shop in the first place.

I got used to my life as it kept repeating itself in a continuous cycle of disappointments relieved only by brief moments of happiness. The trouble was that the brief moments of happiness were getting fewer.

9

Senior school

LEAVING ST JAMES CHURCH SCHOOL for my new senior school was a big jump for me, not only because there were so many more people, but also because I had to cross Fore Street, Edmonton—a busy main road between Silver Street and Seven Sisters Road. Even in those days it was full of buses, cars and lorries all making their way from the North Circular Road.

I was feeling rather sorry for myself. Mum had been flustered getting me ready on my first day. I was ready, but Mum insisted on finishing her fag, and then after all of that she didn't come. Perhaps she thought she ought to take me, and then feeling that she didn't want to be seen by the other parents, she thought better of it.

She shrank back into the house and then, feeling embarrassed and awkward that she had made me late with all her indecision, she sort of shoved me out, and then promptly slammed the door behind me. I felt as if I had been kicked out like the cat.

Being late was a regular occurrence with Mum, and it was little surprise that I had to run all the way along Grove Street, arriving in all the chaos of the London rush hour. The roar of the traffic and screeching of brakes were a little unsettling the first time, although I was determined not to show it. I stumbled up to the curb and waited for the traffic lights to change. I had all the feelings of worry and trepidation, and like all the other children I felt vulnerable.

A trolley bus came in front of me moving slowly, passengers clinging to the platform pole like firemen on a shout.

Ding, ding.

The clippie in her uniform was ringing the bell. The passengers, with their umbrellas, their briefcases, were packed in with things I couldn't tell. A motorbike backfired. I jumped back. I was going to have to get used to this busy stream of traffic every day.

There was a tall, dark haired lady on my side of the road. She was dressed in a nice white coat and matching hat, and as she stood there; she held firmly her daughter's hand.

I stared at her. She looked so beautiful, so fresh, and so clean that I swear I could still smell the faintest hint of her perfumed soap on the air. My mind snapped with hurtful thoughts about my Mum. It upset me. It dawned on me that there were people who couldn't stand the sight of beauty.

I forced myself to move away. I couldn't let myself get too close to the longing. It was eating me away inside. It was enough that I felt forgotten and alone. I felt like an apple with two maggots inside.

If Mum had been there she would have called her 'stuck up', although I didn't see anything stuck up about her; I thought she was just very smart. The little girl looked a little snooty though, clutching her little wooden pencil case and standing in her nice new black leather shoes. She had pretty girls' shoes. Not like mine. They were clumsy boys' shoes: clodhoppers.

Lost in my own thoughts, I watched how the lady behaved. I found myself comparing her with my Mum; checking, searching and yearning to understand what a normal mum was. Mum was different to other mums, and I wondered if I was different in some way.

Although Mum had convinced me that the way we lived was normal I knew in my heart that it wasn't. Yet I simply couldn't resist comparing our ways to the ways of others.

I began to notice more of the world around me as my horizons opened up. The hospital, the Home, and the wedding, all showed me different sides of people. They all stretched the stark contrast between my family and others with whom I came into contact. I knew that some of my neighbours didn't celebrate Christmas because they were Jehovah's Witnesses, but apart from that, everybody else at school did; so why didn't we have Christmas?

Easter was just the same. Life was just as desperate. Nothing changed really, no Easter Eggs or anything like that, except that to some extent I was worse off because I didn't get the free school milk. Mum would be at home on Good Friday and yet spent most of the day round her friend Lill's. I didn't know what they got up to, but I would be left on my own in the house with Jane most of the time.

I hated it when the teacher asked the class to write about what we did for Christmas. I couldn't write anything. We didn't have Christmas like other kids. No decorations, no tree, no presents or anything proper. If I was lucky we had bangers, boiled potatoes with gravy, and tinned Farrows peas. Sometimes Dad might have scrounged a couple of comics for me, *Beezer* or *Topper*, but that was about it.

A large lorry rumbled like thunder and belched out a big cloud of blue smoke. The lady and the young girl were by this time standing next to me. Holding her daughter close, she bent down and gave her little girl a big hug and kiss. She took from her handbag a little lace hanky, and then carefully licking it in the corner, she wiped away the lipstick mark from the girl's cheek. The girl gave a little shudder of protest and tried to push her mother away, pretending she was too grown up for that; she didn't want all the fuss, especially not in front of me.

The traffic at last stopped at the lights, and I saw the lady bend down again and give her daughter another big hug. The girl seemed embarrassed, looking back at me; then, pushing her mother away, she confidently walked across the road. I felt she just took her mother's love for granted.

Reaching the pavement on the other side, the girl gazed at me. She looked back at her mum as she waved to her, just as if she were putting on a show for my benefit. For a brief moment I felt hurt and I didn't really understand why. Perhaps it was the realisation that I didn't have a mum to wave back to, and that I was alone. She had a mum who cared.

It occurred to me that love for the little girl I had just watched, didn't depend on how much food she brought from begging for her family.

As time went on and I got older, I began to notice grown up people more closely, watching them interact with each other. Every morning I would study them arriving at the school. If the other mums bumped into each other, they spoke, and they chatted about their kids and they seemed to enjoy exchanging embarrassing stories about what their children got up to. Somehow, I knew inside that my mum was very different from other people's mums. Strange though, I didn't really question what Mum did. I seemed to accept the way she was, even though I noticed it was different. She didn't just avoid other mothers; she actually appeared to be hiding from them.

I told myself I had more freedom than the other kids. My mum didn't care if I stayed out late, and perhaps it made me feel more streetwise.

At Raynham Road School our teacher was Mr Green. Although I felt a bit lost in the new big school, he really helped me to settle in. I liked him because he was one of the few people I felt had time for me, and I was also eager to learn and do well. Because we all came from a church school they seemed automatically to put us into the 'B' class.

I was quite a bright young thing and would always chat to the teachers in my class. I thought this would be my chance to make new friends, and for once in my life they wouldn't automatically know where I lived; they wouldn't know about the poverty and all that came with it. I thought that if my friends' mums knew about me they wouldn't let their children play with me again, so it was better they didn't know. What little girl would want their friends to see Dad staggering home drunk, or my Mum and Dad shouting and swearing at each other, as if they were on a stage playing it out for the benefit of the neighbours?

My sister Jane used to go to a nursery in Lower Edmonton, and soon it was up to me to pick her up after school. I really didn't want to do it as I was looking forward to making new friends and going round their houses and playing out. It wasn't as if the nursery was on the way home. I would get out of school at 4 p.m. and have to run all the way to Fore Street and wait for a bus to get me there, pick her up and bring her back home and then, after all that, I would have to baby-sit until Mum got home.

I was glad when Jane was old enough to go to school, and she got a place at the local primary part of my school. At least I didn't have to get the bus to pick her up, so I was pleased about that—although I still had to fetch her from the Infants. She got out of school at 3:30 p.m. and so she had to wait in the school playground covered seating area. I say seating area, although I seem to remember it was just a corrugated roof with a bench underneath.

Mr Green was a nice teacher and I enjoyed his lessons, and then, six months later I was put into Miss Dee's class: she was very strict. If we were misbehaving she would come round and smack the back of our legs with her ruler. On another occasion she kept the class behind as long as twenty minutes, until people stopped talking.

I watched as the clock ticked past 4:00 p.m., then past 4:20 p.m. I was too frightened to tell her that I had to pick up my sister, and I started to worry about Jane being left all alone in the school playground. If I told the teacher I had to pick her up, she may well have stopped Jane waiting in the playground for me, and I didn't want that! She would have only been about four and a half years old and Mum would have killed me if anything happened to her.

Eventually Miss Dee let us go and I remember running for all my life to reach Jane's school playground, just in time to stop Jane wandering in the other direction. I guess she had given up on me and tried to walk home alone. Luckily I was able to call her and stop her in her tracks.

Staying in the convalescent home made me realise that other people actually had clean sheets on their beds once a week. I remembered how fresh they would smell, all crisp and clean. I never did get used to the dirty sheets on my bed. To me it was horrible. I couldn't live in that state, and despite my nagging, my mum refused to wash them, leaving them until they were absolutely disgusting. I didn't know how she could have left me in the filth of it—she just didn't seem to care that I found it a problem; to her it appeared normal, yet I knew she wasn't brought up like that. Her parents were posh, owned a house in Chiswick, she went to a private school, and was the youngest daughter of a family of master bakers. On the rare occasion I went to her mother's home, my paternal grandmother's, it was plush, and oozed the quality of furnishing I would have died for. I saw no excuse for the way she treated me; she must have known better, yet everything from her was an embarrassment. She didn't seem to understand a young girl's needs and found it awkward to talk about, until one day as I was going back to school at lunchtime, she just opened the door after I had left and shouted out at me: "You'll get your periods soon!" Then she promptly shut the door again. I didn't understand why she said it. When I spoke to her about my periods, personal things and what to do, she just shrugged her shoulders and wouldn't talk about it, and I was left to figure it out on my own.

I think we had a lesson at school about periods and things. They showed us a cine film and I learned about it all from that. A friend gave me a Tampax, but without the instructions, so I didn't know what to do with it. I got a little scared that there was something wrong with me.

I told my Dad I needed some money. I didn't tell him exactly, but I intimated that I had a problem. He seemed to cotton on straight away. I didn't have to explain further. So he gave me some money to sort myself out there and then. I rushed round the chemist and bought a box of my own so I could read the instructions and figure out how to use them.

That was my Dad. When he was sober he was in tune with me as a little girl, much more than Mum ever was, and somehow I never did understand that. There was a soft caring side to Dad, which softened the hardship and made me love him.

With this seesaw of support it was little wonder my personal hygiene would come into question from time to time, with my friends at school. As I went through puberty I found, as most girls do, that my underwear needed to be changed on a regular basis. Not only that, but I found I now needed a bath at least once a week, and some deodorants. But it was impossible to get my mum to give me anything, and I soon realised she wasn't going to help me.

I used to have to go to the chemist and get Dr Whites towels and Mum told me to bag them up and put them under the bed. When Dad came home one day they had a terrible row. He said I couldn't just put them under the bed—I had to burn them. So after that I didn't take any notice of my mum. I bagged them up securely, and Dad showed my how to take them down the end of the block and put them down the rubbish chute. Dad was there for me during this time, but he was like a chocolate soldier in the sun. The help would soon collapse in a little puddle.

The next day I decided there was going to be no other way of doing it—I would have to earn some money.

I started to run errands for the lady next door, by taking her washing up to the Chinese Laundry. She was a kindly lady and I didn't know if she knew how I lived, but she gave me a shilling each time. (Five pence in today's money.) Determined to do something about it, the very next Saturday I walked up and down Silver Street, and eventually found a modern Launderette that had just opened up. It was just what I was looking for, fresh and clean with a line of modern front-loading washing machines with chairs, tables, and baskets for holding the washing.

Brilliant, I thought! I would no longer have to put up with the filth ever again. I would be able to have clean fresh clothes all the time. Finally I would be able to escape and live the way I wanted; I wasn't like my mum, and I wasn't going to put up with the way the family lived any longer. It was the start of asserting my independence, and I was determined I was not going backwards.

With my spirits high, I gathered my dirty clothes and disgusting sheets and walked to the laundrette. Pushing open the door, I was struck by the hot strong smell of washing powder, and of bubbles that wafted up from the machines, although I wasn't sure if bubbles could smell; however, I loved it! The lady supervisor was really helpful: she answered any questions I asked, then showed me how to put my money in the slot and load the machine with powder. She told me all about the various washes and how to sort my clothes out into different piles, depending on the colour, material and temperature to wash them on.

The shop was bustling, full of people all chatting away like a Saturday market, all sitting there staring at their underwear going round and round in the soap and bubbles. The sloshing noise of the wet clothes in drums, masked amongst the babbling crowd… it was just what I needed, a real morale booster, and I started to look forward to going with my laundry every Saturday morning. Sad, isn't it? It was like a second home, with all the ladies chatting to me, and taking an interest in helping me. I felt a sense of belonging that I didn't get at home.

Despite all the nagging and pleading at home, it was still impossible to get a bath. We had one in the house, with running water and everything, but Mum would complain that she had no money for the meter—again, saying it was all my father's fault because he had raided the gas meter for his drinking the night before. She told me that if I wanted a bath at home, I would have to give her half a crown. The only way I was going to be able to afford that, was by taking on more jobs.

Later I met one of the other girls at school, Janet, and we were chatting away, and I told her about my problem of getting a bath when she suddenly told me that she didn't have a bath at home either. It was the first time that I met someone who shared the same problem! The difference was that her mum cared about her and kept her clean. Her family must have been equally as poor as us because I seem to remember that her family used to live with their grandmother. I was interested in how she managed without a bath and so I asked her what she did.

"Just behind Edmonton Town Hall," Janet said.

"Yeah, really? Well, I haven't seen it."

"Well," she turned to point up to Fore Street, "next to the Town Hall is Edmonton swimming pool, right?"

"Yeah. Well, okay, I've been in there."

"Yeah, so that's…" a motorbike thundered past and her words were blown away "…where it is."

"What?" I couldn't hear. "In the actual swimming pool?"

"No, no," she shook her head, "not in the actual swimming pool yer daft happeth, it's down a little corridor off to the side."

"Ole right."

"Well, look," she said, "if you go in there you pay a shilling, yeah? Like you would if you were going swimming, right?" She paused for a moment and came closer. "And then you just ask for a bath."

"I haven't seen any baths in the swimming pool."

She laughed and stood there shaking her head. "They're in there, Mary. I should know. God, I use them each week."

"How will I know where the baths are?"

"What do 'er mean?"

"Like where are they, where do I go?"

"Yer go in the main entrance like, and turn right through a door and give the geezer a shilling. Tell 'em you want a bath and they will give you a load of fluffy white towels, show you where everything is, soap and stuff, yeah."

"That's it?"

"Yeah, that's it."

"So when's it open then?"

"You'll see the opening time on the board as you go in. Same as the swimming times."

"Right, thanks," I said, then turning to go, "Won't other people be using the bath at the same time though?"

"Yeah, but don't be daft. You have your own room, your own bath, and you'll lock the door. Right?"

That did it for me—I was sold on the idea! "Right," I said, "Thanks, that's really great."

I skipped home on cloud nine: problem solved. I was so very happy that day. I couldn't wait, and I remember vividly the lovely smell of freshness from the fluffy white towels. The spotlessly clean white tiles all decked out with hooks, and bath mats on the floor. I was in heaven. I loved running the bath with lashings of piping hot water, soaking in the soap and bubble baths for as long as I wanted. It was all part of the deal for a shilling!

In spite of the hardship, life began to improve with my Mum working again, and for a short time, armed with my new-found friends from school, I was happy.

The cinema was only a short walk from the house and on Saturdays my friends started knocking, asking me to go to the Saturday morning pictures. Persuading Dad to give me a shilling was difficult at the best of times, although I found it became much easier if I arranged for my friends to be waiting on the doorstep, shouting for me to hurry up. There were a mixture of boys and girls.

For some reason I remember that Mum would insist in putting a wave in my hair. I liked the idea she was showing some interest in me, but I found it irritating. I was getting to an age where I wanted to do things myself and, like all young girls, I wanted to look like everyone else. I was growing up and, like everything she did, it would take so long that it would end up making us all late.

Often we would have to take the shortcut to the cinema, down an alley and along to a wall that was about three feet high. It was a little scary, because over the other side the ground dropped six feet onto a stone pavement. Two boys would wait for me and help me over, then we would all scamper off getting to the cinema just in time. Sometimes one boy would go and pay to get in, and then the rest of us would sneak in through the exit door for free.

I quite enjoyed life for a while, playing with my friends and for once we had enough money and I didn't have to beg for food in the shops. I thought that all the hardship and hunger were behind me. I felt quite grown up and life seemed better, but like everything in my life it was a fragile balance.

It wasn't long before my whole world was to fall apart.

10

TB

MUM ALWAYS HAD TO GO TO THE HOSPITAL for regular X-rays as her sister had died of Tuberculosis (TB) some years earlier. So when Dad told me that Mum had to go to St Ann's Hospital, I didn't think anymore about it. Life for me was a succession of ups and downs. It wasn't all downs, and it wasn't all ups. It lurched from one to the other with frequently more downs than ups.

There were rare moments when Mum got a job. In those up moments Mum would give us breast of lamb, rice pudding and the like, but more often than not, she didn't work and we were left in poverty and porridge. I was worried whenever Mum went to the hospital because without Mum, there weren't any ups at all. I lived in hope, because I refused to look at it in any other way.

I toddled off to school on the morning of Tuesday 13th September 1960, wondering if she would be home in a few hours. It was lunchtime as I turned the corner into Langhedge Lane. An ambulance stood at the end of the block. It was just waiting there, the driver sitting in the cab.

I walked in the house as normal, and trotted up the hallway. There was a lot of thumping and banging in the living room and I wondered what was going on. I peeped around the living room door.

Dad was standing next to an old battered half empty suitcase. The lid was laid open, and I could see some of Mum's clothes lying in a heap. He looked sheepish, as if he were caught in the act of something he didn't want me to see. For a moment I didn't understand what was going on. I know it sounds silly, but I didn't really connect the ambulance that stood at the end of the block, with the suitcase: I didn't know what to make of it. I knew my mum was cold and distant towards me, but she was my Mum! I didn't understand why she was leaving home.

I quickly glanced around the living room. "Where's Mum?" I asked. I walked towards Dad. He bent down, put his hands on my shoulders and spoke tenderly to me.

"She's in the kitchen, love."

Dad was sober. I mean, he was shaved, dressed smart and there wasn't a hint of booze on him. I knew straightaway that something was wrong.

I ran into the kitchen. She looked up at me, her face stained with tears. Then she blurted out, one line at a time. "I'm going to St Ann's." She tried to dry her eyes with a hanky.

"Why Mum?" It was the first time I had seen my mother cry for something other than being beaten up by Dad, and I really didn't know what to think.

There was a strange silence.

Cough, cough. She put another hanky to her mouth.

"Tuberculosis (TB)—yeah." She drew a breath like she was sucking on a straw.

Cough, cough, splutter, wheeze.

"Be away a few months—yeah," she said. "Isolation ward." She doubled up, struggling to get her breath. As she pulled the handkerchief from her face, I thought how pretty the hanky was with its bright crimson spots.

We didn't have any pretty hankies.

Then I saw that the red spots were blood. I gasped!

Now I was frightened. No, *really* frightened, and instead of crying for myself, I felt like crying because I was losing my mum.

My little mind had just cottoned on to what was happening. The ambulance was for *her*.

I really was losing my mum.

I had lost Les, and now this terrifying disease had moved into the house to take his place. I didn't know what TB was, but I had seen what it could do. Mum's sister died from it. She was in the ground, buried in the cemetery, dead and gone to heaven.

"Oh, no! Not again," I cried. I couldn't bear it again.

My world fell apart after Les left. I had to start begging from the shops to feed the family, and now it was all happening again. I was going down into a pit of despair and it was all too much for me. I didn't understand anything anymore. I so wanted to cry and sob, but the urge to cry just dried up.

It was like every time something like this happened in my life it would leave a little scar. I could powder over it with makeup, to hide and bury the hurt, but still it would be there. Every now and then, something would happen to blow my powder away, exposing all the raw hurt underneath and I would be left, worthless and alone once more. What had I done that was so dreadful? I wondered if I was paying the price for someone else's misdeeds? I felt so mixed up in my mind. So many questions left unanswered. I stood motionless: I felt both worried and frightened at the same time, my mind spinning in a whirlwind of haze. When would it end? It was as if an invisible blanket had come between me and the outside world.

The North Middlesex Hospital was only a ten minute walk away—I didn't know about St Ann's.

"Where's the hospital?"

Mum looked up at me from the kitchen chair by the stove. She went through another fit of crying and coughing and, not wanting to risk another coughing fit, she silently beckoned to the note lying on the table. I picked it up and read it.

On one side there was a list of routes by bus and train. I turned it over and saw a simple line drawing that looked like a map.

Sitting down at the kitchen table, I studied it for a few moments trying to work out how far it was. I didn't recognise any of the numbers of the buses or the names of the roads because I never went to London on my own. Most of the time I would go into Edmonton, which was in the other direction. I recognised Seven Sisters Station. It showed the road leading to St Ann's and suddenly I could see that it was at least two train stops from Silver Street Station. At least five miles away. I couldn't walk and visit her there. It would be too far. It would use all my pocket money and I had only just managed to do my laundry, and I was blowed if I was going to give that up. I went back to speak to Dad in the living room.

Suddenly I began to feel strange. Light headed, I reached for the chair. It was the first time I had seen my mum so upset. I couldn't tell if she was crying for us, or herself, but I gave her the benefit of the doubt; she had watched her sister die from TB.

I sat there quietly for a moment whilst Dad carried on packing, until I felt a little better. I slipped back into the kitchen to see how Mum was.

"I've gotta go to the Isolation ward," she muttered, "because—you might catch it—see." She was trying not to cough again.

"What's happening?"

"Yer father will cook yer meals, and," *cough, cough,* "you'll have to look after Jane."

I heard the suitcase snap shut.

The ambulance crew came in and I was brushed aside as they helped Mum out of the house and into the ambulance. Dad left with them to the hospital. The house fell silent and I was left alone.

I went back to school that afternoon and tried to join in with my class. I bumped into Mr Green in the corridor, and as I walked on, he called me back.

"Mary, Mary, come back here."

"Yes Sir." I slowly turned and walked back to face him as the other children brushed past.

"Whatever is the matter with you today, Mary?" he asked.

"Nothing Sir," I said.

I may have been only young but I was one step ahead of him now. I knew that if I told him anything there would be a problem. I didn't want the social workers coming round otherwise I might be taken into care, or something equally frightening.

"You look very pale. Are you sure you're all right?"

"Yes Sir," I sighed. "Just a bit tired Sir."

He bent down and looked at my face. Could he tell I had been crying?

"Red eyes. Too many late nights, I shouldn't wonder. Get an early night. You need it." He waved me away and carried on walking back to the staff room.

He was right; I couldn't concentrate on anything. My mind was a bag of racing worry, but what could I do? I had to soldier on. As I had done so many times before.

The next few days went fine and life carried on much as normal. There was still some food in the cupboard and if I nagged Dad, he would give me half a crown.

I picked Jane up from her school as usual and made dinner most nights in the first week that Mum was away. One day I came home and found there wasn't enough for Jane to eat, never mind the rest of us! She whined and moaned about being hungry. I sat her in the kitchen, gave her a rusk I had found in the cupboard, and made her a drink to keep her quiet. Then I went upstairs and got her some comics that I had stashed in my bedroom.

"Now you stay here," I said, shoving a pile of comics on the kitchen table.

She looked up and nodded before dipping her nose into her cup.

"I'm just going round the shops for some food, and I'll be back in a minute—all right?"

She dragged a comic across the table and dropped her cup on it, then looking up at me she just watched me leave the kitchen. I glanced back and watched her, sitting there swinging her feet against the chair busily lost in her comic once more. I suppose I was a little uncomfortable leaving her on her own, but I didn't have a choice: Dad wasn't home.

I scampered out of the house and down to Lee's corner shop nearby. I managed to get some jacket potatoes and some hard cheese. It had only been about ten or fifteen minutes at the most, but by the time I got back, I found the house empty. There was no sign of Jane—she had disappeared; she was only four years old.

Panic set in. I called out for her, but got no reply. I desperately searched upstairs, pushing open each door, peering under beds, and looking in all cupboards. I searched the toilet and thought that perhaps she had got locked in, or maybe she had fallen in and drowned in the bath.

Frantically searching through the house from room to room, I couldn't think straight. Had the rent man called and had she accidentally locked herself in somewhere? The under stairs cupboard had a little latch which would drop down and lock on its own. I checked—not there! Then the kitchen. I didn't have to check the fridge because we didn't have one, but I did look in the larder, then finally, the living room—she wasn't there.

Bursting out of the back door and into the garden I raced up and down the alley, over Grove Street, and then back down the lane toward the railway. Nothing!

It was getting late. I began to cry. I blamed myself for not taking Jane to the shops with me. Why didn't I think to take her with me? I kept asking myself this question over and over again.

I was running in circles, calling her name until my throat hurt. I searched all the places I knew. Out in the coal shed, over by the church and I even went back to my old junior school, I was so desperate. It didn't seem to matter how hard I searched, she was nowhere to be seen. I didn't want to give up, but I didn't know what else to do.

I thought, perhaps she had been taken by someone, or run away from home or something. I just didn't know. I reasoned that if she had run off she would have talked to me about it on the way home from school; she would have said something about it to me, I was sure of it.

No, I thought, she wouldn't have run away; after all, where would she go?

Then I thought that if she had been taken she would have screamed the place down, and so I ruled that one out. At the end of all my thinking, the only explanation I could come up with, was that she must have wandered off with a friend. The problem with that theory was that she didn't have many friends around where we lived. I didn't know where to look anymore. I didn't think she would go off on her own—she was too young. I ran out of ideas and I didn't see anyone else to ask, until I spotted a young girl my age walking across the green.

"Hello," I said. "My name is Mary. I live just over there." I pointed to my block. "I'm looking for my little sister, Jane, and I wonder if you have seen a little girl wandering on her own?"

"Nay, I have seen naebody, nere a wee bairn. I've jist come down from Scotland, and I doona know anybody. My name is Joyce."

"So you haven't seen a little girl then?" I thought I would try again, thinking she came from a special school or something.

"Nay," she said, "I've na seen a wee girl." That was a waste of time I thought: obviously foreign.

"Thanks." I gave her a little wave and turned away.

It was getting very dark and I was starting to get cold. I sat on the grass verge by the old school playground, alone, shivering and sobbing uncontrollably. I sat there, my mind racing and muttering to myself with my face all blotchy and red, my eyes streaming with tears. I just sobbed and sobbed and sobbed. I didn't know how long I sat there. It seemed like a lifetime. My bottom was getting cold from sitting on the damp grass verge, and without a warm coat I was now starting to shiver.

Eventually I had to give up and return home. With a mixture of deep sobs and open loud crying, I sat on the front step, my head in my hands, my lifeless eyes closed and with the familiar taste of salt in my mouth, I was all alone. I dashed inside, up to my bedroom, flinging myself onto my bed, chucking the blanket over me, and burying my head deep into the pillow.

Something woke me, but I thought I was still in a dream. The smell of hot vinegar on chips, and voices from downstairs. Then I realised it wasn't a dream.

I got up and bounced down the stairs, and there was Dad with Jane standing in the hallway arguing over sweets or something. I ran up to him, smacking him and beating him hard with my fists; I was so angry with him.

"Why didn't you *tell* me you were taking Jane with you?" I screamed, flaying out with my hands and banging him hard. "Why didn't you leave me a note or something?"

He seemed startled and held out the bag of Fish and Chips, and then, shoving the bag at me, he gestured for me to take one. I can't remember if he said anything or he was simply overwhelmed by my outrage and the onslaught of my attack.

"Why didn't you tell me?" I shouted at him again, louder than before—and then—I hit him again with my fists. But he just looked down at me, taking no notice of the blows raining down on him, and holding me off with his long arms.

"I've been all over the place looking for her! You bloody sod!"

"Shorry." The stench of Rum and Blackcurrant caught me full in the face. "Thought you might like some Fish and Chips."

He lurched toward me, and then tipping two packets of Smiths Crisps and two wrapped parcels of hot newspaper onto the kitchen table, he shuffled off into the living room with his meal still wrapped up. Jane and I were left to our own devices to unravel the newspaper and get ourselves a drink. We plonked ourselves down at the kitchen table and wolfed the food down, picking up the hot chips with our fingers.

We sat there and tucked into it. I could never resist the sweet smell of vinegar on hot newspaper. It always wafted through the house and seeped into every room. It was proper food, it was hot and I certainly wasn't going to wait for it to cool down. I was so grateful for the food. I was starving hungry and it was such a treat. We both relished the moment, filling our tummies until we were fit to burst.

He must have won 'on the dogs', and had some money for once. Rum was expensive in comparison with a pint of bitter, less than a shilling, and he would only have a 'Rum and Black' when he was flush with money, and the only time he had money, was when he won on the horses or dogs.

Fish and Chips was a fairly easy food to be able to afford if you were very poor, but it didn't seem to work that way in our house. For some reason it was a very rare treat and I can't remember very many times that it happened.

This was just the first week and we had fish and chips. Dad told me that mum would be in hospital for three months. That left eleven weeks of 'missing Mum' to go before she would be home. I wondered if we would have fish and chips every week until then.

I hoped that things would get better. Perhaps Mum had asked someone to look in on us, or Dad had asked Auntie Alice to help us—I didn't know, but lived in hope. Hope... that I could rely on Dad.

11

Hunger

WE LIVED ON DAD'S COOKING for the first two weeks after Mum had gone, and that was okay. But night after night, it was always the same old thing. Dad had stopped giving me any money for school dinners; he knew I didn't like them much, but now I found my diet consisted almost entirely of mashed potato and cheese.

I would come home and find him in the kitchen mashing potatoes in a big heavy saucepan that he sent back from Germany during the war. He would be there, thumping away at it as if he was beating up someone. I didn't mind him mashing up the potato because he was quite good at that. It was much better than the lumpy stuff we had at school.

"Is that our dinner—mashed potato?" I asked. "Is that it?"

"Yeah, there's a piece of cheese in the cupboard." He nodded at the larder. I fetched the cheese and he started to grate it over the top of the potato ready to put in the oven. I wouldn't mind, but he grated all the green mouldy bits into it as well.

My stomach churned at the thought of all that green mould mixed with the potato.

"Ole, Dad, you just grated all the mould into the potato. Look at it." I retched at the sight of it.

"So, it doesn't matter."

"It's revolting." I peered into the pot. "It's revolting. I can't eat that."

"It's all right, you won't notice it when it's all mixed up." He reached over and smothered it with salt.

"Why can't I have a steak and kidney pie, or Spam, like Mum used to bring in?"

"Well, you can't."

"Why not?"

"We can't afford it, so that's it. Now shut up about it— you're getting this."

"Why not? I'll cook it myself if you like."

"No, you'll have the same as what I'm doing. I'm not mucking about just for you. Now get the table ready and the knives and forks from the draw."

"Why don't you give me the money? I'll do the cooking for you, then."

"No, and that's it."

"I don't want this. I want housekeeping money like Mum, so I can get proper shopping. You know, like bread and milk, steak and kidney pies, carrots, and peas. It's no good dishing up potato mash all the time and then giving us porridge for a change."

I stomped my feet. I wanted to beat the pulp out of him and wake him up, but somehow I just didn't have the strength. He knew very well what I was talking about.

He silently looked up: bewildered.

My fingers curled around the plate as I sat down to eat. I could taste bile rising. Tears pooled up in the corners of my eyes, but I didn't say any more.

He rarely fought back when I was angry and I got the impression I was dealing with a wet fish. Although what I found really strange, was that whilst he was more than eager to give Mum or Les a black eye, he never raised his hand to me. It was always Mum who slapped me.

The very next day he came home earlier than usual and disappeared into the kitchen. I thought he had made an effort and things would be different, and that we might get Spam or corned beef. I crept down the stairs, with my stomach reeling.

With eyes wide with expectation, I peeped round the kitchen door. I half expected him to be struggling with the oven. Not a bit of it! There was nothing, not even a loaf of bread or jam. No. He was making porridge! I just looked at him, boiling with rage. After all my nagging and shouting yesterday, I thought that we might get a change. But it wasn't like that at all.

Each day for Dad was like a goldfish going round the bowl. Each lap of the bowl would be the start of the day again, afresh, and it didn't seem to matter what I said or did, it had no effect. It was like the lights were on, but there was nobody at home. I knew the drink used to make him silly, but I couldn't understand why he didn't do anything to help us; after all, he was the adult and although I would soon be twelve, I was still a child!

He was simply out of his depth. Perhaps mash was the only thing he knew how to cook, and the drink had caused him to forget or perhaps he simply couldn't be bothered to bring in anything else. Whatever the reason, we had to have porridge made with water yet again. I didn't know what the truth of it was and I didn't really care, so long as the cooking improved and we had something to eat.

I found myself pleading with him. "Come on, Dad, we need to eat more than just porridge. Can you bring in some proper food tomorrow? I'll cook it; if you get some potatoes and carrots, steak and kidney pies, or Spam or something? Pleeeeeeaaaaaasssssse!"

I asked him nicely and hoped that I could appeal to his caring side.

The next day I came home from school with hope and optimism, and waited anxiously for him to come home. He ambled in at 6 o'clock with nothing again.

"Not again! I don't believe it!" I shouted at him and beat him with my fists as hard as I could. I lost it completely, jumping up and down and banging my feet against the table with such force that it toppled over and crashed against the cooker. I pulled it back up and set it straight, before picking off the splintered wood in the hope of calming myself. But it was no use—I was just as annoyed, my rage just as furious, and I stood and screamed at him.

"Why haven't you brought us anything to eat?" I swung at him, but he just put his hand up and held my arm, and in the scuffles that followed I knocked off his glasses, sending them spinning across the kitchen floor. He walked over and picked them up and then he just sat there, in the kitchen, and looked at me like a little child lost.

"I am so sick of potato and cheese! Why can't we have proper food?" I punched and kicked him, but he just got up and pulled down a packet of porridge oats, thumping it down on the kitchen table.

That was it. He had had enough. He simply lurched out of the kitchen, collapsing into his chair in the living room, and closing his eyes to the problem.

I followed him, grabbing hold of his jacket. I went right up to his face, and exploded with an onslaught!

"I want to see Mum, I want to see Mum up the hospital— and if she dies—if she dies, it will be all your fault!" I spat in his face, and this time I was determined not to let him go to sleep and fob me off. "Give me some money for the bus fare," I said, but he just lay there in his drunken stupor.

I was determined I wouldn't be beaten and so I went through his pockets, finding old betting slips and bits of fluff, until eventually I found a shilling (five pence). But it wasn't as if that was the end of my dilemma, because, although I now had some money, it wasn't much.

What do I do with it? It would buy a loaf of bread or a pint of mild ale for Dad, or some school dinners for Jane. Her dinner money was half a crown a week. Do I spend it on the bus fare to the hospital?

"Oh! What should I do? What should I do?" Pacing up and down, I started to argue with myself. "What was best?" I needed someone to help me decide—but there was no one. I was all alone—just Jane and me. I put the shilling on the table and looked at it.

It didn't help.

Should I pay Jane's dinner money? At least I wouldn't have to worry about her for another day, and that would be one less problem for me. With any luck I could scrounge the rest of her dinner money from Dad tomorrow. All I had to do then would be to feed myself.

"Yes, that's it." Decision made.

I rushed to give her the money for the morning, so that I didn't have a chance to change my mind. I wrapped it in a note and gave it to her, and told her to put it in her coat pocket for the morning. Then I got myself to bed.

Each day after that I would go through Dad's pockets until I found some money. It was no good nagging him as it seemed to have no affect once the drink had got to him. I didn't have the option of catching him before he got to the pub because I had to pick Jane up from school. So there really was nothing more I could do.

I lived hand to mouth, eating sometimes, and then not at others, most of the time living on porridge and the free milk I got from school. Sometimes I had a thrupenny bit. It was a funny twelve-sided brass coin worth about 3d (one penny today). I would buy a packet of Spangles with it. They were boiled sweets, about half an inch square, the thickness of a beer mat. Each sweet was individually wrapped in paper, and then the collection wrapped to make a stick about two and one half inches long. I would suck one and let the flavour explode on my tongue. It was a waste of money, in the sense that it didn't contribute to a meal;

but if I didn't have the energy or feel good enough about myself, then I realised we would both be done for.

Sometimes Dad would be home at six, seven o'clock, or much later, after I had gone to bed.

I decided on a new approach. Getting Dad to do something didn't work. It simply didn't get anywhere at all. His mind was so screwed up with the drink it was like dealing with a baby. I made the decision to do everything myself. I would do whatever it took to feed myself, and little Jane. I was not going to depend on anyone anymore. I wasn't a quitter and I wasn't going to let them win. It wasn't just the anger at my Dad because I started to realise my Mother was just as bad. Why hadn't she arranged something with some of the family? There was enough of them living in London at the time—Auntie Alice, Uncle Les, Uncle Ron, Auntie Hilda, Uncle Tommy, Uncle Bobby, Uncle Alfred. Where were they when I was alone?

Perhaps it was because of the way I had to stand up for myself, or perhaps it was the sheer fright that I might lose my Mother to TB, I didn't know. It was now a few weeks or so since she went into hospital, and after an awful lot of nagging and rummaging through Dad's pockets, I finally managed to get the bus fare.

Every day I was coming home to an empty house, laying the fire, getting the coal in, getting the shopping, making the dinner, and then finally doing the washing up.

Teachers asked for my homework. Homework? By the time I had got Jane to bed my day was done; I was exhausted and had no trouble sleeping, no matter how cold it was.

I started to wonder when Mum was going to come home. I couldn't live like this any longer, and besides, the food that Dad was giving me was playing havoc with my tummy. I had to find out. I couldn't wait any longer.

I brought Jane home from school, and finding Dad home early I took the opportunity to tell him I was going to visit

Mum. With the money I had managed to scrounge out of his pockets, I left Jane with him, ran up to Fore Street, and caught the bus to Seven Sisters Road. It took me to St Ann's Hospital in time for visiting. I got off the bus just outside the hospital and, following the signs through the maze of old corridors, I managed to find the ward for 'Infectious Diseases'. I grabbed one of the nurses and asked where my Mum was. She took me to the desk, and I waited whilst she searched through a list of names. Finding my mother's name on the list, she quickly showed me into her room.

Gingerly I poked my head round the door, worried that she might tell me off for coming on my own. But despite my fears, she was very pleased to see me.

"Hello Mum."

"Oh, hello love! You on your own?"

I let the question go unanswered.

She kept asking how I was getting on and did I have enough money for food and the electric meter. I didn't tell her exactly the problems I had extracting money from Dad, and I thought it best not to tell her what really was going on. I wanted her to get better and I thought that if she worried, it would stop her coming home early.

She was in a room all alone in her old iron framed hospital bed. Apart from the side cabinet and some newspapers on a chair nearby, there was nothing else. I sat on the bed.

"How are you then Mum?" It was a silly question as she looked very pale. Her hair was lifeless, like her eyes. No shine. Then I realised that she wasn't wearing her glasses. I reached over to the side cabinet and put them in her hand and she put them on.

"Thank you love, that's better." She held a hanky over her mouth as she spoke.

"Are you getting any better?" I had to ask. She looked worse to me.

"Yeah, they've started me on this gold treatment, very expensive they tell me."

"So when are you coming home?" I didn't spare her feelings with chitchat. I wanted to know.

"I don't know. They talk about three months in all," she said, reaching for her drinking glass. It was empty, so I filled it for her and waited whilst she took a sip.

"Three months?" I felt my little shoulders slump. "How many weeks is that?"

"About December, I think."

"Yes Mum, I know, but how many weeks? How many, Mum?" I desperately wanted to know so that I could count them down. I felt like a castaway, as if I had to cross off the weeks to keep me sane.

"Well, I don't know." She started counting on her fingers. "About thirteen weeks, isn't it?"

"Thirteen weeks. So we have about ten to go then?" I felt as if my head had sunk down to my boots. The time was too long. I stifled a tear, pushing it down and turning away for a moment to hide my face from her. I didn't know if I could last that long.

"Yeah, I guess it is."

I recomposed my face, hiding my fear. "Won't they let you out earlier if you do well?"

"No love, they won't let me out because other people will catch it."

She reached over for her glass again, almost tipping it over me in the process. Irritated, I took it from her and got a tray from the side cabinet nearby, setting it down on her lap. She put down her hanky, and took a little sip of water before looking back up at me.

"Does other people mean...?" The glass clattered back down on the tray, interrupting my thoughts. "Could I, or Jane catch it?" I asked.

"Well yeah, that's why Dad has arranged for you to have a vaccination."

"What's a vaccination?"

"It's an injection the doctor will give you."

"Well, no, he hasn't." I shook my head from side to side. Now I knew for sure. It would be up to me to fend for myself from now on.

"What do yer mean?"

"I mean that he hasn't done anything. That's what I mean!"

"You should have had a letter to make an appointment at the doctors."

"Well, I haven't. So what should I do?" I raised my hands as if to show them empty.

"You better remind Dad to do it when you get home. All right?" She grabbed a notepad at the side of her bed. "Do yer want me to write it down?"

I nodded. "Yes Mum."

She scrawled a note, folded it up and gave it to me.

"Thanks Mum," I said. "I have to go now. I promised I would get back to do Jane's tea."

"All right," she said. "Bye love. Nice to see you."

I made the excuse and left. I had found out how long I had to wait for her to come home, and now I knew it was going to be a long time. It made me realise more than anything else, life was going to get tougher than it already was.

In my innocence I still didn't realise how long she would be away. For some reason I thought that if I didn't tell her about Dad, she would be home sooner and things would return to normal.

On reflection, perhaps that was a mistake and I later realised I should have told her earlier—I didn't know—but I didn't understand how bad it was to get.

12

Desperate Times

LIFE CARRIED ON OKAY for another week after my visit to Mum, and I thought that things would return to some sort of normality. I gave Dad the note that Mum had given me, but nothing happened and I guess that it got forgotten.

I had managed to scrounge half a crown from Dad on a regular basis. Nagging at him for food money seemed to work for a while, and I was so happy that the episode of hunger was finally behind me. I continued to buy food from Lee's corner shop, usually fish fingers or Fray Bentos steak and kidney pie. Sometimes I would get Spam or corned beef; anything that didn't need cooking. I didn't know how to do proper cooking, but I knew enough to cook tinned carrots and peas and heat up a tin of Fray Bentos in the oven.

Mum had been away for four weeks now, and I was learning a bit about cooking meals. It was quiet in the house. Jane was lying on her bed, busy with her colouring books, and I was sitting in my bedroom reading a copy of *Judy*, when the front door slammed. It was about four o'clock in the afternoon, and seemed too early for Dad to be home.

I heard a banging on the stairs, and my bedroom door swung wide open.

I jumped up, wondering what was going on. Dad was standing in the doorway, clutching the handle of the door. He shifted to one side, and sort of hung there trying to steady himself.

"Why haven't yer cleaned the house, then?"

"What? What do you mean?"

He was so drunk. The fumes hung in the air like a curtain.

"I give yer the housekeeping—what yer doing with it?"

"What am I doing with it?" I said. "It's not my fault the place is in a mess. I'm at school all day while you're down the pub."

"Well…"

"Well nothing, what time do I have?"

"Well, ish not good…ennuff."

"What do yer mean? You've got a nerve! I spend all the money that you give me on food!"

"Well it ishn't good en..nuff." He was just like a broken record as he stood there, clutching the bedroom door like a drowning man. "You haven't done anything," he said.

I had done everything to keep the family going.

"I'm cooking and feeding you and I've got Jane all the time—she's only little. I'm trying to cope with her all by myself, and that's not easy. I'm not Jane's mother." I heard the echo of my own words, as if hearing them for the first time.

I waited for a reaction, but none came.

"I don't understand…" I felt myself gag with upset. "What do you expect me to *do*?"

"I ex..pect the place to be cleaned. It's filthy." He was slurring his speech badly now.

I walked up to him and spat my words at him, like a flamethrower at the circus.

"Well, why don't you clean it then? I don't have the time."

He struggled to stay attached to the door handle. Suddenly it swung away and there was a little kafuffle as he tried to steady himself.

"It's your job, not mine to look after us," I said. "Why have I got to do everything?"

I cocked my head and forced him to look at me. "Well, isn't it?" I stared straight at his face.

He gave a little cough, and then the corner of his mouth lifted with a half smile. "I'm sorry love, I've lost my job, and I just wanted to have a go. Sorry."

He just scuttled out, staggering off to the toilet. He was still there an hour later. I could hear him snoring. I felt a bit like Mum, let down and worrying about where the next penny was coming from.

It was about 9 p.m. when I went upstairs to put Jane to bed. I knocked on the toilet door to say I wanted to use it. It was unlocked. I opened it gently and peeked in. I was embarrassed and ashamed by what I saw.

I went down and told Jane I was getting her bed ready, and she could read for a bit longer.

Rushing upstairs once more, I found Dad was exactly where I left him hours earlier; sitting on the toilet asleep, his trousers round his ankles and his head slumped down on his chest.

I did what I had to do, took hold of his arms and shook him roughly.

"What, the...?" He started to stir, calling out as if in a dream: "Dummkopf!" I didn't understand what he was saying, but it sounded as if in his dream he was back in Germany during the war.

I helped him get up from the toilet, and getting some newspaper from the top of the low level black cistern, I had to wipe his bottom and clean him. I didn't want to do it, and the very thought of it made me retch, but I had no choice.

I coaxed him along the landing to the bedroom where I helped him fall onto the bed. He lay there like a corpse: dead to the world. I put a blanket over him, and left him snoring and gently closed the door.

All his dignity was stripped away by the drink, and my pride for him shrunk in an instant. I sat at the top of the stairs and hugged myself for a moment. I felt like I wanted a blanket to wrap around me to make me feel warm, and to cushion me from the world. I found it disgusting, especially as he bled. It must have been from all the drink.

I worried what would become of my Dad. Would my Mum get better, and what would happen to Jane and I, if she didn't? I clung to hope.

Dad got laid off. The work he took was casual most of the time and it seemed to me he would alternate between being on the Dole—'sign on the Panel', as Dad called it—and working. Mum worked part time, so I didn't qualify for free school meals. So when she went into hospital for three months, she lost her job. Dad stopped giving me any money, and soon the cupboards were bare.

I didn't understand how he had money for drink.

When I got home from school with Jane, he was already sitting at the kitchen table smoking a fag and reading the paper—the sports page. Checking the racing results, I suspected.

"Dad." I waited for his attention to look my way. "Why do you have to keep going down the pub?"

Silence.

"Don't you know how it makes me feel having to step over you in the morning, lying there in the hallway blocking the door to the kitchen, in your own sick? It's horrible for me, Dad. Can't you see that?"

He kept on reading the racing results.

"You were sat on the toilet asleep. I had to help you to bed. Why do you keep going down the pub all the time?"

He glanced up from his paper. "I don't know, it's just a drink. That's all, you know. A swift half on the way home from the betting shop."

"But you don't get home, do you?"

He didn't answer.

"You go every day, to the pub, the betting shop or both. Why can't you stay in with me and Jane at night? That's what all my friends' parents do."

He turned and spoke to Jane. "Hello darling. Did yer have a nice day at school?"

"She did," I answered for her. "Don't distract! I am talking to you. Answer my questions please!"

He got up from the table and put his paper down. "I've got to go out to see a man about business."

I rummaged through his jacket pocket as it hung on the back of the chair.

"What's this in your pocket?"

He glanced up at me, watching me search. "Betting slip," he blurted, flicking the hot ash from his fag on the floor.

"Look," I said, "here's another five or six!" I pulled out a whole bunch of them and flung them on the table.

"Hmm."

"We can't afford it, Dad. Please, not any more." I pleaded with him.

"You checking up on me, eh? Just like yer bleeding mother."

"No," I said, "I just want us to be a family while Mum's in hospital, and be together. Please can you stop going to the pub and come home, please Dad—please?"

"Hmmm, I'll see."

"And give the betting shop a miss Dad," I added. "Walk past for our sake. If not for me, then for Jane."

He leaned over to me, and whispered, "I'll try. I'm going out, I'll try and get a job." He reached out to me and tenderly stroked my hair.

"So what time will you be home tonight then Dad?" It was four o'clock already.

"Oh..." He thought for moment. "Around half past six, love."

He got up, picking up the old betting slips from the table, and stuffing them in his pocket he quietly slid out of the house.

The next day at lunchtime I returned home and searched for anything to eat, scraping raisins off the bare shelves, until there was absolutely nothing in the house at all. I had to come home at lunchtimes, I didn't have a choice. If I hung around at school then questions might have been asked—about why I wasn't staying for school dinners. I didn't want to draw attention to myself, otherwise the Social Workers might get to know about our circumstances.

There was some mail on the hallway floor. I decided to open it. We had a 'red' Request for Payment of rent, and I wondered what was going on.

It was three days before I saw Dad again.

I started to realise Dad must have been giving me money for food, from the rent money. It didn't come out of his drink money. Oh no! Suddenly I worked out why he had stopped giving me anything for food.

Was there an arrangement between my parents to divide up the responsibilities?

Who paid for what?   Perhaps Dad was responsible for paying the rent, and Mum for the food?

It was the only way I could explain why the rent hadn't been paid.

Dad must have carried on paying the rent, spending the rest of the money on drink as he always had. So when there wasn't any money for food because Mum was in hospital, it didn't seem to register with Dad that he would then have to pay for the food as well. As far as he was concerned, it was up to Mum. The fact that she was in hospital wasn't his fault, until, that is, I nagged him so much. Then what he did was to give me the rent money, and spend the rest on drink in the usual way.

This explained why we were getting the notices to quit. He hadn't paid the rent, he had given it to me, and I had bought the food with it—until it ran out, of course.

I hadn't had any money from him for about three days, when one night his mother, Grandma Alice, came round knocking on the door.

My Dad's mum was definitely an East Ender and drank quite a bit, as I understand. She didn't have the nerve to beg for drink when Mum was at home, but she knew Dad was a soft touch. I was ironing in the living room by the window when she knocked on the door. She stood on the other side of the room, chatting to Dad, and I was quietly listening.

"How's Nellie then, she getting better?" She made herself comfortable in a chair by the fire.

"Still in hospital," he said, lighting up a fag and wafting great clouds of smoke. He got up and slung the empty cigarette pack on the fire.

"How's she getting on then?"

"Ole, all right, she'll be a few months getting better." Dad shuffled in the chair.

She gazed over at me. "Yer helping yer dad with the housework, are yer dear? That's nice."

I gave her a passing glance, and smiled, but said nothing and buttoned my lip. I suspected she had come round to scrounge off Dad, and I was watching for it.

"She's a good girl, isn't she Jimmy, helpin' yer out an' that."

"Yeah." He took a drag from the fag. "She doing…" He stopped to clear a bit of tobacco from his lip, spat it out on the carpet and then carried on, "Doing well at her new school."

Sidling up to Dad, she whispered in his ear. I thought she was going to scrounge a cigarette, except that he had thrown the packet in the fire. I didn't hear it all.

"Could yer see… lending… little money… drink for ages."

Well, that was it! I had had enough. She was asking Dad to lend her money—give, more likely.

"Nan, I'm sorry, but we don't have any money," I butted in. "Dad's not working, Mum's in hospital. We can't give you anything, we don't have enough for ourselves, and besides, I've got Jane to feed as well."

She looked startled, but I didn't care.

"You should be helping *us* out," I continued. "We've got nothing. I'm living on the free school milk. Look at the cupboards if you don't believe me. Come on, look at them." I walked to the door and beckoned for her to follow. She got up and followed me into the kitchen.

I opened each cupboard in turn until they were all open. I wanted to show up Dad in front of his own mother—to let her know he hadn't got us any food. To show her, in the hope that it might prick her conscience.

"What do you want me to do, Nan?" I said.

She didn't say anything.

Staring at the empty cupboards she stood there, whilst Dad sheepishly lounged against the kitchen door.

"I've got nothing, and you want me to share it with you?"

"Right," she said, "I think that I had better go home."

The cupboard doors slammed like a machine gun as I punched them closed with my hand.

She made her way to the front door. Dad followed closely, but I watched to see that he didn't give her anything.

I smiled from the doorstep as she disappeared out of sight, then closing the door I brushed past Dad. I was making my way back to the living room to finish the ironing, when he grabbed me by the arm. I shook him off and ran into the living room. He started shouting out at me from the hallway.

"Yer shouldn't be talking to my mother like that, she's your Nan! Have some respect, who do ya think you are?"

"I'm the one doing all the housework, that's who! I told your mother because she was coming round here to scrounge money for drink, and besides... she needed to know some home truths."

He followed me into the living room. "Well, I don't care what you think." He moved over to the ironing board. "You're not talking to her like that, do you hear? I don't know who you think you are!"

"I'm the one running this place, and I'm not having you giving money away." Grabbing the iron firmly, I held it up and threatened to smash it into his face.

He went to grab the iron and pull it out of my hand.

"Mind, it's hot!"

He let go.

"If she dies in hospital I shall never forgive you, you know. I will find you and make you pay!"

Suddenly he backed off.

"And, what are all these red demand notices I've been opening?"

"What notices?"

Walking over to the radiogram, I selected one from the pile.

"Here you are, like this one."

He looked at it for a moment in silence.

"Aren't you paying the rent, Dad?"

"Just don't open the door to the rent man. Remember, don't open the door, okay?"

"Why?"

"Look, just don't open it, okay? You won't, will you?"

"All right, I won't"

I was no longer frightened of him. I had put up with so much—there was nothing worse that could happen to us.

A couple of days later after I got home from school I heard someone ringing a bell. I went out to the end of the block to find the Rag and Bone man sitting there on his horse and cart. I walked over to talk to him, giving the horse a wide berth. I hadn't seen a horse close up before, and the size of it made me a little nervous.

The large grey mare stood still in its shafts, the blinkers mirroring each side of its face. I thought that its owner looked frightening. He sat high up on his wooden seat, his mean eyes peering out from beneath his old cloth cap. His scarf was tucked tightly around his unshaven beard, and he held his little crop tightly in his right hand.

"Excuse me mister, how does this work then?"

"What do ya wanna know then? He's an 'orse, and this'en here's a cart."

"Well," I said, "do you buy clothes and things?"

"Yeah."

"Would you buy clothes from me?"

"Yeah. You bring out some old clothes, or rags or the like."

Suddenly the horse made a rasping noise, and then there was this awful smell. I stepped back and held my nose, much to the amusement of the driver.

"It's all right my darling," he chuckled. "Bessie's just farted. Come on round this side."

I walked around the cart.

"What do you mean, like from a dress, shirt, or coat or something?"

"Yeah, that's right, then I weigh it on these here scales over there, see."

"Right."

"Then we agree a price and I give you some money for it."

"Are you going or will you wait here for a minute for me?"

"I'll wait for yer. Don't be long."

I rushed indoors and got Dad's old coat out from underneath a pile of clothes that littered his bedroom, and scurried back to the waiting cart.

"What will you give me for this?" I held the coat up for him to see.

"Let's have a look, shall we." He took it from me, bundled it up and placed it on the scales. He mumbled something I didn't hear, then he spoke loudly. "Two and six."

"Thank you then," I said. "I would like to take it if that's all right with you."

Dumping the coat on the pile of clothes behind him in the cart, he counted out two shillings and six pence into my hand.

Brilliant, I thought, now I could get some food for the whole week! I never told Dad that I had sold his coat. I didn't think he would be very pleased, but I was in a devilish mood and the gloves were off. Keeping things afloat with my own money and the bits I scrounged out of his pockets put me in control and I didn't have to rely on anyone. I put aside the half crown for Jane's dinner money, and took my chances with the food.

From the jobs I did for the neighbours I managed to get a little food for Jane, sometimes sweets like a packet of Spangles as a treat, a packet of biscuits or a large potato. But it wasn't long before there was no money for the electric meter and the gas had been cut off again.

I got used to candles and did the best I could. It didn't matter if we had any carrots or peas. We had no way of cooking them. In desperation I managed to retrieve some coal from the railway tracks and lit a fire. I put the potato in the ash tray of the fire and cooked it in that.

For a short time I managed to keep Jane and myself fed, but no matter how hard I tried, or how many jobs I ran, there came a time when I didn't have enough for myself.

Dad kept coming home late, completely drunk and not a penny in his pockets. He lay in the hallway, between the front door and the stairs. He didn't even make it to the living room, only a few feet away. He lay where he fell, in his own stinking vomit. In the morning I had to step over his body in order to get into the kitchen.

I got Jane up, made sure she washed and dressed, and took her to school out through the french windows at the back, so that she didn't have to see Dad. I gave her my last money for her school dinners, and went to school hungry, hoping I would be able to get something during the day.

It was now five days since I last had a meal and I found that I didn't get hungry any more. I stopped going to the toilet. I had not eaten any solid food, and so my body just shut down its normal functions. We both still got a third of a pint of free school milk at the morning break, and that served to keep me alive. I told myself that I could survive if I could just keep going, do more jobs, and take more washing to the laundry at the weekend. In that way at least I could keep Jane fed, most of the time.

I suppose that in my little mind I realised that if Jane complained she wasn't having anything to eat, then the authorities might ask questions, and perhaps they would take her into care. It was my responsibility to make sure she was all right, or I would get the blame, so in my mind it was better to give her the money for food, and go hungry myself.

My twelfth birthday was coming soon and with it the start of winter. The weather was closing in as we approached November, and it was starting to get cold in the house.

Realising I couldn't keep up with the need for coal, I began hoarding what little I had, lighting the fire only on the coldest nights, and burning any wood I could find. Scrounging along the railway track for the odd chunk of coal could make the difference between lighting the fire, or staying in bed. But it was a risky business.

Running round the back of the church, ducking under the wire fence, I would scurry down the shallow embankment by the railway tracks and pick up what coal I could find. It was the main Liverpool Street line to the north and sometimes trains hurtled through at breakneck speeds. I wasn't always lucky of course, and on occasions I would come home empty-handed, curl up in the chair and cover myself with a blanket.

As the days went by, I became more tired. I started to notice that my skirt, once too tight for me as I was growing up, was now becoming a nuisance falling down whenever I ran across the road to school. I couldn't afford to wash my sheets and clothes, and we didn't have any money for soap; so when it ran out—that was it.

I had to make choices about every last penny, and how it was spent, until there wasn't a choice to be made.

It was the weekend and I knocked at the neighbour's house as usual, to take the laundry and earn a shilling, but I didn't get any reply. I went back a little later and tried again, but she wasn't in. I was relying on the money I earned to be able to buy some food, and I hadn't expected this. I sat on her step for a little while, feeling more upset as the hours ticked by.

Mrs Wilderspoon, bless her, she didn't know that I depended on her money for food. Had I told her she was keeping us fed she might have saved us. But it had to remain a secret. It was so important to keep quiet. People don't understand why. They don't understand the fear.

I knocked again—nothing.

Again and again I went back and knocked until one of the other neighbours nudged passed.

"Mrs Wilderspoon isn't in, she's gone to her sister's for a week."

"Do you want any washing taken to the Laundry for a shilling?"

"No!" She looked down her nose at me, turning away.

"Do you need any errands done?" I pleaded, once more hoping somehow to change her mind.

"No thank you!" She vanished into a wall of twitching curtains.

Walking back to our house I tried not to cry, but inside I knew our situation was dire. I didn't know what to do.

I recall sitting at the kitchen table, my head in my hands. It was the weekend so there was no school milk. I had done so well up until then. I had found a way of coping, living on my wits, but I began to wonder if this was the end of the road for Jane and me. I wanted to just curl up and die, and it would have been so easy. If life had been hard up until now, then without the money from my errands, life was going to get a whole lot worse.

I didn't know why I didn't try stealing some food from the shop, but it never occurred to me. I guess it was the sign of the times. I was more frightened of being caught than of starving.

Dad continued coming home late at night with nothing, and although I frantically searched his pockets, I found they were empty more often than not, and I began to wonder if he was hiding money somewhere. Darkness and cold descended on the house. We had no electric, gas or coal. Finally we had hit the buffers. Nothing, no money or food.

I just took to my bed, hid under the covers and slept for most of the weekend. I can't remember getting up for anything other than the odd whinge from Jane about being hungry. I gave her a Spangle I found in my coat pocket and let her lie on my bed, fully clothed and we huddled together to keep warm. I read her a story from the light of the candle until she fell asleep, and then, lifting her up, I gently put her back into her own bed for the night. She was too young to know the hunger and pain I suffered, and I tried to shield her from the horror of it as best I could.

Despite the worry about being kicked out, the fear of the rent man and the anxiety over food, I seemed to have no trouble sleeping. I welcomed sleep as a way of forgetting my worries and losing myself in the dreams of happy times. Occasionally I would wake up and as if still in a dream, I would see a roast dinner, piping hot, lying there on the chair, but every time I reached out, it would vanish. Soon all my dreams would be about food, save one. Perhaps it was because I found an old picture of Dad in his uniform, I didn't know, but this dream used to haunt me so many times. It always started the same way—Dad as a soldier sheltering in a muddy war-torn trench, explosions all around. At that moment in the dream I am not sure where I am, but I hear Dad's voice. "Stay here," he says, "I have to go love," and then I swear I feel something, as if a kiss on the cheek, and then I watch him disappear over the top. He stops and glances back, waves, but when I wake up, I find myself alone and the house empty.

Come Monday, I walked Jane to school as usual, but this time I had nothing to give her for the school meals. In desperation I mentioned that I didn't have any food to my friends, Margaret and Christine, but rather than be interested, I found that they didn't really want to hear it. They told me not to keep moaning about it. I never understood that, but I took the hint and didn't mention it to anyone ever again.

At one time I remember a teacher asking me if everything was all right at home. Perhaps he had noticed I wasn't looking so happy, or maybe he had noticed I couldn't concentrate on anything. He probably saw a deterioration in the standard of my schoolwork, my clothes and general appearance, and then he might have seen that I stopped keeping up with the shorthand, concentrating just on typing instead.

There were a whole bunch of clues that were there for adults to pick up on, despite my attempts to hide my life from the world. I was so frightened of the family being split up—that was the fear that was so great; it was more important than even food. It was the secret that was the important thing, and yet, I almost yearned for someone to notice and lift me up and out of my situation. But the fear of being taken away was so deep rooted.

I was not sure we would survive this one hurdle. I was going downhill fast and I no longer had the strength to cope anymore.

13

Winter Chill

MUM HAD BEEN AWAY nearly six weeks. It was 25th October 1960 and things had become far worse. It had been relatively warm through September, but it didn't last. Black damp was the curse Jane and I now endured, and without coal, electricity or gas; it chilled our very bones.

No longer could I choose which shops to use. I had to do whatever I could to keep us alive.

I couldn't steal. I wouldn't tell lies like the other children. Mum always knew whenever I tried to tell fibs. I would blush and then my little knot of deceit would be unravelled, and my pride laid bare. But more importantly the price for failure would be high. If I were caught and sent away, then what would become of Jane?

I decided to go and fetch some coal from Mr Roberts, the greengrocer at the top of the road. Mum hadn't paid him the last time so I didn't look forward to it, but it was Hobson's choice. It was that or nothing; really no choice at all.

Quickly, I got Jane ready, but she didn't want to go.

"Do we have to go, out? It's so co..old," she shivered as I wrapped her up with a scarf.

"Yes darling, I know," I said, "it's cold, but we have to try and get a fire lit."

"But it's sooo co..old, can't I stay here?" She looked up, pleading, stamping her feet to keep warm.

"No darling, we have to go. Come on, we won't be long, I promise. I'll give you a Spangle, will that be okay?"

"All right then," her face lit up, "but you promise?" She glanced up at me with a cheeky grin. "Not long...and a Spangle?" I bent down and gave a little reassuring hug.

"Okay, come on then." I took her hand in mine and held it for a moment. I needed her to trust me.

Grabbing the pushchair before she changed her mind, I trotted up to the greengrocer at the top of the road, and gave Jane my last Spangle as I promised.

The greengrocer's shop was set out with fruit and vegetables, leaving a small path to the door. Jane stood by the pushchair outside on the pavement, as I sneaked a look inside.

Was Mr Roberts on his own? I signalled to Jane to wait there.

Marching into the shop, I found Mr Roberts standing in his white overalls by to the till. There was no time for mucking around or mincing my words.

"Please could you let us have a bag of coal? Mum will pay when she can—she's in hospital." I blurted it out, stood back and waited.

He looked at me and I could sense the rejection. He shrugged his shoulders and shook his head, then looked down trying to avoid catching my eye.

I glanced sideways to hide my tears, and then I looked back, holding the stare a tad longer.

"Thank you anyway," I said.

I dreaded the rejection. I couldn't take the disappointment anymore. Everything was an effort for me, and I found even putting my shoes on a struggle. I wasn't even sure I had the strength to lug the bag of coal home, even if he had given it to me.

Turning away, I dragged the pushchair back out of the shop and into the street behind me. Then, glancing back one more time, and as I blindly reached for Jane's hand, I caught his eye.

I saw something. I couldn't put my finger on it, but it might have been a slight hesitation as he turned back. It was as if something unspoken had passed between us, and then I watched as his eyes slowly glistened, until he was forced to wipe away the moisture with the back of his cuff.

I must have looked such a sorry little mite, my lifeless eyes now haunted and distant, my little dress and coat dirty from making fires and picking up coal. I couldn't remember the last time I had a meal, and my face was looking gaunt, my once thick hair hanging in a shaggy heap. It was all a reflection of how I felt. Jane had at least been getting the school meals. I managed to fund some of her school dinners from my odd jobs, but I had not eaten solid food myself for over a week.

Without warning, he beckoned to Jane to bring the pushchair back into the shop. He picked up a bag of coal, heaved it into the pushchair, and then unexpectedly, he placed two large potatoes on top.

"Thank you Mr Roberts," I said.

"Go! Quickly now—before I change my mind." He turned away and shrank back into the shop.

I scampered out just in time to see his wife appear. He turned towards her and shooed us away behind his back with his hand.

I scuttled away as fast as I could, stopping just a short distance round the corner, but far enough so that we couldn't be seen. I waited and listened. Jane crouched beside me, clinging to the pushchair.

At first, all I could hear was my pounding heart, and then as I calmed I caught a snippet.

Mrs Roberts was in full fight, screaming at the top of her voice.

"I hope you're not giving more coal away to those children, are you?"

I didn't hear his voice, but she was still going as we scurried away along Grove Street.

Lugging the bag of coal in through the front door, I quickly made up a fire, lighting it with just enough coal to take the chill off the air. Then, taking one potato I quickly put it in the ash tray to cook for Jane, and hid the other in an old shoe at the back of the under stairs cupboard.

At lunchtime the next day I came home from school as usual, and started searching the kitchen cupboards looking for food, although it was futile; I knew there was nothing.

Bang, bang.

I stopped what I was doing and listened. I looked along the hallway; through the crack by the hinge in the kitchen door. Peeking through the letterbox, I saw a pair of eyes.

"Hello!" he shouted.

A few minutes went by and I saw the shadow appear at the back of the house. He was looking through the windows, cupping his hands on either side of his face to look. He then stood on the concrete step by the old drainpipe; peering, tapping and calling my mother's name. It was the dreaded rent man!

Mum had told me not to be seen by the rent man; I didn't fully understand why—I just did as I was told.

I was trapped in the kitchen. The kitchen door broke into the hallway a few feet from the front door. If I turned right, I could run down the hallway, past the stairs and meter cupboard, straight into the living room. From there I could escape out the back through the french doors and into the garden. Turning left would take me to the front door and into the arms of the rent man.

I darted back and forth, from the kitchen to the hallway, dodging the darkness of his shadow, and then hiding carefully so that my own shadow couldn't be seen, I stood still, petrified that he might have seen me.

Could he hear me breathing? I didn't know. I was aware that my heart was pounding loudly and I attempted to hold my breath just in case.

I edged my way to the front window, and then, catching a glimpse of his shadow, I worked my way back through the hallway to the stairs. I couldn't go upstairs—that wouldn't help me because I had to get back to school. I had to sneak out the back of the house through the french doors.

"Open up, I know you're in there!" his voice bellowed through the letterbox.

Clap, clap!

The front door shook under the force of his knocks and the windows rattled in their frames.

I ducked down behind the meter cupboard, which nestled under the stairs. I was close to the living room, its door slightly ajar, but I had to cross the hallway to get there. From the letterbox the rent man had a clear view down the hallway and could see the living room door.

"You're going to have to open the door to me some time you know." He let the box snap back with a loud thud that made me jump.

Darting out from behind the gas meter, with my shoes firmly grasped in the pillow of my skirt, I shot back into the hallway. The front door was now behind me, and in front of me the living room directly ahead. I dashed in, clinging to the handle on the inside and keeping the door slightly ajar.

Clap, clap.

I was trapped in the house. After about a minute, the letterbox snapped open again and this time cigarette smoke wafted in. I peeped out from my hiding place in the living room, looking up the hallway to the front door; then I saw my shoe.

"Argh, the bloody shoe!"

I couldn't believe I had dropped it in the hall! Could he see the shoe? A shoe that wasn't there before? My heart was thumping. I was in sheer panic, not knowing what to do. On top of that I would soon be late for school.

I lay down flat on my tummy and tried to tease the shoelace into my hand, but it was too far away. Instead, my finger burst with pain as a splinter from the rough edge of a skirting board jabbed into my flesh. I muffled my startled cry, and tried to pick out the splinter with my teeth.

I was lucky, the splinter was big enough to grip, and I was soon able to draw it out.

Licking my finger like a wounded cat, I sat nursing the wound in the living room, one eye on my finger, the other on the shadow of the rent man.

We were well matched, hunter and hunted. I wasn't a quitter, but neither was he. It was obvious that if he got to the back of the house before I did, I would be caught.

I found a brush left by the fireside. Mum used it to sweep the coal dust from the grate. I slipped it out from behind the living room door, and managed to pull the shoe back a little. Then it rolled over onto the sole.

Thump.

I froze. He froze. He must have heard!

He moved back to the front window. Then the kitchen window tapped continually as he went.

I couldn't wait anymore. I ran into the hallway, snatched my shoe like a baton in a relay race and returned to the living room, this time closing the door. Grabbing my coat, I slipped my shoe over my heel and trod it on. I dropped the latch on the french doors, and quietly closing them behind me, I scampered through the garden, along the path behind a neighbour's coal shed and up to Langhedge Lane at the end of the block.

I was almost free. There was one more path to cross—the path that led to the front of all the houses in the block, including ours. The last time I saw the shadow of the rent man he was standing in that path, knocking on the front door.

I took a quick peek to my left, down the path. He was sitting on the porch, his back to me, scribbling in his little book of papers. I slipped silently by. He turned and looked at me, but I was already well away.

Once back at school I sat in class and nursed my finger in the relative safety of the warm classroom.

14

Starving: Final Struggle

IT WAS ON SUNDAY 30th October 1960, my twelfth birthday, when my desperation became absolute. I got up about nine o'clock. Dad was still asleep after the night before. The house was cold, damp, and the windows glistened with the misty chill of little Jack Frost, as Dad used to call it.

He used to tell me that little Jack Frost had painted the picture on the window during the night. Of course it was nonsense because I knew the pretty patterns were caused by the condensation of moisture from our breath, freezing on the inside of the glass. I asked our science teacher. He told me that instead of the water molecules flowing from gas, to liquid, to solid, the molecules are converted from gas to solid, which are the ice crystals of hoarfrost.

From my bedroom window, patches were now clearing. The misty blur gave way to the sight of smoke, which billowed above the chimney pots; like firing cannons in the still morning air. I sat there in the silence until the 9.30 trail of cotton steam to Liverpool Street thundered by.

I wandered downstairs and sat alone on the bottom step, staring along the hallway passage at the pile of envelopes still lying on the hall floor. I was wondering why they were still there, left where they fell the day before. Dad must have walked over them to get in last night, yet he didn't bother to pick them up.

I felt strange, I didn't know why, but there was something different about me. It wasn't because it was my birthday, it was more than that. There was something unsettling, a restlessness that I couldn't explain.

Had Dad left them for me? Was there a birthday card for me? I didn't think so. I don't even think that Jane knew, and I never reminded her. I didn't want anyone to know because it would make me so sad inside, with so many thoughts washing around my mind as I walked over, and picked up the letters.

Each envelope was exactly the same, each neatly written, each carrying the same message, and each message beginning the same way: "This is a notice to quit..."

Quit notices. These were my birthday cards.

Mum had been in hospital almost two whole months, yet I still managed to keep the secret from all my friends. It was a testing time and I had learned much about myself, but there were still parts of me I just didn't understand. Why did I believe my father?

I didn't know. He always let me down. Every time I doubted my own instinct and trusted him, things went horribly wrong.

The hard lesson came to me quite unexpectedly, or was it my birthday present after all?

I went back upstairs, sat on my bed and slipped my coat around my shoulders, but I wasn't left on my own for long. Jane had woken and wandered in.

"What's the matter?" I asked.

"I'm cold," she wailed.

"All right," I said, "I'll get you some socks to put on your feet. Would you like that?"

"No, I want something to eat—I'm hungry!" she shouted.

"Shoosh now, you'll wake Dad." I searched my coat pocket and found a fruit gum. It had fluff all over it, but I didn't think she would be bothered. "Here you are, do you want this?"

She didn't say anything, she just snatched it out of my hand and rammed it into her mouth as fast as she could.

I walked her back to her room. It was no wonder she was cold, the house was freezing. My heart went out to her, seeing her standing there in her pyjamas and her little feet bare. I got her to sit on her bed, tucked her up with blankets and slipped a pair of my thick woollen socks on her feet. For a moment we chuckled when they came up to her knees. Finally I draped her coat around her shoulders and propped her pillows behind her back.

Putting an old wooden tray on her lap, I gave her an old well-used colouring book, and some pencils from my schoolbag. With her mind elsewhere and the sweet I had given her from my coat pocket, she eventually settled down.

With Jane settled, I took the opportunity to sneak into Dad's room and rummage through his pockets for any money I could get. It wasn't as easy as I thought; he was still wearing his trousers. Like the Artful Dodger, I pulled each pocket inside out. I searched through his jacket, his wallet, and his outdoor coat. My efforts were in vain—he had nothing.

I sunk down on my knees and looked at him. I felt so helpless and I was so close to tears. I began to wonder what was the point. I had to get through the day and crying wouldn't help.

I shoved my arms in my coat and wandered downstairs and made myself a drink. The living room was still warm from the fire the previous night, so I took my drink and an old copy of *Judy* magazine and huddled on the settee. I sat there reading amongst the smell of spent coal and of old newspapers that were piled in a heap in the corner of the room.

For a moment I was lost in a story of a little girl locked in the classroom by some naughty boys. As I read the words staring out at me from the page, I realised I needed help too. I couldn't do it alone. Woe betide if I tried to come between my dad and his drink. He couldn't help me and I couldn't help him.

I reached up to the mantelpiece, taking the pencil I found lying there. I started to write my thoughts on the side of a page of the magazine. Tearing it out, I folded it and stuffed it in my coat pocket, stood up, put my cup on the mantelpiece and strode over to the french windows.

I stared out into the garden. The patch of unkempt grass and weeds was divided down its length by a crazy stone path that tee'd into the narrow path to Langhedge Lane. On the left-hand side, a wooden pallet rested against the rickety picket fence that separated our patch of weeds from the neighbours.

I said to myself, "Today I am twelve. Today I have a grown up plan. I have to fight this on my own. We will not go hungry. I will not give in."

I took out and unfolded my checklist, and read it to myself. At the top I had written 'One bar of soap'. Soap was the lifeboat of my survival. So strong was my feeling that I would have fought for it, and if I died, they would have had to prize it from my frozen grasp. Safety had to come before food. If I didn't keep up the image to the outside world, then someone might notice. A teacher, a doctor, or other adult would notify the authorities, and one wrong step and Jane and I could be taken into Care: I couldn't have that.

Second on my list was money. Without money we had no heat—the engine of my bones. Without heat we could not cook, or dry our clothes from the continuous damp of winter. Every day now it had rained without relief—depressingly so.

It came to me. I had to make a decision. I was like a shipwrecked sailor, on the rocks and sinking fast.

I wrote down my last comment. Choice.

I had to choose between staying and starving, or breaking out and getting help.

I was now so scared that the rent man would come at any moment and throw me out of the house. What if the he came whilst Mum was in hospital? Would she return to an abandoned house? Would I be lost in some Care Home with Jane for ever?

I was wasting away alarmingly, although somehow in my confusion, I didn't realise how bad. I was now very weak—everything was an effort. Living on just one third of a pint of milk was simply not enough to keep me going, and now I didn't even have enough for Jane. It was the weekend and I had nothing at all.

I could no longer shield Jane from the crisis; moreover, I was scared in case someone found out. I needed Mum now more than ever. I didn't have the money for the basics, let alone laundry and the house was returning into filth once more. I made the decision to go and get help from Mum. It was my only hope and I was determined to confront Dad and get the fare money.

The next day Dad was home about five o'clock and I saw my chance. Sitting at the kitchen table, he was drinking a beer and reading the racing results in the late edition of the *Evening Standard*.

"I'm going to see Mum," I blurted.

"Ahmm." He was engrossed in reading.

"I've got to tell her what's happening to us," I said. "We're starving here. I can't carry on!"

"Go on then." He didn't look up.

"Give me the bus fare." I snatched his paper.

He got up, swung round and reached out for it, but the sound of tearing paper was lost in the noise of the scuffle. The racing results page was in shreds. I stood back facing him, holding the torn remnant behind my back.

"I haven't got any money." He just stood there.

I dropped the paper behind me and pounded into him. I suspected he had gambled it all. Why else would he be looking at the racing page?

"You've lost it all on the horses, haven't you?"

The corner of his mouth flickered up in a nervous twitch.

"I knew it! I flipping well knew it. You've lost all the money, haven't you?" I wanted to shake him like a rag doll, and perhaps if I had been a boy like Les, I would have.

Was that why my brother Les had to be kicked out all those years earlier? Had he suddenly realised what my dad was really like, and rebelled against it with such anger that Dad was forced to get rid of him?

"I will have to walk all the way," I said, "unless you give me the fare now!"

"I haven't got it. Really." He pulled out his pockets and I saw they were empty.

Picking up the torn page, which I had dropped on the floor a few moments earlier, I walked into the hallway. Dad followed me out. Jane started crying as Dad and I scuffled over the racing results. His elbow struck me a glancing blow on the side of my face.

"That's it," I wailed, "I've flipping well had enough, I'm going up to see Mum and tell her."

He couldn't see my misery, or feel my pain. I realised I would have to go. I was making mistakes and falling over unexpectedly. It might have been my imagination, but I swear my teeth were getting lose, my hair was falling out, and I was convinced that if I didn't do something I wouldn't see another week.

I had to leave Jane behind. I didn't want to, but I had no choice.

"You'll have to look after Jane," I shouted from the Hallway.

I slammed the front door behind me in a strop, and raced up Langhedge Lane as best I could. I really wish I hadn't, because I tripped, striking my knee on the pavement. Nursing my knee I heard a noise and glanced over at the house nearby. It had a little picket fence by a low brick wall. An empty R.Whites lemonade bottle rested next to the old metal rubbish bin. I sneaked it out through the gap in the fence, hid it under my coat, and carried it to the corner shop, where I offered up the bottle. My nose was so close to the counter that I could taste the smell of fruit pastels, wine gums, liquorish and so many others that I couldn't describe.

The shopkeeper examined the bottle. There was a brief moment when I thought he would reject it, or say it wasn't his, and hand it back to me. He turned and dropped it into the crate behind the counter, went to the till, and tipped a thrupenny bit into my outstretched hand.

"What do you want with it then, Miss?" he said.

I didn't say anything. I picked up a packet of Spangles I spotted on display at the front of the counter, handed back the thrupence and scampered out.

When I got to Fore Street I slowed down and started the long walk along Tottenham High Road to the hospital at St Ann's Road. It wasn't long before I crossed White Hart Lane, then Lordship Lane and past Bruce Grove. Following the route the bus had taken some weeks earlier, I was able to remember the junctions. It wasn't the shortest route, but it was a simple way that I could follow without getting lost. I kept telling myself that all I had to do was get to Seven Sisters Station, and then look out for St Ann's road on the right-hand side. At each passing bus, the smell of the warm exhaust fumes struck a contrast against the cold air. But It was no use longing—I didn't have any money.

Such a long time passed before I reached the junction for Tottenham Hale, and that was despite walking as fast as I could. As I drifted in my mind, I found myself counting the paving stones, sometimes trying to distract myself from my pain, and at other times, so that I could get some idea of the distance I had travelled.

Reaching the Junction with Seven Sisters road I reckoned I had travelled about two miles: roughly about half way.

My heels hurt, my soles hurt, my legs hurt, but more than anything, my toes hurt. They rubbed, they scraped, and they blistered, until I had blisters on blisters.

Spotting the entrance to the Underground Station, I sat on the little wall by the railing to take a quick look at my feet. My toes protruded from the blisters, my toenails like gravestones, all alone between pockets of swollen flesh, but there was nothing I could do.

I unwrapped my new packet of Spangles and sucked one slowly. My mouth pumped with moisture as the flavour flooded my tired muscles. It was so powerful, as if I had never tasted anything throughout my life; and now, all that exotic tang of pleasure gripped my entire body.

Starving myself—I could cope with that. I felt a calmness—perhaps it was the Spangle, I didn't know, but it was as if I didn't matter any more. It wasn't about me, or my pain—it was about my responsibility. I couldn't let Jane down. It was my responsibility and Mum had told me to look after her, and I was determined we were going to survive.

For a moment I sat still in my numbness, and let myself hope that this nightmare would end. Strangers brushed past me, scrambling down the steps as they rushed for their train. I was left, discarded like the wrapper of my Spangle.

Every step I took was an effort, and when I reached traffic lights, I found it almost a blessing because it gave me relief, an excuse to lean on the railings so I could take the weight off my sore feet. I would stand there, rocking and briefly hauling myself up by my arms, freeing myself from the pain. My feet now felt like clumps of stinging meat hanging on the end of stick-like bones.

As if in a trance, my mind rambled as I stood alone waiting for the lights to change. I ate a Spangle in the hope it would boost my energy once more. I should have been thinking about the way to the hospital; instead, I was day-dreaming about Mum coming home; of jam, the taste of thick cut bread covered with butter; the smell of it, so vivid I could taste it, there in the street.

The lights changed. I dashed across to the island in the middle of the junction. The pain, from my blisters, was now excruciating. I stopped, crippled.

The acrid smell of screeching blue smoke coming from the tyres should have given me a clue, but such was my dulled and fuddled brain, I didn't see the lorry now bearing down on me. I glanced up at the driver and looked right into his face. It was screwed up, his eyes narrowed as if to shut out the impact that was yet about to come.

I tried a quick sprint. My foot gave way. I plunged sprawling into the kerb. I reached up for the traffic post and tried to haul myself clear of the road, but I slithered down, trapped between the lorry and the kerb. Its enormous back wheels bore down upon me, crushing the skirt of my coat. I couldn't get up.

The driver leaned out of his cab. "What do yer think yer doing?"

I looked up at him, silently nursing my knee.

"Look where you're bloody going—bloody stupid girl! You'll get yourself killed, you will—mark my words!"

The lorry rushed past; uncaring, roaring and belching smoke in my face, like some fire eating dragon.

Clambering up the traffic post, I stood there once more, shivering, waiting for the lights to change.

I hobbled, exhausted, across to a large tree growing out of the pavement. I was tired beyond belief; my legs ached, my feet were sore and painful, and my knee was now grazed and weeping. I didn't know how much farther I could walk. I felt my head swim with the pain of it all.

I fell down beside the tree, my whole body shaking uncontrollably. I felt so tired that I could have just lain there and gone to sleep, despite the noise of the traffic and people passing by.

Was this my end?

Agonising over my decision to walk, my mind exploded with worry. Should I give up or carry on? I wasn't sure if I could make it any further. It might have been okay if I were fit and well, but now, without solid food for over two weeks—yes, the hunger pains had gone, but I didn't have the energy to continue; all I had was my stubborn pride and determination.

I was sure Mum would be able to help me, and I hoped she had some money to give. This time I had to tell her what was going on at home. I had nagged and begged and still Dad didn't provide for us. What could I do?

I got myself up and gave myself a good talking to. "Now pull yourself together, Mary," I told myself. "I hadn't come this far to quit now." I soldiered on, my mind resolute, my body; I wasn't so sure. I was thirsty, but I didn't even have enough money to buy a bottle of drink. I kept asking myself if I had made a mistake in walking all the way. Was there anything else I could have done?

Cold, dark and now with a biting wind, my very bones ached beyond belief. My shoes had rubbed and rubbed and the pain was now so bad I just had to rest. I sat down on the nearby wall, undid the laces of my shoes, and let the cold air dampen the pain.

My shoes came from a catalogue, they didn't fit properly, but I did not dare complain for otherwise I would have had nothing. For a moment I sat there still shaking and ate one of my precious Spangles. I lost track of time and rested. I tried to get my shoes done up again, but they wouldn't fit. Instead, they scraped the skin off my left heel making it bleed. I tucked my sock down with my finger in the hope of stopping it rubbing, and carried on walking, but as I reached the junction with St Ann's Road, the pain became unbearable. I stumbled for a moment, stopped and put my finger down my shoe to see if there was anything else I could do to relieve the pain. There wasn't.

I told myself I wasn't a quitter and I had to be a good little soldier, like I had read in the books at school. As I reached a 'fish and chip' shop, I found the smell of chips almost overwhelming, yet I had to get to the hospital.

A group of boys tumbled out. They had Brylcreemed hair swept back with a quiff at the front. They wore black leather jackets, denim jeans, black leather boots with white socks, which were rolled over the tops of the boots. One had a white scarf dangling over his jacket. I thought they were rockers, although I didn't see their motorbikes. They were larking about, when the one with the white scarf strolled over to me.

"Do you want a chip love?" he baited, holding one out teasingly.

I brushed passed as quickly as I could, but the others followed. I spun round to avoid them, but it was no use and eventually they all herded me in, like cattle. I reached out for the chip in his hand and he snatched it away. A big cheer went up.

"Want a chip love?" They all stood there laughing and joking at me.

I tried to push my way through them, but I didn't have the energy and they jostled me back. It was now dark and I was frightened they might turn on me.

"Go on Tommy, give 'er a chip then," one shouted from the back of the crowd.

Tommy came over to me and pushed 'white scarf' away. He put his arm around my shoulders as if to take possession, then he started chatting me up.

"Where are you going love?" He put his face so close to mine that I could smell the vinegar on his breath.

"To the hospital to see my mum." I pushed him away.

"Why don't you come with me then?" He pulled me back.

"Why, what do you want?" I pushed him away.

"He wants to give you something love," one of the lads shouted. I flicked my head round nervously snatching a glance. I wanted to find out where they were in case I had to make a run for it.

"Do you want me to come to the hospital with yer?" He pushed me up against the wall.

"No—now leave me alone." I shoved him away.

"What's the matter with yer mum then?"

"She's got this illness that spreads awfully quick. Leave me alone otherwise you might catch it. I'm not very well myself."

That was it. He didn't want to tease me anymore and suddenly he backed off and turned away.

"Come on," he rounded them up. "There's Jimmy over there with a bottle of beer."

Soon they disappeared into the night chasing after some old drunk, and I was left with a feeling of relief.

Now I was safe again I started to count the paving stones on the street, setting little targets for myself, and promising rewards. If I got to the bus stop I would stop for a minute, and at other times I would set a target for the telephone box. They were my favourite because I could sit inside and rest, and with the light switched on, it was warm, draught-free and a momentary escape from the cold night air.

I kept thinking of just how far I had come. It had taken me over two and a half hours so far, and it seemed an awful lot further than I remember on the bus. My pace was painfully slow.

I collapsed on the pavement by the side of the fence, exhausted, and impatiently chewed another Spangle until all the flavour had gone. Then, taking the empty sweet wrapper, I put it up to my mouth and licked every last drop of flavour until my tongue could lick no more.

As I stood up I caught the attention of a postman walking towards me. He looked smart in his uniform and neat cap.

"Excuse me Mister, could you tell me where St Ann's Hospital is please?"

"Yes Miss." He stopped and pointed. "It's just round the corner there." A white sign stood on the corner.

I couldn't see it because it was partly hidden by the trees. I breathed a sigh of relief. It wasn't far.

I walked into the hospital grounds, followed the signs, past the mortuary, and down the long corridor leading into Mum's ward. I just sat down beside her bed, exhausted.

"Hello Mare, are you all right love?" She called me Mare as if she couldn't be bothered to pronounce my name properly. For a moment I thought she was caring about me.

"Hello Mum."

"Yer Father was up the other day. Yeah?" She seemed all excited. "He brought me up that long box of fake pink pearls. You know?" She nudged at me with her elbow.

"Yes Mum." I was hoping she would hurry up.

"The one from the drawer at home. So as he could pretend to everyone he gave me a present for my birthday. Bloody cheek!" She shook her head.

I didn't comment.

"Brought a card with it. That was something. Thought he was doing me a favour, he said. Bloody cheek."

"Yes Mum."

"You know that young girl of twenty-one, two rooms down, with the dark hair I pointed out to you last time?"

"Yes Mum, I remember."

"Well, she just haemorrhaged."

I didn't say anything.

"It reminds you just how fragile life is, yeah."

What I struggled to understand was why she had to unload all that on me? It scared me. I knew full well how fragile life was and I wondered why I had come.

"How are things at home then?" she asked.

The question woke me up.

"There's nothing Mum—I haven't had anything to eat." I felt myself getting upset. I looked away and swiped away my tear.

"Hasn't yer father cooked anything for you?"

"No—nothing," I said. "Not for over two weeks now, and Dad isn't giving me any money," I went on. "I've been doing all the cooking, cleaning and looking after Jane, and he's out of it. Sits down the pub, or betting shop all of the time."

For a moment we sat there in silence. I didn't know how she would react. I was scared.

She looked puzzled.

I looked at the floor.

She reached over and took a sip from the glass of water on her bedside cabinet. "So how did you get here then?" She glanced round to see if anyone had noticed.

I glanced up at her. "Walked all the way."

"Walked all that way!" She had to catch her breath. "You couldn't have done! It must be about four miles. What? *All* that way? Didn't you have anything for the fare? You... you must have had something!"

I took my shoes off and showed her my feet, all red and blistered, and then lifting my skirt I showed her my knee, all grazed from the fall I had at the traffic lights. She could see that my clothes hung from me, my little face listless.

"No Mum—nothing. There's nothing at home." I paused. "No porridge, no cheese, nothing."

"Nothing?" She didn't believe me. "What about gas and electric?" she asked again.

"Nothing," I shook my head, "no food, no gas, no electric and..." I stopped myself at the last minute. I was going to give her the notices to quit, but I changed my mind. "I haven't had anything to eat for the last two weeks and there's nothing in the cupboards. I come home from school each lunchtime, and go back hungry."

"What's happening to Jane then?"

"I give her money for her school dinners from the money I get for my jobs," I said. "The lady who I do the laundry for, Mrs Wilderspoon, has gone away for a week's holiday to her sister's. That's why I've had to come here to see you." I took off my coat and laid it on the bed.

Her face changed, her eyes wide and mouth frozen open. She didn't say anything.

She looked down at me, my skin all dry, and my hair scraggy. My skirt was all dirty from the tumble I took with the lorry, and my face had lost its fullness; my legs were like cricket stumps and my arms as thin as bamboo canes.

She reached over to the cabinet beside her bed.

"That's my last half crown. So you get a loaf of bread, eggs and some jam and get the bus home. Now be careful," she said. "My nurse was run over on the way to work tonight and has died, so be careful."

"Thank you Mum. When are you coming home?" I scratched my head nervously.

"I don't know, but I don't think it will be long now as I am up, and walking each day. They were giving me some pills at the start. Made me sick all the time, so I didn't take them."

"So what did the doctors do when they found out?"

"They were all puzzled, then they gave me different ones, antibiotics or something with a long name."

"Did you take them?"

"No, I hid them under the pillow. That is, until some young nurse, nosey parker, came and found them."

"So what happened?"

"She told the doctor, and he came down with all his mates. Gave me a telling off, he did. All that nurse's fault, bloody nosey cow." Mother didn't like taking pills.

"So are you taking them now?" I worried that she wouldn't get better if she didn't take the pills.

"Where's yer Dad then?" She asked.

I shrugged my shoulders. "He just comes home sozzled and sleeps. I keep searching through his pockets but he doesn't have anything." I hoped that she would tell me some other way of getting money out of him, but she didn't—she just glanced out of the door into the corridor. She seemed to be worried in case someone had heard.

"All right—well, there's nothing much that I can do for you until I can get out of here."

As I went to leave, she turned to me and said quietly, "I will try and come home as soon as I can."

I could see a look of worry on her face and she gave me a drink of orange juice in a glass. I took a sip or two but I just couldn't drink too much without feeling sick. I had lost a lot of weight, and I think she was genuinely shocked, but didn't want to overreact in case I got upset.

Visiting time soon came to an end and I had to leave. We didn't touch and she quietly waved goodbye.

There was something very comforting about a London bus on a cold night. I indulged myself and soaked it up as I lay out on the back seat. As soon as I got to Langhedge Lane I dashed into the shop to get some bread, jam, a large potato and packet of Spangles. I didn't get any eggs because I didn't have a way to boil them. I had some coal and that meant I could put the potato in the ash tray of the open fire and that would give me a much needed hot meal. But one thing was certain—I was determined that Dad wouldn't have any of it.

I crept into the kitchen with the food and tucked it out of sight in the cupboard and then cautiously checked to see where Dad was. As it happened I needn't have bothered—he was asleep in his chair.

Quietly I dashed back into the kitchen and splashed the jam generously onto a couple of slices of bread and wolfed it down with a glass of water—something I later learnt to regret.

15

Coming Home

MUM HAD BEEN AWAY for over two months and during that time it continued to be a battle of wits, what with the juggling of money, the notices to quit and dodging the rent man.

Walking all the way to see Mum the last time, I was determined to be self-sufficient. I started to hoard food, hiding a little each time until I had a little stock squirreled away, like a refugee in a war camp. Not to keep it for myself and Jane, but to make sure that Dad was hungry. I thought that if I could keep him hungry, then he would be forced to get food for himself, and therefore us kids as well.

Things began to improve. Mrs Wilderspoon had returned from her week away from her sister's, and perhaps she had noticed how thin I had become; I didn't know, but she carried on giving me a shilling each time I took her laundry. It was such a relief to get my earnings back. I could keep my independence, and I could pay for Jane's school dinners and still manage something for myself.

Dad continued to roll in drunk. I had given up nagging him; I just went through his pockets each night extracting what cash he had. I started to notice he didn't have much money on him, as if he were making sure he spent it all. Even my little slush pile was starting to get smaller, and the food supply slithered to a halt. I needed a new approach.

We were sinking again so I took to going to the Coach and Horses. That was his favourite pub. If I went there late at night and stood outside the door I would be trampled by the drunks; occasionally some would vomit over me, and at other times they might flick their cigarette into my hair. It was safer to go just after evening opening time. Dad would have moved from the betting shop to the pub and would still have money in his pocket.

I came home as usual after school, and sat around at home until pub opening time. Then I got Jane ready in her coat, wrapped her up with a blanket and got her into the pushchair. Giving her a sticky bun I had bought earlier, we set off up Langhedge Lane to the Coach and Horses.

I crossed the road and then stood outside the door, and patiently waited for someone to go in. An old man in a cloth cap and tweed jacket brushed past me. He grabbed the handle and went to push the door, but I spoke to him.

"Please Mister," I shouted. He pushed open the door then turned to look in my direction. The cigarette smoke billowed out, filling the air with the drunken talk of unemployed men arguing over points that didn't matter.

"Yeah, what's the matter love?"

"My dad. He's up at the bar." I pointed.

He looked down at me, followed my finger's direction and nodded.

"Okay love," he said.

"We don't have anything to eat at home. Can you send him out to give me some money?"

It was another way of putting pressure on Dad.

"All right love."

I jammed my foot in the door.

Bottles clanked amongst the chatter. Two men were sitting playing dominoes in the corner, another two sitting up at the bar to the right.

Jane sat kicking her heels in the pushchair at the front of the pub.

I watched as the man in the cloth cap walked over to Dad. He spoke to him, then turned, pointing at the door. Dad glanced round, and leaving his half finished pint of beer on the bar, he tottered over to see me.

One of his cronies, as Mother used to call them, shouted out: "Who's that Jimmy, yer girlfriend then?"

He spun round, raising his left hand as if to take an oath on the bible, and then let it fall forward from the elbow, flicking the finger forward as if to throw their remarks away.

"It's me daughter, ain't she pretty?"

Then, turning back to face me, he held the door open.

"I need some money Dad, can you let us have half a crown?" I held out my hand.

"Here you are." He dropped half a crown in my hand. He rubbed my head with his rough hand and returned to the bar, letting the heavy pub door close behind him.

Got him! Delighted, I pushed Jane gleefully along Fore Street to the shops. I needed a bar of soap, some deodorant, and some food. What I wasn't going to do was stock the shelves of the cupboards at home. I was determined he would find nothing until he learned to bring some food home himself.

He seemed to be proud that he had a daughter and how pretty she was, but that didn't stop him neglecting me or Jane and I am sure his mates would have given him a good beating if they had known how we all lived. Getting him when he was drunk was good for me on the one hand, but on the other, it highlighted his problem; he didn't seem to have any priorities. He would give money to anyone.

I would have to tell him I needed money for food or for school or something, and he would give me what he could and I recall that he was very generous in that respect. It was such a shame he couldn't do it when he was sober, because I could cope with the drinking if he brought in enough money for us to live on.

After the first week of my new approach I managed to do quite well. I was eating again, although I found I could live on less, probably because my tummy had shrunk so much and I found that even a small amount of porridge was enough to make me full. Sometimes I would have a craving for butter or cheese, and then it would make me feel sick, and I would have to rush to the toilet and throw up.

After a few days I began to get better. As we approached the weekend I was determined to wash my bed linen and clothes properly. I got up bright and early on Saturday. Leaving Jane happily playing in her room, I rushed up to the Laundrette. I sat there amongst all the other ladies, watching my washing and having a laugh and joke with them. They never asked why I was doing all the washing, or wondered what was happening in my life. It didn't seem odd to anyone that I was doing this on my own. Nevertheless, we had clean linen again—such a treat!

Of course I was only young and despite all my efforts at budgeting, I could not make it stretch to the weekend and soon the cupboards were bare again. What money I got from Mrs Wilderspoon I put aside for Jane's dinner money and I couldn't use that.

Dad hadn't come home, and I started to get tummy pains that appeared to hurt more than before. I was worried for my own health. I was either dashing to the toilet, or bunged up, or a mixture of both, and sometimes I just felt sick. I didn't know what was happening to me, when Dad rolled in with a whole basket of food. He had been down to see his sister, Auntie Alice, and managed to scrounge it all from her.

She was a real switched on businesswoman, and didn't suffer fools lightly, but she couldn't see us all go hungry. I didn't know what he said to her, but whatever it was I was grateful I would have something on the table to eat.

I didn't know if Auntie Alice had given him a good talking to or not, but he got a job and things got better. We had the electric and gas switched on and at long last we could stop using candles.

Although the job wasn't a proper job, in the sense of forty hours per week Monday to Friday and all that; no, that would be too much commitment for him, and wouldn't fit in with his casual lifestyle. It would be temporary work, hourly paid factory shift work.

On some occasions Dad got casual work with Lyons, the bakers. He would have to go there at nighttime, queue up and wait in line to see if there were any jobs for the night shift. Sometimes he would be lucky and get a job for the whole shift. The downside was that we were alone in the house all night, but the upside allowed us to return to some sort of normality. It didn't always work, of course, despite all his hanging about in line, and we would all suffer again.

I think the idea was to confuse Mum as to what he actually got paid. In his mind if Mum could figure out what he got paid, then she might demand a proportion of it, rather than accept whatever he gave her. But as it was, he was able to convince her that he had no money, and she simply had to live with what she was given.

Mum finally came home from the hospital after three months, and with her return a final end to the starvation. I never did tell Mum what fully happened whilst she was in hospital and I didn't know why; perhaps I just wanted to forget it and, besides, I didn't want her and Dad to have any more arguments.

I was so pleased to see her back. She appeared so much better and had put on a bit of weight. I rushed to put the kettle on and make her a cup of tea as Dad was fussing about unpacking her bags. I cried silently on the inside. She didn't know the immense relief I felt, as the burden was suddenly lifted from me, or the full horror and trauma I had been through.

Mum had been very lucky and allocated a home help. Jesse, her name was. She would come in, do all the housework and clean the place up so that Mum could rest a little and concentrate on getting her strength back.

Jesse lived in our street and Mum knew and trusted her. The good thing for us was that Dad had to keep giving us food money, and for a while it stopped him drinking so much. He was working nights, and sleeping during the day when Jesse was there. He knew that if he didn't behave, the authorities would find out: Jesse would tell them.

Dad was pleased to have Mum home, but at the same time he was expecting a bit of a problem when she read the notices to quit. Well, I wasn't wrong—when Mum saw them she went ballistic and they were at it hammer and tongs, shouting and screaming at each other.

The next day Mum went to the local housing department. They were sympathetic and listened to her tell them that she had been in hospital with TB and that she hadn't any money. She seemed to be good at sorting it out, and life soon returned to the same old routine. When the home help stopped, Dad would be off down the pub, but at least the bills got paid and we got fed on a regular basis.

Was I the same after that? No—I didn't think I could ever be. My life was forever changed. I had joined a very select club of children who had known real hunger and this was in 1960's England.

When I asked Mother about her TB and her time in hospital, she recalled the visit I made. She told me she remembered that I had walked all the way, and that she had parted with her last two and six pence (Half a Crown) for me to get the bus home. I was so successful in those three months in shielding Jane from the horror of it all, that she recalled nothing of the hardship.

Was I abused? I didn't think so at the time. I wasn't physically beaten or attacked and Dad didn't belt or threaten me. Mum could slap me at times, but it was relatively rare.

I don't know what would have happened in a Care Home. Perhaps it would have been worse at the hands of a stranger, for all I knew. At home, at least I had the freedom to do something about it.

I could have run away. That would have been the easy way, but I chose to stay. It wasn't about me or my needs anymore, it was about staying together. I couldn't abandon Jane—we were sisters and I had to help her.

16

Books and Orphans

IT WAS A SUNNY DAY in July 1961 when the school holidays started. I was twelve, as I recall, when Mum first got a job at the Orphanage in Bush Hill Park, cleaning. Each day she would take me there, drop Jane, now five years old, at her friend's house, leaving me to play with a little orphan girl called Katherine. She had short club cut straight hair, like a basin cut all the way round, fresh faced, dressed in a mauve and white checked dress, with a little white Peter Pan collar.

The tall ruddy faced woman who ran the Orphanage was called Mrs T—I didn't know her real name. She wore a white blouse, bottle green cardigan and pleated skirt, her hair in a fringe and bun at the back.

I hadn't seen a woman with a moustache before and I found myself staring up at her all the time. Perhaps I was a little afraid of her when she asked me to stay for lunch, although I felt I dared not refuse.

A long dining room was fitted with two trestle tables, each with a white tablecloth and napkins. There were eight wooden chairs placed on either side for the children. It looked so lovely, each place laid out with cutlery and a glass of water.

"Come on," Mrs T walked Katherine into the room, and I respectfully followed.

"Sit down Mary," Mrs T pointed to a chair. Katherine sat on my right, and we waited quietly.

"Hello girls," someone opposite called.

We both nodded.

"Hello," Katherine said.

Soon the room filled as children streamed in, sitting down at the table quietly waiting for lunch to commence. I expected the children to be chattering, but they appeared to be muted in the company of Mrs T.

I glanced up to see hot plates being brought in. Mrs T carried two herself. I was dreading it, until a huge plate of roast lamb, boiled potatoes, carrots and peas suddenly appeared, and was placed down in front of me.

I just looked at it and dared not move, thinking it was surely for someone else. I looked up at her, puzzled.

"No, this is for you," Mrs T said. "Go ahead."

I felt like I had been commanded to eat. I glanced up at her. "Thank you," I said, hoping my eyes didn't give me away, for they must have been as big as saucers—and I swear I was dribbling at the sight of it all! Steam rose like smoke from a cigarette and my tummy couldn't wait to start. It was like Christmas had arrived for the first time, and I began to wonder how long Mum would stay at this job. As far as I was concerned, she could have stayed for ever.

I cannot tell how wonderful it was—such happiness all in one day: food piping hot, and… with gravy!

"What's that?" I pointed to some green liquid. It was sitting in little pot with a spoon sticking out of the lid.

"That's mint sauce, isn't it Kathy?" a boy opposite shouted.

"What's yer name?"

"Mary," I said quietly. I was shy.

"My name's Kevin, and that's Kathy; her real name is Katherine, but we all call her Kathy." He pointed to Katherine who was sitting on my right.

"Is that what they call you?" My question went unanswered.

"Would you like some?" Kathy pushed the mint sauce toward me.

Taking the spoon, she dropped a little of the sauce on the side of my plate, and then she carefully replaced the spoon in the pot.

"Thanks." I tried it.

They both stared at me, waiting to see my reaction.

"Brilliant!" I turned to Kathy, my face beaming.

She passed the pot over to me. I took some before passing it over to the next child.

It wasn't long before the room was full of chatter and clatter, as knives cut into crisp roast potatoes and gravy. Oh, Bisto! This was proper food!

As I got to know Mrs T, I found that she was not so frightening. She was so organised, and I guess that with so many children it would have been difficult to accommodate all their individual needs.

Kathy and I used to run all around, into every nook and cranny, and even the washroom, with its overwhelming scent of green Palmolive soap. I marvelled at the facilities they had, their little sinks, their names labelled above their own little coat peg; individual cleaning kit; the little round tub of Gibbs Tooth Paste; little tooth brush; all neatly set out for each child; an identical life in an identical world.

We didn't have toothpaste at home. I had to use salt and water with my fingers.

They had clean clothes, nice meals and although they had chores to do, I could see how clean the place was kept, and how well it was organised. It was a home, and I began to realise the difference between a home and a house.

How heavenly it must have been, to be cared for in that way. The smell of the dormitory, its freshly changed beds all lined up like chocolate soldiers on parade. To me, well, all I could see was love and care.

I started to wish more than anything else I could be an orphan too. Had I lived in the Home, perhaps I would have seen a different side and envied people with parents; but then children at the Home had no idea what life was like for me; their expectation would be much greater.

The following week my little friend Kathy, with whom I had become quite attached, had an interview for adoption. It saddened me that she had been taken away, especially as I found out later she was split up from her younger brother, but I never did find out what happened.

Shortly after that Mum got a full-time job at the Jameson sweet factory, and the world of the Orphanage was swept aside. She didn't stick at the sweet factory for more than a few weeks before leaving. I think she found full-time work too demanding. She got a job working for Page's Paints, but it was only part time and she didn't get the same money she got at the sweet factory. By the time she had taken out her fag money, there wasn't a great deal left. Certainly not enough to cover the electricity and gas, and they continued to be cut off from time to time. When we had no gas, she would put money in the gas meter, and then I would have to get food, begging from the shops again.

I had done a lot of growing up, and I guess I had enough of scrounging for food on tick. I refused to go to the corner shop. Mum asked Jane, but she was so stubborn she flatly refused to do it, and that was that. I had to back down and go myself, but I had made my stand, and I let them know I wasn't going to do this any longer.

I joined the Girl Guides at the Salvation Army Citadel at Upper Edmonton, and I used to get the bus there, when I had money. Or if I were hard up, then I would walk with another girl, Anita, who lived three doors along.

The bus stopped by the sweet shop as I recall, and sometimes I popped in there if I was early. On one occasion it was raining, and when I looked up something caught my eye. It was a tall imposing building next door. It had a big sign— 'LIBRARY.' I had never been in a Library before. We had one at school, a small affair, so I knew what a library was. Mother didn't have books at home, and I wasn't sure that my mother would know what to do with a book because I never saw her with one.

I went in—wow, it was massive! I found it overwhelming. The scent of wood polish and the lovely smell of the books! Perhaps it was the glue used in the book bindings that I could smell. The mustiness of old paper, subtly blended with the pungent aroma of the shoe-squeaking highly polished floor, seemed to waft up into every corner of the large room. There were hundreds of books on shelves, and shelves upon shelves all the way around the room.

Stunned, I couldn't believe what I had found. Not only was it warm, cosy, and inviting, but very quiet. I found the whole atmosphere intoxicating. Their sheer number stifled even the noise of the librarian stamping the books; it was as if this was the temple of books—cathedral-like, silent and revered. It seemed to me the books were held up to be worshipped. So many books—walls and walls covered in them! Oh, I was in heaven—what joy! I couldn't get over it—the sheer excitement of it all.

Enid Blyton and *The Famous Five*, *Just William*, *Heidi*, the *Adventures of Tom Sawyer* and *Huckleberry Finn*—it was overwhelming! I had never seen so many books. I started to devour books as if I had been starved of stories all those years, and I marvelled at the lives of those fictional characters.

On returning home, through my excitement, I couldn't wait to tell Mum that I had found a library. I shouldn't have been surprised by her response. She said we don't have books in this house and that was it.

I never saw either of my parents read a book, although Dad would read a newspaper. It wasn't because they couldn't write—they could both read and write quite well, and Mum in later life took a great interest in politics, but still never ever read a book. I found that very strange. I never questioned it again.

I spoke to the librarian on my next visit and she seemed to take an interest in me. She didn't have a moustache! Instead, she was a small woman with spectacles, and a slim boyish figure. She spoke very posh, like the teachers did at school and very particular as I recall. Fussing about the bindings of the books, she examined every tear as if they were as precious as petals on a rose. Olive Drab, I think her name was; I had to laugh, when she told me. I thought the name suited her—like some comic strip joke.

She started to show me how to find the books by using the Dewey index. Locating my favourite authors became my passion, and soon I started to devour them like a swarm of hungry locusts on finding a field of wheat. From the stories I read, I got an insight into the lives of people. It might have been the *Famous Five* or perhaps *Just William*, but in all these stories the child characters were always 'looked after', and kept from harm. They were always 'called in for dinner' and were 'tucked up in bed'. Those make believe children never ever went hungry like Jane and I did, and despite all their adventures, there was always the sense they were loved.

Each time I visited the librarian told me how I could join the Library and borrow books. She asked if I wanted to join.

"I don't know," I said nervously.

"Well," she said, "you get four books for three weeks and then you can bring them back and get them renewed."

"What if I don't bring them back in time?"

"You get a small fine for each day that it is late," she said.

I thought for a moment. Could I trust my family? I didn't think so. I worried that Dad would take it, to what he called, the pawnshop, or chuck it out and then I would have to pay a fine.

"No," I said, "I'll just come and read the books here if you don't mind."

"All right," she smiled. "Let me know if you change your mind." She carried on stamping books. I could see she was disappointed. I was too.

I had to keep my world separate from my parents, and I hated that, but it was the only way I could become myself. I wasn't like them, and I began to think I was an orphan, adopted by this family, as if I had been found alone in the street. I might have parents and live in a house with them, and to all appearances I was a child in a family, but to me it felt like I was alone.

17

Clacton

I FIRST BUMPED INTO LINDA when I was thirteen. She got off the bus outside Woolworth's when I was walking home from school with Jane. We started chatting, and talking ten to the dozen, as we walked the same way home. I found out she went to a different school to me, but she used to get off the bus in Fore Street outside Woolworth's. I recognised her.

"You live in the house above me, don't you?" I asked.

"Yes."

"What's your name?"

"Linda."

"I go to Raynham Road School. What school do you go to?"

Each house in the block of Maisonettes would have an identical layout, and so Linda's house was the same as ours, the main difference being the way it was furnished. As soon as you walked into her house, the smell of freshly cut flowers drifted along the hallway, making the house so bright and sunny. The house always seemed happy, and entering it was like walking into a dream.

The living room had a thick pile carpet, a sideboard of polished wood stood by the french windows. It was decorated with framed photographs of Linda, her brother and other family members. They were neatly positioned between pretty porcelain figurines, each placed on a neat lace doily.

In the corner was a matching display cabinet with ornaments and crystal glasses. A smart radiogram was positioned along the wall on the right-hand side. It had two cupboards, one in which the records were kept, the other filled with bottles of drink. She took out some of the records—her records from amongst all the others that were stored there. I could see that her family all enjoyed music.

What was it like in my house at this time?

I lived behind closed curtains, where naked bulbs of meagre light glimmered in the darkness. Linoleum spread throughout the house like lilies on a pond, exposing large patches of raw floorboards extending onto the landing and stairs. The living room, an oasis of comfort, had a lonely shrunken rug by the fire. We had a radiogram, like Linda's, but ours came from the junk shop, and the record player didn't work. It didn't bother me; we didn't have any records.

Linda was a little chatterbox of a girl, with lightly streaked curly brown hair that just covered her ears.

I really liked going to her house; she had a gramophone. We were dancing to 'Poetry in Motion' when her mum popped her head around the door. She was dressed in a freshly starched white apron worn over a bright flowered dress.

"We're going to Clacton on Saturday, Linda," she shouted above the music with a cheery smile.

"Do we have to?" I think Linda wanted to stay at home and go out with me.

She didn't turn the music down and went to carry on dancing, when her mum turned to me. I felt a little awkward, and stopped dancing for a moment. The music continued blaring out.

"Do you want to come with us, Mary?"

"Yes please," I nodded and glanced back at Linda.

Her face screwed up like a squirrel finding nuts.

"Oh great, yes okay!" She jumped up and down, grabbed both my hands in hers, and pulled me towards her, nodding frantically.

"We'll have such fun together, won't we Mary?" We both jumped up and down.

"Okay, that's arranged then." Her mum closed the door and we carried on dancing.

I understood Linda's parents were going to meet with friends at Clacton-on-Sea and they probably wanted someone to be company for Linda whilst all the adults talked.

Saturday morning arrived; I got ready, and knocked for Linda at about 8 o'clock. Her dad answered the door and left it open for Linda.

"Linda!" he called. "She won't be a moment." He turned and left me standing on the step.

Mr Bistow was a very tall man, slim build and broad shoulders. I thought he looked a little strange with his balding dark hair, and his face framed with spectacles, but he was really very nice. Her mum was well rounded, motherly, and she wore a starched pink and blue flowery dress.

Linda ran up to the open door and pulled me into the living room. We sat down on the sofa, chatting about the trip as the adults fussed to get ready.

Linda and I squeezed into the back of the little two-door sky blue Morris Minor. I sat behind her dad who was in the driving seat on the right, and Linda sat behind her mum. Clacton-on-Sea was about sixty miles from London, and it took us about two hours on winding roads, and something called a dual carriageway. I wasn't a good traveller and felt sick on the way, but I wasn't going to let that spoil it for me.

It was about 11 o'clock when we arrived at the car park just across the road from the pier. An old man, dressed in a cloth cap, and mackintosh, sat on a wooden seat at the side of a small shed. Linda's dad wound down the window and gave him a shilling. He pointed and we parked at the end of a row of other cars. Linda wanted to get out as soon as the car was lined up, but her mum was determined she should wait.

"Come on mum!" Her mum took no notice. Instead she sat calmly applying some lipstick and powder, using a little compact she kept in her purse. Her dad opened the door and held the seat forward for me to get out whilst Linda's mum continued to take her time.

"Come on mum!" She thumped the back of the seat with her hand.

Her mum didn't react.

"All done," she said, and dropped her compact and snapped her purse closed. "Just be patient." She slowly opened the car door, but Linda didn't wait for her. She shuffled across the back seat and clambered out the driver's side following me out. Dashing round to the back of the car, she retrieved her bucket and spade from the boot. As we both rushed across the road towards the Pier, her mum and dad were left to lock up the car.

Linda led the way, full of fun and mischief. She held her wooden spade in the air like an over enthusiastic tour guide. Her mum and dad took their time strolling along behind, seemingly unconcerned. She took us to this monument in the middle of a formal garden; a war memorial, her dad called it. I thought it looked a little sad. It had a big square stone base mounted on steps; above was a bronze statue of an angel. Her face was covered in white streaks from the seagulls. Her large wings were spread open, as if to take off. In her right hand she held a wreath and in her left a twisted vine. Carved on one side of the square were the figures '1914—1918', and below it '1939—1945', and on the other, there was a wreath, and weathered brass plates with the list of people's names.

The flowers were so pretty, some in borders of bright blue, tightly packed about the base of the palm trees. Others formed into large carpets of pink and white, the scent of which I found overpowering.

Untangling his camera from its strap, Mr Bistow lined us in front of the war memorial. We looked like sisters as we posed for the picture, me in my green and white striped dress, Linda in a yellow checked dress with a smart white leather belt.

"Right now, girls, pay attention," Mr Bistow snapped. "If you get lost," Linda mimicked the words as he spoke, "this is where we will all meet up." He looked at his watch. Linda looked at me, giggling and making funny faces behind her dad's back.

"Stop showing off," her dad pulled her in line. "Now pay attention, will you? Linda, show Mary where things are, and make sure you don't get into any trouble." He added: "Back at the cafe by 3 o'clock. Right?"

"Yes dad," she shot off. "Come on, Mary."

"Bye," I said. "Where are we going, Linda?"

"We're going off to the beach by the Pier." She waved to her mum with a flick of the wrist, but didn't turn round. I snatched a glance back to see where her parents had gone. Linda grabbed my sleeve and tugged me as we ran away towards the Pier. She seemed to know her way around very well, and was well used to the routine of it.

The entrance to the Pier had two giant white towers, one on each side with a big union jack flying overhead. To the right was a large ramp that led down to the beach. There wasn't any water like there was when I was at Hastings. Instead, there was a vast expanse of flat smelly sand that stretched as far as the eye could see.

Linda was larking about, looking at some boys and giggling as she took me past the candyfloss stall. We stood and watched as the man spun the sugar onto a stick. We didn't have one; instead, we wandered over to the hotdog stand nearby. I was busy looking at the Pier and all the people milling around, when Linda thrust a hotdog in my hand.

"Do you want anything on it?"

"Like what?" I said.

"Onions, tomato sauce, HP sauce or something?"

"No thanks," I said. "How do I pay you for this?"

"You don't have to. Mum told me to buy you lunch and gave me a ten bob note, so we can do what we like."

"Thanks."

I bit into the hotdog. It was really nice, and we sat down on one of the benches along the promenade by a small garden. I could have eaten another one, but I didn't say in case she thought me too pushy.

"That was great. Do you want another?" Linda asked.

"Yes please!" I could hear myself sounding too keen.

"It's all right, I'll get them, and you wait here with the bucket and spade." She shot back to the hotdog stand whilst I sat quietly, breathing in the fresh air.

The sky was blue, clear and crisp. Seagulls drifted aimlessly in the breeze above, and as they breathed in the subtle blend of seaweed and salty mud, they practised bombing the sunbathing people, spread out like linked sausages roasting in the sand. I say sand; but the beach was a mixture of sand and shingle, which seemed to form in layers down the water's edge. Further out I could make out great clumps of black seaweed that clung to the large stilts that supported the Pier.

Linda returned in no time and we sat and munched another delicious hotdog in silence, sharing a bottle of Tizer. I soaked it all up, the sun, and birds: bliss!

As we retraced our steps back to the Pier all the smells intermingled. I remember the sickly sweet smell of candyfloss, the overpowering savoury aroma of choking onions, all competing with the flavour of the hotdog still lingering on my tongue.

Walking down the large slipway to the right of the Pier we stopped by a little stretch of sand. We sat down and made sand castles with Linda's bucket and spade for a little while. She kicked my one down, and so I stamped on hers until we had destroyed them both in a fit of fun and laughter. We both made a little tunnel and bridge, scraping the sand away with our hands until it was about two feet deep. Linda decided to walk across it to see if it could take her weight. It didn't, and she collapsed, laughing, into the hole we had created.

We started to tire of the sand games, and as the sun was starting to get very hot, she suggested we move somewhere cooler.

"Do you want to go and collect some mussel shells?" Linda asked. "It'll be cooler out there."

"Yes, all right," I said.

We took off our shoes and socks and placed them in the bucket. She carried the bucket and I the spade. Wandering out onto the hard sand, we dug around in the rocks collecting any small little shells that we found. We wandered aimlessly, until soon we had reached the Pier.

Linda went under the stilts where the sand was cold and muddy. I looked up at all the giant pillars that criss-crossed in a tangle of metal and concrete, some twenty feet above us. She started picking off much larger shells she had spotted on the giant girders of the Pier. She was telling me how her mum would cook them in a saucepan and how the shells would open up. I was fascinated with it, and she showed me where she had picked them, when suddenly I felt the cold trickle of water rushing over my feet.

"The water's coming over my feet, Linda."

"The tide's coming in—we ought to get a move on." I didn't know what tide was.

"Isn't tide a washing powder?"

"Don't be soppy, it's the water, it's coming back over the sand."

I looked up at the Pier, its giant legs stretching up above me. I knew enough to realise that Piers, being on legs, usually had water underneath, but how deep I didn't know.

Well, that was it. Linda struggled to free herself, and instead sank up to her knees. She couldn't budge, and as soon as I went to help her the same thing happened to me. The more I struggled, the more I stuck. Black cold, oily mud squelched up between my toes as my feet sunk down into it. After much pulling and poking with the spade I was lucky enough to ease myself free.

When I first went into the shadow of the Pier the relief from the hot sun was welcoming, but now it was starting to get surprisingly chilly.

"Come on," I beckoned with my hand.

"I can't, I'm stuck!" She frantically tugged at her feet, but she made it worse.

The warm water was coming in fast, splashing against the pillars, and making the mud suck even harder.

"I can't stand up!" She lost her balance. Her hands stuck almost as deep as her feet.

"Hang on," I said, "I have an idea."

The water was about six inches deep when I first spotted a plank of wood floating nearby.

"I'm not bloody going anywhere, Mary." She was now talking to the water on all fours.

I grabbed the wood and attempted to drag it over to Linda, but it was too heavy for me.

"It's too big, Mary!" she screamed. "I'm scared."

I looked across. I could see Linda shivering, her eyes wide, her face begging me to do something.

"I've got another idea—hang on."

I slipped the spade under the plank and tried to lever it. It didn't budge. Splashing the water with the spade, I created little waves. It was enough to float the heavy plank, and using my foot I was able to slide it across onto the more solid sand behind her.

With the water swirling and gurgling round the big iron pillars at the base of the Pier, I started to panic as the cold numbed my toes. Would I have to leave Linda and run for help? It dawned on me that if I didn't get her free soon we would both be in trouble. I wasn't sure if the plank was wide enough to support both of us.

Gingerly as I worked my way along the plank, she somehow managed to get one hand free. I needed to get behind her where the sand was firmer. If I could get behind her and onto the more solid area I spotted earlier, then I thought I might have a better chance.

I stretched my arm out as far as I could.

"Grab my hand."

Gripping hard and giving her a big heave, I managed to prise her foot free and then pushed the plank further towards her, where she was eventually able to get a firm foothold with her good leg.

"Okay, you pull," she said.

Standing there with one foot on the plank and one in the mud, I grasped her arm. "One, two three—go!" I pulled for all I was worth.

Sluuurrpp—plop.

Her foot broke free from the gungy black sand. The water was now swirling almost up to our knees.

Quickly she made her way across the plank, and grabbing her bucket and spade, we scurried out from underneath the pier and into the daylight.

Although clear of the Pier we were still fifty yards from the beach. The water was rising so fast that it was now up to my skirt, gushing between my legs with little waves. They were shallow at first, then rushing torrents that almost pulled my legs from under me.

There was no time to lose. We dared not wait for the water to get any deeper; otherwise we would have become stranded. Linda started picking out the high ground and darting from one island to another until we reached the safety of the shore.

Dropping to the beach I nursed my toes, picking out the mud and trying to wash myself clean. That was until Linda pointed to her watch and shouted out that it was now ten minutes past 3 o'clock. We quickly put on our shoes, gathered our things, and raced back up the ramp by the Pier and back to the cafe.

Arriving at the cafe we must have looked a right sight, our legs covered in sand and mud. Linda's parents didn't look best pleased. Mr Bistow frowned, and shook his head. Then he went over to the owners and asked them if they had a bucket of water that the girls could use to clean themselves up with.

"What have you been up to?" I didn't think he expected an answer because he could see the sand still firmly stuck to our legs. We cleaned ourselves up in the little yard out at the back.

Everyone on our table was immersed in discussion, excitedly talking about what we could all do with the shells. As we passed them round for all to see we didn't draw attention to the fact that the tide had nearly caught us.

I had a great time and Linda and I remained friends through the summer, until strangely one day, the whole family completely vanished. They seemed too well off to be living in Langhedge lane, and I wondered if they had bought their own house.

I never found out where they went and I never heard from Linda or her parents ever again.

18

Meeting Joyce

AFTER THAT I USED TO GO AROUND WITH MELANIE, an outgoing and lively girl who sat in front of me. It was one of those occasions when arguments just seemed to happen—when girls are all together and have to muck in. This was how I first got to know Joyce.

I grew up a bit by the end of the summer, and it was then that I was drawn to Melanie. She was very confident and had an answer back for anything. She seemed to like me and I guess she took me out of myself and away from my home situation. I visited her house only once or twice. She never came to mine. Most of the time we met at school, or outside her house.

She came from a family with a very comfortable home. Mine would never compete and I felt I could never let Melanie know of it. She had all the nice fashionable clothes. Her mum seemed to spoil her with everything. I didn't mind that because she was fun and I enjoyed it.

We used to meet in the milk bar or coffee bar, talk about the boys, walk along Fore Street and look in the shops, before going on to the cafe. The mods would hang about with their Vespas and Lambrettas, and the rockers with their motorbikes.

I had seen Joyce around the school, and once before when I was searching for Jane. We hadn't spoken much but we knew of each other, and sometimes met through mutual friends.

A few weeks later she was sitting in the Wimpy Bar with a couple of other girls. Melanie and I walked in. Joyce called over and asked Melanie to come and join them. I sat opposite Joyce. Apparently Melanie and Joyce had gone around together before. Joyce and I got on very well, swapping jokes and we really had a good laugh.

Suddenly we ran out of money and time; we all got up and went our separate ways, and said we would all meet up at the Quabana milk bar at the weekend.

The next time we met was in the changing room for PE (Physical Education). I noticed her bra was grey, and some of her clothes the same. I wondered if she, too, was neglected by her family. Was that the common bond? I kept those thoughts to myself.

Joyce, bursting into the room shouting with her broad Scottish accent, instantly sucked out the silence, her big brown eyes, like her dress, vibrant and sparkling.

I was sitting there all alone when she came right up to my face, her cheery smile beaming at me. She said I had such a pretty face, with my full lips and bright green eyes. No-one had ever told me I was pretty before, except my Dad when I was very little, and so I guess I was a little flattered by it. I didn't know if it was Joyce's intention to flatter me and draw me in. But whatever it was, it worked and it certainly endeared me to her, and from that moment on Joyce and I clicked like sisters.

Soon we found ourselves bumping into each other more frequently, especially at break times when we would be chatting for ages, as if there was never enough time to say everything. I wasn't sure if she wanted to make a new friend, or whether she had recognised the signs of poverty. We both understood what poverty was all about; she didn't ask about my home life, and I didn't ask about hers. The comfort in poverty was that you knew that the other would protect you from those embarrassing questions.

In my case, "Why is your house in the dark?" and in her case, "Where's your mum?"

One evening I went into the changing room for Badminton after school. It was full of the usual group of girls from the school. Melanie spotted us together, and I got the distinct impression she was jealous.

Joyce was in the corner talking to Melanie; then she got up and both sheepishly disappeared almost as soon as I arrived. Joyce bounced back into the changing room with new blue eye shadow on, doing more fussing around the mirror than a hornet on a jam jar.

"What da ya think?" she shouted, giggling and doing a twirl; then glancing back at me, she tossed back her head, eyes sparkling and her cute nose twitching with mischief.

I got up and wandered over to the sink. "Hello Joyce," I said. "Like the eye shadow—really fab!"

Turning her head, she put up the back of her hand close to her face and whispered: "I wanted to tell you that Melanie has been saying nasty things—no, don't look round—she's been spreading rumours about you behind your back."

"What's she been saying then?"

"Says that yer Dad's always drinking, and yer doon tha pub wi 'im?" she said.

"Oh, did she?" I didn't know what to say. I didn't know Joyce that well, and I was a little taken aback.

Later I spotted Melanie talking to one of the other girls over by the bench. She certainly clocked me talking to Joyce, and I could see from the look she gave me, she was not a happy bunny. Although she did not realise that Joyce had a sting all fired up in her tail.

Melanie started. She looked across at Joyce as she stood by the mirror.

"What yer got on then?" Melanie teased. "Looking like a clown running away to the Circus, are yer?" She turned to the crowd as though she were some sort of stand-up comedian.

The room erupted like someone had just thrown in a grenade of laughing gas, and despite the insult Joyce just couldn't help joining in, stifling a rye smile that made her rub her eye.

"Oh shit!" Joyce said.

"What's the matter?" I glanced back at her.

"Eyelash—oh no! Oh bugger it—would you no' believe it!" Joyce stood in front of the mirror trying to get the lash out. Pulling her lashes up with one hand and trying to catch a glimpse in the mirror somewhere between her elbow and her wrist, she juggled amid all the chatter of girls at a hockey match.

"That'll teach yer to show off!" Melanie shouted, making funny faces behind her back and prancing around the room.

Joyce glanced back over her shoulder, corkscrewed round, and fixed her stare at me.

"Da ye nay know what Melanie has been saying about yeah?" she said, her arm outstretched, pointing accusingly at Melanie, then glancing sideways at me and nodding. "Been spreading rumours about ye and calling ye a slut." She faced Melanie and screamed at her: "Stuff that'n up yir arse!" She swung round and beckoned to me with her hand, then flicked her frosty gaze back to Melanie.

I looked at Melanie. "No… I didn't," I said.

Joyce and I glared at Melanie, like two lions stalking their kill.

Suddenly I started to make sense of what was going on. Joyce had only told me some of it and she wanted me to hear it from Melanie, but even I was shocked at the speed and ferocity of the events that followed.

I crooked my neck over to look at Joyce, but she wasn't where I expected. She had flung herself away from the mirror, her legs outstretched, her arms waving out, her red face screwed up, and I thought for a moment she was ready to tear Melanie apart. Unexpectedly she turned on me.

"Well, go on then, Mary! Go on! GO ON THEN!" She shouted again and again, louder than before. "Go and BLOODY ASK HER! GO ON!"

She spooked me with a fit of fury so powerful that it took everyone by surprise, especially Melanie, who was unnerved; the saucy smile that had been emblazoned on her face now wiped clean.

"So what's she been saying?" I asked, flicking a glance back between the two of them.

Joyce egged me on as the hushed room waited for the executioner's axe to fall.

"Okay," I said, "what've you been saying about me then?"

Melanie squirmed superficially, flung me a glance, her face flustered as if she hadn't expected the fight.

"I haven't said anything!" she said.

She started to back-pedal, excuse it all, saying how she couldn't be sure that it was me she saw going into the Coach and Horses with a young bloke; none of it true of course. Then finally leaning backward she spun round on her heals like a tango dancer and delivered her one liner to Joyce.

"What's the matter Joyce? No boyfriends then? Lonely cow?"

Joyce didn't wait. She pounced on her as fast as a bug on heat.

"Not like you, yer dried up ole biddy!"

I could see Joyce, her eyes narrowing. She was going to crucify Melanie now and any friendship that might have been before was suddenly swept away. Raising herself to her full height, Joyce went for her!

"Gonna tell Mary what ye said, ye lying bitch," she baited, first raising her clenched fists, then thrusting the point of her finger directly at Melanie as if to stab her there and then. Her tongue was sharp with rage, and precisely at that moment there was a gasp from the retreating crowd, as if she was going to punch Melanie full in the face.

I flinched as Melanie stumbled back, cowering down. "I didn't mean to say anything nasty, it's just that..." She stuttered, before turning round to look at the crowd, her eyes lowered, realising her support was ebbing away. She started to gather her belongings from the bench. But the mob wasn't going to let her go. They were there for the kill.

"So what did you say about me then?" I said, squaring up to her. "Come on, tell me to my face."

But she didn't seem to be scared of me and her arrogance snapped back like it was on elastic.

"Bloody well ask Joyce, she seems to know all about it!" she said, spitting in my face and jabbing her finger at Joyce.

"Oh NO! NO! YOU tell me NOW!" I demanded, prickling with anger. "Well, YOU bloody tell me what you were SAYING about me? I don't need to hear it from Joyce, I NEED TO HEAR IT FROM YOU?"

She sank down a little and then, trying to appeal to my better side, she spoke softly.

"Well... I didn't really..." she began, flustered and embarrassed, her face crimson.

Lurching forward, Joyce grabbed Melanie roughly by the shoulders, held her there and then spun her round to face me.

"GO ON, tell her what you said to me!" she insisted, thrusting Melanie's head forward, making it clear she wasn't going to let her off lightly.

Melanie ducked down and snatched herself away, and then grabbing her things from the bench, she barged Joyce aside and stomped off out of the changing room, much to the amusement of the crowd.

Something about Joyce drew us into a hidden Velcro-like bond, so strong that it took my breath away. She stood her ground beside me, and she brought me the adventure I needed. I toned down her reckless streak, and so between us we had danger within control. It was like I had only lived in black and white and suddenly Joyce had shown me the world in extravagant brilliant colour.

Her family lived in a maisonette above the Heralds Department Store, now a Weatherpoons pub, 'The Gilpins Bell'. She had an older brother Ian, a younger sister Lesley, and brother Tommy, who was about eight years old at the time.

I didn't think she ever realised how difficult life had been for me because she didn't have to worry about money like I did; she was hard up and she had a difficult time, but she didn't have the trauma of begging or the shame of it in the same way.

We both had to cook and clean and look after our siblings; her father worked—mine drank. But like her, I had to keep my secrets from schoolmates. We didn't speak about it much but the implication would always be there, and somehow, we simply accepted it in each other; she didn't ask why I was sitting in the dark and I didn't ask about her mum.

Her mum was a handsome woman. She had Joyce when she was only seventeen, and perhaps that was her downfall. I was told that she had a friend in Montrose, Scotland, who died falling from scaffolding on a building site. I didn't know the details of it, but tongues wagged in the closed community. It forced the family to move to London to start afresh. Sadly it didn't work for them, and Joyce ended up running the house, not her mother who was rarely there; her marriage had broken down and perhaps she searched for a new life for herself.

I really liked her mum, because despite her difficulties, she took time out to take an interest in Joyce's schoolwork, something my parents never did. I was drawn to people who cared, and despite her mum having her own problems; I felt a warmth from her that I never got from mine. Perhaps in my childish way I wondered if love was like pollen, and that if I got close enough it would brush off onto me.

So that is how Joyce and I got to know each other. She had to adapt at a very young age, trying to blend in like me, trying to hide her background and keeping secrets. Joyce had a broad Scottish accent that would always be difficult to follow. Joyce didn't have the support of her relatives as she would have had back home and I guess she was a little adrift when I met her.

19

The Milk Run

BOTTLES OF FREE SCHOOL MILK were delivered to the classrooms during the morning break. Students would take what they wanted, leaving the rest in the crate. Never one to miss a trick, Joyce suggested we go round nicking the bottles of milk.

"Aye, come on." Joyce strolled down the corridor.

Suddenly she disappeared behind a classroom door.

"I'm not sure about this, Joyce." I looked through the window.

I didn't want to join in. I didn't have the face for it, and I wouldn't lie.

She was frantically waving with one hand, and holding up a bottle of milk with the other.

As I opened the door she pulled another bottle from the crate, clanking it loudly. It echoed down the corridor.

"Oh, that's really great," I said, "so I'm falling for this one, am I? On the vague promise that we won't get caught?"

"You will if you doon'na shut up! Now get yourself over here."

"You're bleeding mad!"

"There is an alternative, then?"

"Well out with it, Joyce!"

"We stand here arguing you'll get spotted, then I'll stand here accusingly telling the headmaster how I caught you in the act, which will certainly happen if ye doon'na shut up!"

"I'm not happy doing this, Joyce." I felt my stomach flutter.

"Stop the fuss'en, will yer!" She shoved the bottles at me. "Now dump the bloody bottles in your bag."

"Why don't you put them in *your* bag?"

"Och, it's not big enough!"

She grabbed me. I stood up. She pulled me down. Someone came out of another class; a prefect I think it was. I didn't feel at all well.

"Now stuff this in!" Creasing up with a fit of giggles, she tried once more to push the bottles into my bag. I snatched my bag away from her.

"Shut up." I held my hand over her mouth. "Someone's coming."

Joyce bobbed up and sneaked a glimpse out of the window.

"It's okay—it's only a first year."

"What do you suggest we do then? Clank our way past the headmaster's office trying to pretend everything is fine, lift yeah skirt or show yer tits?"

The classroom door opened into a large hall. To the left led to the headmaster's office, to the right, a door guarded the stairs, cloakrooms and the assembly hall on the floor below.

"Doon'na be stupid!" She glanced back at me, her eyes big and wild with excitement. "No—we slip out the back through the cloakroom—go on." She shoved the bottles in my bag and bundled me out. She held the door ajar. I squeezed through as quietly as I could.

I ran for all I was worth, the bottles dancing like two rampant ferrets in a bag.

Where was she?

I had a clear view to the headmaster's study. I felt exposed. I couldn't risk opening the door for fear of dropping a bottle.

"Come on, Joyce." She was slowly closing the classroom door.

I waited by the exit to the stairs clutching the bag in both hands.

"Open the door, for Christ's sake, before we get caught! I'm standing here like I'm pregnant!"

"Okay, whatever you say." She let the door go.

Slam.

The classroom door echoed loudly across the hall.

"Oh! Right! That's really great! Fine friend you are. Remind me—I'm the one with all the stuff and you're throwing a strop."

"Well?"

"Before I drop like a pregnant cow, get down here and open the flippin' door before the egghead we call headmaster comes out with his big cane!"

"Come on!" She rushed across the hall, snatched the bag, spun round and swung through the doors, dropping down onto the stairs. I shot down after her as fast as I could, trying not to make any noise until she caught me by the arm. Together we tumbled out of the door into the playground. Joyce slung the bag back at me, and we both ran back to her house, giggling and laughing as we went.

Thinking the house was empty, Joyce ripped the tops off, lit the stove, and threw the milk into the saucepan. We chilled out and chatted, smoking 'Rothmans King-size' cigarettes in her kitchen, and drinking hot chocolate. Tommy, her younger brother, must have heard the noise and wandered into the kitchen. He had come home at lunchtime not feeling well, let himself in and gone straight to his bedroom.

Joyce made him a drink, put him on two chairs with a pillow, and covered him with a blanket so she could keep an eye on him. Usually we had the house to ourselves, to sit and chat about things, boys and plan for our nights out.

20

Best Friends

ONE DAY JOYCE'S MUM left the family home and went to live in a flat in High Cross, Tottenham. She had apparently met another man. I didn't know the truth of it. Joyce's dad used to give her money for housekeeping, and she was forced to do everything else like her mum.

Joyce's dad was a short, slim, and quiet man. He had a regular job, so she didn't have a problem in the same way I did. At least she had money coming in for the family, and she was able to buy her clothes, and food. Sometimes her dad would give her a fiver as we were getting ready to go out together.

We wore the same dress size, and although Joyce's clothes were a bit louder than mine, we used to swap. I thought it was really great because I would be able to expand the range of clothes I had. Lovely 'shift dresses' she had. One was white with blue scalloped edging round the hem. I really liked borrowing this dress because it suited me. She had an outrageously shiny bright purple coat with a long fur collar, belted at the waist. She loved to shock and make a statement and I think she saw me as a challenge, with my conservative pinks and blues.

I must have been about fifteen years old at the time, because I recall dancing with my friend Margaret to 'Love, Love Me Do', which was the 1962 release from the Beatles. The following year, 1963, President John Kennedy was shot, and my brother Les had just moved out from my Auntie Glad's house. He had moved to a second floor flat at 102 Edith Grove, London, living with Keith Richards and Mick Jagger, who were starting up a band at the time which they called the Rolling Stones.

Mum said she was going to see Les at Edith Grove and would I like to come? I hadn't seen him for about six years and I thought it would be lovely to see him again, and find out how he was getting on. When we got there Mum knocked on the door and a girl answered in this big cowboy hat. Mum asked for Les.

"Phelge—it's for you!" the cowgirl shouted up the stairs as loud as she could.

"Who is it?" He was standing at the top of a long flight of stairs.

"I fink it's yer Mum."

"What does she want?"

"What do yer want?" Cowgirl asked.

Mum shuffled, looking at the floor.

Cowgirl turned round.

"Don't know."

"All right." He dropped down the stairs.

He wasn't best pleased to have his mum arrive on his doorstep in sight of all his flatmates. I learnt later that he had decided to use a different name—I didn't understand why, but he started to call himself James Phelge. I thought I was going to get invited in to meet all his mates and have a nice afternoon but it didn't happen that way.

"How are yer?" Mum asked.

Grunt.

"Haven't got any money—could yer lend us something for food?"

I wondered what was going on. Mum had the money for the train fare to get there, and yet she was asking him for money. I was confused. I thought she was seeing him because she missed

Les; he was her only son, after all. Yet it sounded more like a business trip. There was no tenderness or affection of any kind. No tears, no laughter, no longing, no love. Mother was an empty shell of emotional bankruptcy.

"Right, er, right." He rummaged in his pockets and gave her what he had, which was about £1. "Here—that's it." He promptly closed the door.

I did wonder if it was worth all the train fare getting over there in the first place. I didn't think it was really about the money; I think she thought he was a lot better off than he really was; and besides, she probably thought that she might milk it for a bit; or perhaps she may just have been curious to see him again.

In any event, it was a bitter disappointment for me. I would have liked to have seen Les again, find out how he had managed after being slung out, and catch up with him because I still missed him being at home. All Mum wanted was to scrounge money from him. I was devastated.

When we got home, Mum turned to me as she walked into the kitchen, and then almost as an afterthought, she said, "Mare, erm, can you go down the shops for me? Get some food on tick?"

It came completely out of the blue.

"What about the money you just got from Les then? What about that?"

"Well, er..." She shuffled her feet and looked down at the floor. "I've got to put that in the gas and electric meter. I don't have anything for food."

"Why not? Yer found the money for the train fare to Les's place all right." She looked up briefly.

"Yeah, well..." Her head sank down as she was having trouble looking at me. She shuffled her feet.

"I'm not doing it anymore," I said, and walked back out to the hall.

"Well, we won't have anything to eat tonight if yer don't go."

"Why doesn't Jane ever go? It's her turn—she's done nothing." I pointed to Jane sitting in the living room.

"She's too young, she ain't old enough yet."

"What do you mean, too bloody young? It was all right to send me at her age—you didn't have any problem with that."

Jane heard the commotion from the living room and sauntered out into the hall. She spoke almost adult like.

"I don't care what happened, I don't see why I should have to do it—it's not my job."

"What do yer mean it's not your job? Do yer want to eat or don't you?" I asked.

"I don't care—I am not going and that's that."

"You can't make her go if she doesn't want to, Mary."

Mum shuffled over and sat with Jane at the kitchen table.

"We haven't got anything for tonight though." She looked up at me standing by the door.

"Look—I am warning you," I said. "This is the last time I'm doing this—right?" I put my coat on, snatched the note out of her hand, and stomped to the corner shop to scrounge food for dinner. I was damn sure I was not going to put myself out for those two and decided to get whatever I wanted to eat. They would have to put up with whatever I brought home.

I found it very embarrassing at my age, now fifteen, and Mum did not really have any sympathy for me, or realise the humiliation I had to bear whenever I passed the corner shop. I knew, and he knew, he wasn't going to get paid. He would look at me, and it made me feel ashamed.

Dad had got a job at the gas factory where they make the slot gas meters. He was probably working as a fitter or machine operator or some such role, and was involved in the assembly of the meters at the factory. He must have had a pretty good knowledge of how they worked and how they were assembled.

I never found out how he did it, but he had worked out how to break into the meter and take the money out without being caught. I would have thought he would have fed the money back into the meter so that we could have the gas for free. Not for us, he took the money out and went down the pub and spent it. So when the meter ran out—we didn't have any gas until he got paid, or I put the money in the meter from my earnings from Mrs Wilderspoon.

Sometimes I would have boys walk me home from school, but when they got to my house my dad would come staggering past completely drunk, and I would be so very embarrassed and ashamed. At other times when the girls from school came round to see me, I couldn't let them see the squalor. They would ask why the house was always dark and the lights were not on. They didn't understand why, and more importantly I couldn't tell them. They assumed that because I went round their houses and danced to records, that they could come round to my house and do the same. I guess it was a reasonable assumption on their part. I couldn't let them see into my life. There was no furniture and what little we had, was completely ruined by burn marks and stains from fags and drink. There still was no carpet, even after living there for more than six years. Life for me had not changed a bit as I got older. I was able to earn a bit more money with the part-time jobs, and make sure I could keep myself clean and fed. I gave the rest to Mum. Dad had spiralled down into drink, messing himself in his drunken stupor. Mum started coming into my bed in the middle of the night. I hated it. She refused to wash his clothes as a form of punishment. I didn't believe her, until on more than one occasion I saw him walking to the bathroom in his bloodstained soiled underpants. I found it revolting especially when I realised he would put them back on in the morning. I caught him washing out his own pants. I felt sorry for him, but disgusted at the sight of it all. It made me even more fastidious about keeping fresh, and soap became my personal pleasure. Like me, Joyce loved to keep herself clean, and perhaps that's why Mum never liked her, but then Mum was always spiteful to my friends. Joyce had seen my dad. She was the only friend who had ever been in my house enough to know what he was really like, but she never said a word. Nothing marred our friendship.

Joyce and I used to travel all over the place. She was very generous with her money because she knew I couldn't afford it. Up on the bus on a Saturday to Alexandra Palace where they had a big roller-skating rink. We used to hire the skates for a shilling, and then if we didn't meet any boys, we would go to the Wimpy Bar, or at other times, catch the bus to Stamford Hill Bowling Alley and play Ten Pin Bowling.

Joyce was so full of extremes that we never had a dull moment, although sometimes I found it a bit of a problem reining her in, she was so wild. On one occasion we were in the Wimpy Bar and we hadn't been there long, when suddenly the waiter brought over two coffees to our table. We told him we did not order any. He simply pointed toward some older coloured men at the other table and said they had paid for them.

We did not know what to do and thought they might have been a bunch or perverts or rapists of something, so we both got up and ran out leaving the drinks sitting on the table. I guess we were a bit frightened of them.

Then as we walked home, Joyce started chatting to some Greek boys. She obviously knew them and introduced me. We all went out off down the road as a foursome. Typical for Joyce, we missed the bus home and had to sleep at their place. I made sure that nothing was going to happen, and told them I was going to sleep and that was it. I wasn't sure what Joyce did. She went off and slept in the other room.

As we walked down the path in the morning discussing the boys, we discovered that Joyce fancied mine and I fancied hers. We were talking about swapping, when they jumped out of the bushes at us, and we began to realise they must have heard. Well, that was it! If they heard us then we had to dump them. We couldn't have boys thinking we fancied them, but it was more difficult getting rid of them than we thought. They would keep hanging around where Joyce lived, and we would keep bumping into them in the street. Joyce was blunt about it.

"Why don't you just Fuck Off!" she shouted.

I never saw them again.

Because my house was so bad and the embarrassment of having boys bump into my Dad, Joyce and I got used to lying about where we lived. We would tell the boys to drop us off at some posh house and tell them we lived there. Joyce would tell them that she lived just a little farther up the road. We would walk the other way for a little while, and suddenly hide in the bushes until they had driven off. Then we would both come out from the hiding places and have a good laugh. I didn't know if the boys came back or not, but Joyce and I found it much better than showing them where we really lived.

As I got out more, I started to take notice of other friends and how they lived. There was Christine, Janet and Vivian. Each lived in a different house, yet something was common: happiness.

Christine came from a large family and I could tell they were not as affluent as Margaret. Their house was well furnished, and the front room a little older fashioned in style, but very clean and smart. As I recall her mum was always washing, ironing or cooking.

"Hello, and do you want a cuppa? Christine's somewhere so why don't you go through and find her, love," her mum would say. "She's probably in the living room."

Walking in through the kitchen door, I would be greeted by rows of hanging washing. The whole house had a comforting belonging feeling of warmth and homeliness. I didn't know if that feeling came from the friendliness of her mum, or the decoration of the house.

Whenever I arrived home there was no greeting from Mum. Sometimes Jane would say something, but she was only a little girl. Dad would say "Hello Mary", never calling me Mare, like Mother did. She couldn't even be bothered to pronounce my name. God, it was short enough! Most mothers called their children by their full name; not mine.

Janet had one sister and lived in a quiet comfortable house. Another girl I met when younger was Vivian, who arrived in our street one day on a scooter with big wheels. I became her friend and would go to her house opposite White Hart Lane, close to where my mum worked for Charles Page. They made kiddies' paints, later to become part of the Windsor and Newton group, an artist material manufacturing company.

Vivian lived in an apartment in an imposing house with big stone pillars at the entrance, tall iron gates and tall railings. Her mum and Auntie were as posh as the house, and they really liked me.

The sad thing was that all of my friends had nice homes with the exception of Joyce and myself.

Then one day I went there to play as usual, and found they had vanished lock stock and barrel—just as they had arrived. I was shocked.

At fifteen I found a Saturday job at Cope's Pools in Bridport Road, working in the cash office. They asked me to work a new contract extending my shift into the evening until 7:30 p.m. In addition we got time and a half, increasing my earnings for the Saturday to £7.50p, almost as much as other girls got in a full-time week.

I loved working there because, although I would have to pay for lunch, it was so much better than I got at home. Rice Pudding and Custard was my favourite, and then because we worked into the evening, they would provide free sandwiches, cream buns and a cup of tea.

The money was great whilst I was still at school because it meant I could go out with Joyce, who was working full time. Of course it wasn't all mine. I had to give £5 to my mum each week for housekeeping, which left me with only £2.50p.

Joyce loved to get me to open up, do something risky and be a bit more like her. She always considered me too safe, and so one day she dragged me along to Turnpike Lane Station.

"Come on Mary," she said, "we're going on a shopping trip."

I gave her a glum look. "Can't afford it, Joyce."

"It's okay, I've already got the train tickets." She was like a child with a new toy.

I should have suspected something, but maybe inside I needed to be taken to the edge. The train arrived and we leapt into a lovely warm carriage, and sat chatting away about the shops she wanted to visit. She almost bubbled with excitement as the train moved off.

"There's only one problem, Mary." She drew two tickets from her coat pocket.

"What?"

She looked down at the two tickets as she showed me.

"I snatched them from the porter's hut." She glanced up to see the look on my face. "They're yesterday's tickets."

"Oh, that's bloody great, Joyce!" If blood could boil! "So what do we do now?"

"It's all right," she said. "The tickets are valid for three days."

I wasn't convinced myself and I was even less confident when we got to Wood Green and saw that there was an Inspector waiting at the gate.

"It's all right." She tried to be reassuring, but I became flustered, and as I approached the ticket office, I dropped my ticket.

She was so good at bluffing, and there I was, grovelling on the ground for this ticket, frightened that I would be found out. Joyce had already gone through of course and blagged it and didn't understand why I had a problem. Still, that was me. No matter how hard I tried, I simply couldn't be as bold as she was, and I really struggled with it all.

Of course, what did she do?

Joyce simply hovered on the other side of the gate jumping up and down with a mixture of begging, frantic waving, and what I can only describe as some sort of Mexican dance routine. As I stood there frightened, she became more and more animated, desperately trying to show me what to do.

Eventually I picked up the ticket and concentrated on looking straight ahead at Joyce. As I walked through she was still making funny faces and waving her hands in the air.

I always wondered what the ticket inspector thought of Joyce, but the distraction seemed to work and we managed to get away with it again.

21

Last Year at School

IN THE LAST YEAR AT SCHOOL, we all had lessons on how to behave at an interview and learnt about the techniques on how to get a job. Smart clothing, clean hands and clean language. Fingernails were scrubbed, and suits pressed, and shoes polished, and all the other tips and tricks of securing the first job.

Many of the girls at our school were encouraged to go up town and work for big companies.

I found the prospect of London exciting and I went for a job at Lyons.

Scrubbed up as smartly as I could, I travelled into London on the train and went to my first interview at Oxford Circus. I remember reciting the words of wisdom that were drummed into me in school lessons. The interview went very well, although I was a little uncomfortable with all the attention I attracted from the boys at the office. They kept staring at me, and smiling whenever I bumped into them, like lovesick puppies.

I returned home and waited anxiously for the job offer to drop through the letterbox.

One of the other girls, who made a suit for her needlework project, wore it to the interview. She looked absolutely immaculate and she was one of the first of the girls in my class to get a job up at the Haymarket. It made the wait for my letter seem all the more distant and I started to doubt my ability.

It was more than a week later before I received a letter offering me the job at a wage of £7.50p per week. It wasn't the money so much as the fact that I had got the very first job that I went for. I was over the moon and couldn't have been happier. I rushed down to the phone box and accepted the job.

It was absolutely brilliant because I was the happiest girl alive. I could belong to the grown up world of working, and even though I was only a copy typist, it was a start. I really looked forward to starting my very first job, and up town! I was so excited that I scampered back to school and told everyone in my class that I met. At the end of the day, I rushed home.

"Mum, Mum!" I shouted as I bounced into the house. "I've been accepted! I've got the job up town with Lyons!"

"Why couldn't you get a local job rather than having to go up town?" she replied.

I felt completely deflated. The stuffing had been knocked out of me—the pride at getting my first job swiped aside with her few painful words. Why couldn't she just let me have something for once? For a moment I couldn't speak. I recomposed myself and turned to face her.

"I want to work up town, Mum, and anyway, the school said that once I had accepted the job I couldn't turn it down!"

She spun round and snapped at me: "Well," she said, then paused for a moment. "We'll see about that."

I was in class, when I got a message that my mum had come up to the school and I was asked to go to the headmaster's office.

My mum didn't come up to the school for anything, not prize giving, not open evening, not unless it was to complain about something. Now I was worried.

"I'm here about me daughter Mary. Being sent off all that way to Lyons in London! Why can't she get a local job like the other girls, eh? I don't see why she has to go all that way up town, and what about all the train fares, eh? She'll have to pay

them out of her wages. By the time she has finished with bus
and train fares there won't be enough left to buy a biscuit."

The headmaster, Mr Evans, shot a glance over at me to see
my reaction. I was just as horrified as he was. He tried to
answer back but she wasn't having any of it.

"Err, Mrs..." he began before being interrupted and shouted
down.

"And another thing!" she added, now shouting at him even
louder than before. "What's in it for you then?"

He didn't know what to say to her. He hadn't done anything
and I am sure the school was doing it's best to get the girls
good jobs and a good start; after all, Lyons was a big company
and could take quite a few girls each year. It was probably a
good deal for both the school and the company, because
ultimately it would enhance the reputation of the school and
improve the chances of the girls getting better jobs in the long
term. Anyway, I wanted to work up town and it was exciting to
travel with all the other interesting people on the train.

"I reckon that you're all getting paid by Lyons for all the
girls you send up there and making loads of money for
yourselves? Yeah! That's what I think."

His face was so red as he fidgeted like a child wetting itself.

"I think all of yer teachers 'er getting backhanders or
something, and I think that yer all on the take!" she added for
good measure. "Sending all these girls up there. Just for your
cheap labour and then ripping them all off! Don't know why
you're so keen to send them all up there otherwise, and anyway,
I'm not having it!"

"Just a minute, just a minute there—I think..." he said.

"All you teachers are the same! Sitting there behind yer big
desks, lazy sods. Yer only work part of the day, while the rest
of us all skimp and save to make ends meet. And you? Making
money out of the poor girls for yourself! Yeah. Lining yer own
pockets! Yeah. That's what you're doing, ain't yer?" She

scowled, pointing her finger and raising her voice again like some wild animal snarling and gnashing her teeth at him.

"That's unfair." He raised himself to his full height and was clearly preparing to ask Mother to leave.

"You should be ashamed of yourself! She will have to get a proper job locally and I'm telling yer!" She exploded: "I'm not having my girl sent all that way!" She paused to take a breath. "So that's it!" she shouted defiantly once more, almost spitting in his face as she got up from her chair. Clutching her handbag she turned and left as suddenly as she came.

The headmaster turned and looked at me. I didn't know where to put my face, I was so ashamed and publicly humiliated.

Normally she was like a mouse, frightened to show her face on the street and never—and I mean never—came to the school to see my work or anything like that. She even walked down to the shops with her head looking at the ground, didn't talk to anyone she met on the way and would normally ignore them. In terms of communication, my mum was normally a non-starter. I didn't mean she wasn't educated, not that, because she was brought up with a posh mum and had a good upbringing. No, it was something that developed later and appears as a result of being with my Dad.

Perhaps it was the shame of living with the poverty and hardship. I had to give up the job I loved up town and look for another locally.

After that I managed to get a job with United Dominions Trust in Bull Lane. The money was about the same except that I was paid monthly, and of the £32 per month that I got, I had to give my mum £21 for housekeeping money.

Now that was the problem. She wouldn't have been able to ask me for £21 if I had been paying for all the train fares to get up town. It didn't matter whether I was happy or not, it was all about the economics of the issue from her point of view.

One of the rules the school taught us was to stay at a job for at least six months, and that's what I did.

I got a job with Taylor Woodrow Construction at Northumberland Park Road that was paid weekly. I could pocket the month's pay because I would get paid from the new company the following week. It was like a little windfall of three weeks' money. I realised that this little bonus would solve another problem for me.

I wasn't allowed to bring anyone back to the house. Mum said it made it awkward and she didn't want me to invite people in because she didn't have much furniture. Well, I thought, I had this money saved, so if I could buy some furniture for Mum she would let me bring someone back to the house, like I saw all my friends doing.

I gave Mum enough money for a deposit on new carpet and chairs. She went to the shop with Dad, and picked what they wanted.

I asked to bring a friend back to the house.

No, she said I couldn't have anyone back to the house.

I was furious with her. It was all a pack of lies. It wasn't about the furniture, it was about her, and she didn't want anyone coming into the house, regardless of what I did.

22

Rape

IT WAS DECEMBER 1965 and the shops were full of decorations. They were so pretty, all decked with tinsel and lights everywhere, ready for Christmas.

Banging on my door, Joyce appeared out of the blue; she was giggling and laughing, and she was full of it.

"Got a great idea—we go to Scotland for Hogmanay—just for once we doon'na tell anyone."

"All right, let's get a coffee and you can fill me in," I said.

We wandered over to the Wimpy Bar.

"Just run away—come on—it would be exciting! Go on, make a New Year's resolution to do something unplanned for once."

"I'm not sure about..." I stopped. I thought, here we go on some madcap idea.

We strolled over to the front of the cafe, ordered some coffee and drifted to the table with Joyce still all bubbly and shouting. She grabbed the arm of my coat and snatched me close to her; she excitedly barked in my ear like a puppy.

"Come on! It'll be a laugh—just on the spur of the moment."

"It will be a laugh—will it?" I asked. "Us getting caught stowing away on a train miles from anywhere, cold and hungry—tell me about it!"

"Nay—doona be daft—us both going to Scotland for the New Year!" Her excitement was boiling over.

"I'm not sure," I said. "It's a long way and, besides, how will we get up there?"

"Well, it's all arranged, it's…"

I didn't let her finish. "Oooh nooo," I shook my head slowly.

She kicked the table. The clatter of slopping coffee cups broke the conversation. I reached over and grabbed some serviettes to mop up the mess on the table. "If you think I'm going to stow away on some train of yours…" I wasn't finished before she interrupted mid-flow.

"No—its no' going to be like that, it's…"

I cut her off. "Like the last time? Then you'd better think again!"

"No Mary." She flicked the hair from her face. "We don't have to."

I didn't answer. I picked up my coffee cup in both hands. I needed to think about this one.

The earthy smell of freshly brewed coffee burst into my face, like a break in moist summer clouds; it made me feel deceptively cosy against the coldness of the drab winter day.

I should have turned it down in that instant, but she made the whole idea so exciting, and sound so attractive. It began to wear me down.

She reached across the table and took my hand in hers.

"Look," she said, "my boyfriend will take us by car and they want me to come wi' them. Awe, I did no' want to go alone— and besides, it'll be better wi' the two of us!" She, like an expert salesman, had made her pitch and now she leaned back in her chair.

"I don't know." I leaned back, sucked in a breath and blew into my hot coffee. "Who is the 'them' that we're going with?"

Joyce cupped her coffee mug in her hand, and, taking a sip, she left the familiar half moon of her pink lipstick on the rim.

She glanced up at me, peering over the cup and grinning; her eyes so wide that they dazzled like diamonds.

"Aye—that'll be me boyfriend's mate! He's the one wi' the car, an' so he'll be coming wi' us." I thought her face flushed a little, but I couldn't be sure. I glanced up from my coffee.

"But it's such a long way, and besides," I said, "where will we stay for the night?"—half expecting her to have some vague idea of us all sleeping in the car or something equally maverick. There was no way I was going camping or sleeping under the stars in midwinter Scotland.

"It's all worked out, do you no' trust me?" she said. "Aye— look now, I have arranged for us to stay at my Nan's place in Montrose." She added: "Now all you have to do is keep ya little mouth shut, ya tell nobody and just come wi' me." She looked up into my eyes like some child asking for sweeties. I glanced back at her in disbelief, questioning her again.

"What about the boys—where will they sleep while all this is going on?" I tried to find out once more what was going through her head. Perhaps I was hoping she would lose interest and drop it, I didn't know, but the thought occurred to me that it was possible that the mate would be driving the car because her boyfriend had already lost his license. So I had a clue to the type of person he might be, although I told myself that his mate might be a nice guy, who knows?

"All sorted!" She finished the last of her coffee. "And besides, there's only four of us. So are you coming?" She looked up at me, her face beaming.

I looked at her and just ran out of questions to ask, but inside I just didn't want to go. I had a sense that it was all a horrible idea to go off four hundred miles or so with no preparation. But that was Joyce, flickering around the flame, chancing her arm; she loved it so much and I guess that's how she got her jollies. I couldn't deny her the fun.

I had not met the boyfriend and never had a clue what he was like. I had not been impressed with her choices so far because she would dump all the nice boys she met. Nice boys were always cast aside in favour of others who treated her rotten, and for some reason I did not understand, she would chase after the rough ones all the more, as if to bury herself in more hurt.

Sitting there a little blank, I pondered. Just for once, should I do something outside the box?

I thought that because there would be four of us, it would be safe; although it did occur to me that I was always playing it safe. Perhaps this was a time to be different, and maybe Joyce was right for once. Something different and against my better judgement; yes, I thought, safety in numbers—that's okay.

I was uneasy about keeping the secret, but it promised to be a laugh and I suppose it made it all the more exciting in a dangerous way.

Sharp intake of breath. "Oh—all right," I said, "I'll come."

"Oh great!" Her face shone like she had been given Christmas for the first time: childishly impish.

I guess that Mum thought I was staying at Joyce's for the weekend, and I suspect that Joyce's Dad thought that she was staying at my place. I never told Mum and I didn't think that she ever asked where I was staying. I packed a little overnight bag and walked over to Joyce's place.

Tony and Keith were waiting in Tony's Black Ford Zodiac when Joyce and I arrived. Tony took our bags, Keith opened the doors, and we both piled into the back.

As Keith drove off, I could feel my stomach churning. I didn't have a good feeling about this from the moment I met the boys. They were not the type I would have gone out with. There was something of the night about them. I couldn't be sure, but they made me uncomfortable.

I struck up a conversation with Joyce's boyfriend Tony.

"Tony," I said, "is this your car?"

He swung round, looked up my skirt, and placed his arm over the seat.

"Yeah, nice motor, what do you think?" His eyes flicked up to my face.

"So why aren't you driving then?" I made sure I caught his eye.

"Keith likes driving." He looked up my skirt again, then flicked his eyes across to Keith.

I thought he was looking for Keith to back him up. I didn't believe him.

"Joyce tells me you lost your license," I lied.

"Ahmm, did she?" Tony shuffled back in his seat.

Joyce stayed quiet.

"So do you have a car, Keith?"

"Not at the moment," he said. "I smashed it up and the Insurance Company didn't pay out. So I don't have a motor at the moment."

I didn't have to ask any more. The answers I got made my spine prickle with trepidation. It was just as I thought. Keith would not take Joyce, unless she found another girl to come with them.

It left me feeling a little uneasy with Keith, and I didn't care for Tony that much either. There was something about him that bothered me. I couldn't pin it down; call it intuition if you like, but it was the way he would look away whenever I asked him a question. It didn't seem right.

Tony kept sneaking a glance at me whenever Joyce wasn't looking, glancing down at my legs and up my skirt. Making suggestive remarks, and running Joyce down. I didn't like that; after all, he was Joyce's boyfriend, and I felt it was a bit of a betrayal that he should be trying to make out with me.

Joyce seemed not to notice, or if she did, she didn't mention it to me. Anyway, I didn't want to make a fuss and spoil the relationship she had with Tony, regardless of how I felt about him.

It was a complete day of driving before we eventually came to a dingy flat on the edge of town. I didn't know what town; in fact, I didn't know where the hell we were. It was up north somewhere, but I didn't think we had driven as far as Scotland.

Eventually, we went in, up some narrow stairs, where we were greeted by two other boys. Three young girls were dancing in the living room as we brushed our way through. Tony dumped our bags in one of the bedrooms at the back whilst Keith waddled off to the toilet.

Joyce and I were alone in the bedroom, Joyce laughing and joking to me about the boys, although I was feeling more than a little nervous when Tony and his mate burst in. Tony strode over to Joyce and grabbed her arm.

"Fuck off down the road to the shops and get lost for an hour, will yer love?" He pulled her over to the door.

I couldn't believe it. I turned to Joyce and looked. She just waved goodbye and walked out of the room without saying a word.

"Joyce!" I called out to her, but she just kept going, leaving me alone with her boyfriend and his mate.

I often wondered if she was in on it and that they had planned to do this to me together, I didn't know. She just walked off as if she knew where she was, and I was left there to be raped, murdered or God knows what.

I didn't have a good feeling, deserted by Joyce, and with all my worst fears about Tony. The sneaky looks, the jokes and sexual innuendoes and pointed remarks. They all added up. Had something been set up and was I going to be the patsy?

Inside, I was churning with anger—anger at Joyce, leaving me to face them, all alone.

God knows what they had in mind, but I imagined that sex was pretty high on the list. After all, they got Joyce out so she didn't spoil anything. Now they thought they were going to have me, one after the other.

As soon as she had gone, Tony came over to me and tried to kiss me. I pushed him away gently but firmly. I told him I wasn't interested, and that he should wait for Joyce to come back, watch the television or something. But he carried on trying to kiss me and then I knew the set up.

I knew all along what was going to happen the moment that Joyce mentioned it in the Wimpy Bar. The mate had to come because the boyfriend didn't drive and then the four of us all going to some remote place from which we couldn't get home. Not telling anyone where we had gone.

Tony turned round to Keith. "It's all right Keith, you can leave us and get something to eat."

Keith didn't argue. He turned and left. Tony was clearly in total control.

How could I not listen to my every instinct of survival! I should have listened to my inner self—all that I had learned from years of begging for food, and now...this awful mess!

If I was raped, killed and dumped, no one would find us. No one would be looking for us up in Scotland—even if I were able to escape.

I swallowed hard. How on earth would I get home? No transport or train fare. It was my worst nightmare and there I was, abandoned and alone, again!

I wondered how many times in my short life I would be tested in my survival skills? How many more times would people I trust forsake me?

"You're Joyce's boyfriend; you shouldn't be doing this!"

He paused for a moment. But he didn't say anything. Instead, he grabbed my arms and pulled me toward him. Again

I shoved him away and told him I wasn't interested in him, or his mate, and that I only came to be with Joyce.

"I don't fancy you!" I screamed at him. "Don't do it!" I struggled to break free from his grip, but he wasn't listening to anything I had to say, and he wasn't about to take no for an answer.

He slid his hands up to the side of my face and stroked my hair. I grabbed his hand and took it away.

"I'm not interested. You shouldn't be doing this," I shouted.

He paused for a moment, then tugged at my blouse. He pulled my shirt blouse open, started to fondle me with one hand, and then, holding me back with the other, he spun me round so quickly that I toppled backwards down onto the bed.

He was now on top of me. "Just do as you're told and you will be fine," he whispered in my ear.

Thwack.

I smacked him one on the side of his ear, but it didn't make any difference. He became even more aggressive, as his rough hands locked round my throat. If I didn't know better, it felt as if he had been waiting for this moment all day, and he wasn't about to give up. I didn't know if Joyce had told him something about me, but I sensed an air of expectation. It was almost as if he had been waiting to do this for some time.

I began to wonder if Joyce had told him I was a virgin, and that a good fucking would be good for me; whatever she had said to him certainly turned him on, and he seemed hell bent on getting his leg over.

"We will see about that," I muttered under my breath. I was just as equally determined that he wasn't going to get anywhere. Not with me, he wasn't.

Each time he tried to fondle me, I just kept pushing his hands away. He kept up the pressure of kissing me and playing with my breasts, no doubt hoping I would give in. But he hadn't counted on my resilience, and besides, he stank of body odour and sweat.

There was no way that I would have sex with someone smelling like that, even if I liked him—which I didn't. I was brought up with filth, I knew what it was like, and anyone who came near me had to be spotlessly clean: Tony had no chance!

Despite my best efforts, he gradually succeeded in pulling the buttons from my blouse; then pulling my bra down to my waist, he lifted my breasts and started stroking them. I didn't know if he thought that I was somehow going to lose my mind with erotic pleasure, but it didn't happen. He straddled my legs, kneeling on top of me when I spotted my chance.

Thump.

I brought my knee up into his crotch with as much force as I could muster.

It made no difference. The groan of surprise didn't come as expected, and he just carried on regardless. Perhaps my aim was not accurate enough to cause the desired effect.

He propped himself on one elbow and put his hand on my stomach, then slid it down and pulled up my skirt. He forced himself on me, kissing me, licking my nipples and trying to pull my legs apart until eventually I could stop him no more.

I tried everything—everything I could to prevent him raping me. But he was physically too strong. He forced his knees between my legs, and in no time at all he had unzipped his trousers. He was pushing himself onto me.

I made things as difficult for him as I could, but with his knees in the way I found I could no longer cross my legs.

"Why do you want to do this?" I gazed directly into his eyes. "You've got Joyce. Why do you want to do this to me?"

He continued the struggle. Then he looked up at my face.

"She's all soft and flabby," he grunted. "You're all firm and fresh, and I bet you're a virgin?"

His eyes seemed to widen. I wondered if the promise of virginal sex excited him. Silly mistake of mine—it focused his mind on the rape. I didn't want that. I wanted to prick his social conscience, not excite him.

"But don't you care about what Joyce will say when she finds out?"

Outside I heard the sound of music and laughter, as the other boys were all drinking, and I wondered if they knew what was going on in the bedroom. I didn't know if it would be better to scream, or just talk. I decided to talk.

Fiddling with his zip, he started to masturbate. He moved his knee. I crossed my legs. He tried to get his knee between my legs and force me apart. I grabbed at his hair and jerked his head back.

"Won't she be upset with you?"

He didn't say anything; instead, he concentrated on penetrating, grabbing hold of me with one hand round my throat and forcing my legs apart. But his hardness softened as he struggled to rise to the moment.

Half choking, I pushed him away. It was no use; he started to pull my panties to one side and use his rough fingers.

"You won't want to live with it after this," I spat words at him.

Grunt.

"How will you get a girl's respect after you do this to me?"

Grunt.

He paused for a minute and started pushing himself onto me. I let myself get upset. It was a mistake I corrected quickly.

Whack.

I caught him on the side of the face once more—I was determined not to give in. What else could I do?

"You seem like a nice lad, Tony. Why do you want to rape me?"

Grunt.

"I am a real person with feelings!" I caught his eye in the hope that I could soften him, but he opened me and tried to enter. He made no response to my question.

"People don't want to be dominated, Tony."

He glanced up at me and fiddled with himself again.

"How can you face some girl you like—after raping me?" I tried the broken record technique.

"How, Tony—how?"

Suddenly he lost his erection and he fell back on his haunches. His face was flushed.

For the first time I began to realise I was getting to him with my questions. It was forcing him to think about what he was doing. He shot me a sudden glance and then looked away: I sensed his guilt.

"I am a real person, Tony."

He took no notice.

"My name is Mary—I am not just someone to fuck."

He fiddled with himself again.

"How are you going to live with the memories, the shame of it all? How will you deal with the consequences of this?"

Leaning back onto his knees, and resting on the bed with the other hand, he tried to regain his erection. For the first time I noticed that both his hands were occupied.

Masturbating with one hand and supporting his weight on the bed with the other, I realised that this was the last opportunity for me to break free. Besides, if I were right, then his mate would soon be banging on the door wanting to rape me as well.

I glanced over at the door.

He saw me look. Grabbing my throat once more, he held me down.

Summoning all my courage and strength I struck a sideways blow across the bridge of his nose with my fist. I pushed him away once more, grabbing his hand as tightly as I could, and pulling at his little finger until I succeeded in breaking his grip on my throat. For a brief moment, I was winning.

Gasping for breath, I shouted: "Sounds to me like you haven't thought this one through at all, Tony."

He didn't answer. He grabbed at me again, holding my hair this time, pulling it back and holding it tight in the hope I would give in. No chance, I thought to myself.

"I don't care!" he shouted. "Now do as you're fucking well told!" he screamed.

"Girls don't want to be dominated, Tony! Are you prepared to live with the memories of hurting me?"

He grabbed my free hand, and pinning the other down with his knee, he tried to force me into position, but he couldn't keep me down. As he struggled to get an erection once more I saw my chance. I raised my leg into his groin and snatched my hand away from under his knee.

"You fucking bitch!" He grappled to regain control.

I pulled at his little finger again.

"Now you just do as you're told before you get hurt!" His hand clamped round my throat, squeezing hard, until suddenly the room was in black and white.

I pulled his finger as hard as I could, and I swear I heard something snap. My vision returned once more.

I sucked in a deep breath.

"You"—gasp—"going to dump me somewhere. Tony?"

He didn't answer.

"What do you think...." my voice strained as I pushed against his weight "...that I will do.." gasp "...after this?"

He stopped the attack and started to listen to what I was saying to him.

"Most girls don't give a damn," he said.

"It matters to me a great deal and I want to make love to the person who loves me, cares for me as a person. I don't want to be dominated and raped."

"It seems to matter to you a lot though," he said.

"How will you face some girl you want to marry after raping me?" I turned and looked at him directly until our eyes met.

I held him there with my stare. I demanded an answer.

He glanced back at me, then out at the door, and the noise outside.

"I don't know!" He shuffled his knee.

I felt a crunch as my knee caught him off-guard.

Bang, bang, bang.

I didn't know which was louder, the sharp intake of breath, or the groaning noise from Tony desperately nursing his balls.

Keith made a sudden appearance, stripped down to his white underpants and black socks. He stood by the door.

"Come on Tony, you said we could both have her."

Tony was still on top of me, his jeans down at his ankles, nursing his crotch. My blouse was all undone, and my breasts naked for the entire world to see. It didn't look good for me, but Keith looked pleased.

I didn't know if Keith was aware that Tony hadn't got anywhere with me or not. But he grabbed hold of Tony and started to argue with him.

"Come on Tony, why don't we take it in turns?" Keith suggested. "You hold her down and I'll have her, then I'll hold her down and you can have her."

The idea seemed to excite Tony, but it worried me.

Not with the two of them! I couldn't win against them both.

Tony was distracted by the conversation with Keith. It was stay and die, or break for freedom.

I grabbed his balls in my hand and squeezed as hard as I could, digging my sharp fingernails in until they sunk deep into his flesh, my knuckles clamping shut like a mollusc shell.

I broke free and ran over to the window, and picking up the nearby wooden chair I held it close to the windowpane.

Tony jumped off the bed and quietly pulled up his jeans.

"I'm going to smash the window if you come any closer." I lifted the chair as if to swing it.

Tony grabbed Keith by the arm, pulled him over to the side, and opened the door.

"Now fuck off!" He shoved him out and closed the door behind him.

All this time I stood by the window.

"I'm going to jump! Don't you come any closer! Else I'm going to smash this window and jump."

"Don't—we're on the second floor."

"Then stay away. I'm warning you..."

"Don't do anything," he said. "All right, calm down, I'm staying here." He jumped back holding up his hands, palms open and fingers spread wide, as if desperate to get me to stop. "You don't have to do that," he said calmly. "It's all right, I won't hurt you." He was still holding his hands in the air as if pushing against an invisible wall. "It's okay, I won't do it!"

He backed away.

I lifted the chair higher in the air.

"I won't do it!" he shouted again, as if somehow trying to reassure himself. "You seem like a nice girl, Mary," he said, "not like all the others that I've met."

I lowered the chair, not because I had surrendered, but more because I was growing tired.

"All right," he said, "get dressed. I'm not going to hurt you." He did up his jeans and stared at the ground like a little boy caught out in a lie.

I had won. He knew that he couldn't force me to have sex with him. I did up my blouse and straightened my clothes, gathered my things from the bed, and stormed out to the toilet, promptly locking myself in.

I didn't know if it was the shock, but I found myself shaking so much that I couldn't do up the clasps on my bra. I couldn't stop myself from shaking. I just sat there for what seemed ages. Thoughts were tumbling around my mind, like particles in a cement mixer. One minute it felt like panic, then fear, and sweating like I was on fire. Then my whole body trembled, my heart pounded, and fingers tingled so much, that I couldn't control anything...

I reached up and grabbed my head with both hands, pulling my hair in an attempt to make it all stop. It didn't.

Silently, as if held in a dam of all my life's sorrow, my tears burst out like blood dripping from a wound so deep I would surely die.

I took hold of myself, until once again I was calm. I dried my eyes as best I could and told myself I would soldier on.

There was a banging on the toilet door.

"Have you finished?" It was a man's voice.

"I'm coming." I unlocked the door and peered out.

It was one of the other guys who was dancing with the girls in the living room. I checked down the hallway to find out where Tony was. I couldn't see him, so I assumed he was still in the bedroom. I could hear the music, but I didn't know if Joyce was back yet.

The thought of going back into the bedroom terrified me, and yet I had to do it.

As I reached for the door my hands trembled uncontrollably. The handle was shaking and clanking like the clappers on a fireman's bell and for the first time in my life, I felt helpless. One of my hands had rebelled against my mind. It must have been the sensible one. It voted not to go in there again, but it was Hobson's choice. I didn't know where I was, let alone be able to get home.

The door burst open. Tony was sitting on the chair by the window, fully dressed smoking a cigarette. He was calm. Keith sat on the bed, and they chatted as if nothing was wrong. They both swung round to look at me.

I could see Tony didn't want to let Keith know he hadn't raped me— because he asked Keith to go and find Joyce. It stopped Keith from asking questions, which Tony didn't want to answer. Well, certainly not answers that I would confirm. He couldn't risk letting his mate know he lied to him; after all, he depended on Keith to drive him home!

Tony sat in the room for a little while. We chatted about things. He told me a little bit about himself and the girls he had known up until he met me. For some reason I didn't understand, he felt comfortable talking to me. It was as if somehow I had shown some understanding of his world and his struggle to make relationships. He started to ask me about how to deal with women, seeking some insight into the way to treat a girl, and their needs.

I wasn't sure if he was winding me up or not, but I went along with the chat and stayed friendly; after all, I wasn't home yet.

It must have been about half an hour before I heard all the commotion when Joyce entered the flat. I raced out of the bedroom, found Joyce in the hall and pulled her outside and into the road.

Furious, I flew at her with so much anger.

"You bloody knew! You bloody knew, didn't you? What he was going to do, you knew, didn't you?" I waved my finger at her, thrusting it into her face.

"Well, I was frightened what he was going to do to me—I didn't..." She flinched and darted back as I waved my fist at her.

"You bloody well knew and you left me with him! Didn't you?" I clenched my fist and held it close to her face, as if to smash it into her.

"I didn't have much choice."

"What do you mean, you didn't have much choice? You had every bloody choice!"

I was certain in my mind that Joyce knew fully well what was going to happen, and I discovered a new facet of her character that I didn't like. She skulked off back into the house and avoided eye contact, which was just as well, for otherwise I am sure I would have torn her, limb from limb.

Tony suggested that we all sleep together that night for safety, just in case the other guys came in, and we all agreed. So that night we all slept together in the same bed, Joyce, Tony and I. But nothing happened.

The details of the journey home were a bit vague. I didn't speak to Joyce for some time after that. At least not until the bruises between my thighs had gone.

When I got home, Mum didn't know where I had been or anything, and as far as I know she never found out.

If this was growing up—I wasn't sure I wanted to.

23

Elsey's Sports

I WENT TO WORK as a general secretary for Elsey's Sports Shop, which was just down from the Spurs Football Ground at White Hart Lane. I say secretary, but I was also responsible for serving in the shop from time to time. I also used to work in the mail order department, preparing the football kits ready for despatch to customers.

The shop sold sports clothes, and all things connected to football. It had two departments, one that looked after the ancillary materials, bats, balls, and other paraphernalia necessary to play the sports, and a boot department. Upstairs there was a toy department, which sold a full range of children's toys, quite separate from the sportswear. On the opposite side of the road, there was also a Scaletrix car showroom. It was owned by two brothers who reminded me of Laurel and Hardy: the slim one looked after the shop side of things, and the other looked after the office and accounts.

I got on really well with both managers, although sometimes it was a battle. Laurel used to like me working in the shop because he noticed that sales went up whenever I was in the boot department. Hardy, on the other hand, always wanted me in the office to do his typing.

I didn't know why, but Laurel always sent me up the ladder. I think he liked looking up my short skirt, and perhaps the customers, who were mostly fit young men in training full of hormones, probably thought the same.

It was a hot sunny morning as I quietly waited outside the shop. I was busily eating an ice cream as part of my breakfast when the brothers arrived. Hardy put the key in the door and turned to look at Laurel.

"You pregnant?" Hardy said.

"No, I don't think so! Why?"

"Well, it's..."

"It's what? You think I look fat?"

I looked down at my tummy.

Laurel fumbled with the door, toppled in, disappeared into the office, and switched on the piped music.

My day was immersed in the smell of leather, of dubbin, and the subtle blends of polished oak that I remember from the library. I listened to the pop music that was piped throughout the shop.

Rob, one of the guys who worked with me, came in looking a bit glum. The managers were in the back office. I was alone in the front shop, singing along to the hit, 'Glad All Over' by the Dave Clark Five.

"Hey Rob," I said. "Did yer know Mike Smith lived down my street? Me and Joyce looked up his house and knocked on his door one day."

He didn't answer.

"So what's up then?" I soaked up the lively music playing, singing and dancing behind the shop counter. "Boom, boom, glad all over... yer!" I was singing out loud.

"She's just packed me in!" His head sank like a dead parrot.

"Oh no!" I stopped singing.

He ran off into the stock room and I was left alone at the counter once more. Rob was a bit quiet for the rest of the morning. I took him a mug of tea.

"Have you got any lunch?"

"Forgot it."

"Come on then, let's go and get a Wimpy burger together."

We were good mates, Rob and I. We talked over lunch, and he seemed a little brighter after that.

It was quiet in the shop when, suddenly, a group of lads tumbled in off the street, making a load of noise and generally larking about. This good-looking young guy came up to the counter, stroking his hair with his hand, beaming and full of confidence. I thought he was about to chat me up, chance his arm, and ask me for a date.

"Hello." He casually lent on the counter top. "Have you got a Jock Strap?"

"Yes sir," I said. "What size would you like?"

He just stared at me. The room went so quiet I swear I could hear his brain, like some clockwork toy cranking up what to say in front of his mates. A bright crimson rash slowly spread across his face. It was like the sort of shaver's rash I had seen on one of the guys in the office.

Quick on the pitch and scoring a goal might have been a strong point. But he didn't know what to do with the question. He stood at the counter alone; he didn't know what to say in reply.

I heard a bit of a shuffle and muffled laughter coming out from the back office. All his football mates, who up until then were just browsing, stopped spontaneously and a hushed fog like silence crept across the crowded room.

Only one person failed to turn and look at the lad as he stood at the counter—me.

The room was like a crowd from bonfire night watching a damp squib—simmering, farting and spluttering until, suddenly, it reached a dry patch, and exploded in laughter louder than Spurs winning a goal on home turf. The whole place cracked up.

I died there and then. I felt my embarrassment rise and I slid down behind the counter refusing to come up.

"Where's she gone?" they all asked, probably thinking this would be a good laugh.

"Don't know," one said. "Maybe she's looking for a bigger one." The sound of another rousing cheer followed a bout of giggling, winking and nudging.

I was still in hiding when one of the managers came out of the office.

"Watcha doing down there?" He knew full well what had happened.

Roars of laughter erupted and someone reminded him what I had said.

"She wanted," he paused for a moment to contain his laughter, "to know his size!" He blurted out the words quickly before his face screwed up into another laughing fit, and pointed to the Jock Strap now lying on the counter.

Soon the whole shop deteriorated into pandemonium as they all doubled up in agony, rolling around as if an unexploded grenade of laughing gas had been thrown amongst them.

Hardy came over behind the counter and bent down to talk to me.

"Get up here!" He beckoned with his hand, splitting his embarrassed gaze between me and the customer, like someone at a tennis match.

"I can't." I refused to come out of hiding. "I don't know what size to give him!" I was frantically waving for him to go away and leave me alone.

"I think he wants a big one, love!" another shouted out. Well, that brought a smile to Hardy's face, and he was unable to help himself and soon joined in the fun, and at the same time tried to cajole me into getting back up.

"Come on, its okay," he said reassuringly. "Just get them out and let him pick one." He handed me the tray for good measure.

Reluctantly I rose from my hiding place amidst all the applause from the little crowd that had now gathered.

I placed the tray on the counter for the customer to choose and promptly disappeared into the back office. I heard his mates still making comments as they all bundled out of the shop and spilled into the High Road, laughing and joking.

I thought it was high time I changed my job!

24

Leaving Home: Just 17

I **WAS SITTING IN THE WIMPY BAR** in Fore Street, Edmonton, sipping my coffee and waiting for Joyce. It was about six o'clock in the evening. I had come straight from the office, dressed in my pretty white blouse and navy blue skirt. She said she wanted to meet up and talk about something. It was the time of the sixties, and Joyce and I changed jobs quite frequently, getting more money each time, and I thought she simply wanted to talk about a new job.

Much of the time we used to go out to the Royal at Tottenham, where we would dance, dressed in the Mary Quant look, mini skirts, white boots, and shift dresses. Listening to live performances of The Animals, the Dave Clark Five, who were based there, or occasionally get a lift on a friend's Vespa to the Cooksferry Inn. It became another regular haunt, and I remember saving up for tickets to see The Who in March 1965.

I was daydreaming about my plans for the future when Joyce rushed into the Wimpy at about ten past six and sat down at my table.

"I'm going to Scotland!" she panted, as if she had run all the way from home.

Coffee slopped onto the table as she drew up the chair.

"Okay," I said to her. "You've got my attention!"

"I'm going to stow away on a train and I want ye to come with me."

"Not sure about that, Joyce!" I felt the warning signs.

I saw the look in her face that spelt danger. The moment when her eyes were so clear, they glistened like morning dew.

"Aye, come on!" she said, flicking the hair from her face. "Do you no' want a laugh?"

"Still not convinced." I stared into my coffee cup.

"Why?"

"Well...you said that the last time, and look what happened. I still haven't got over that, Joyce." My eyes narrowed.

"I'm sorry about that." She looked down at the table.

I glanced back up and looked round the room.

"You were a rotten cow leaving me with your boyfriend. I am not sure I have forgiven you yet."

"What ye nay sure of?"

"Not sure it's the kind of laugh I want right now." I was trying to be polite for the sake of the friendship, but underneath I wanted to tell her to fuck off.

I was friends with her, God knows why, and the truth of it was that I didn't know why either. There was something about Joyce that was like a drug and I was drawn to her like a fly to a spider's web. But not this time. Things were going on at home and I had my own plans.

She reached across the table and grabbed my hand, pulling me over to her.

"Och come on—let's run away without telling anyone, not ye Mum, naebody—let's just go!" She put her face close to the table and looked at me, pleading.

"Where are you going then?" I glanced up from my coffee.

"Montrose," she said. "I've a Nan up there and she'll put us up at her house. Awe, come on, it'll be a laugh."

"Oh. No, no, no, Joyce, I am not going." I glared at her, shaking my head slowly.

The prospect of doing something shocking gave her a great buzz and she could talk about nothing else. She knew I was not one for madcap schemes. Not after last time.

I had left the job at Elsey's Sports and she knew I wouldn't want to lose my new job at the claims department of the insurance company in Finsbury Circus; after all, I was only just seventeen years old.

"I'm sorry Joyce, no. You can forget it."

"But Mar..." I stopped her saying any more.

"Joyce, I am *not* going, but if you want to rush off up to Scotland, then that's up to you—but read my lips!" I pulled back from the table. "I am *not* going!"

The loud scraping of my chair broke the awkward silence. I got up.

Her shoulders sank. I saw the disappointment on her face and I knew she was determined to go, with or without me, but I didn't want to take the risk. Not anymore—I had grown up and Joyce was too dangerous, not only to herself, but also to me. She brought those around her down in her rush for excitement, but like a child, she never knew when to stop.

We finished our drink and left the Wimpy Bar to go home. I wondered if that would be the last time I would see Joyce. I didn't know if she had argued with her dad—Her mind seemed in turmoil. I didn't think that anyone knew what to do with Joyce—she was so exuberant, and so full of explosive energy at times.

It left a bit of a gaping hole in my life because we shared everything, our innermost thoughts, our worries, our fears, and I guess that we were very supportive of each other and, of course, we were soul mates. There were other things we didn't talk about, and perhaps accepted that there was a darker side to both of us. It was that which bonded us together, the fact that there were things we never discussed.

I never spoke of it to anyone, about how poor my life had been—about the struggle I had endured, and the starvation Jane and I faced at the time of Mum's TB. I didn't mention it to Joyce, and I am sure there were things in her life she didn't want to tell me. We understood that there was something unspoken, and that was okay.

With Joyce, she didn't need to know. The friendship was unconditional on both sides.

Maybe it was the absence of Joyce that made me do what I did next. I was earning a reasonable wage and was determined to leave my unhappy home.

Life hadn't changed much. I serviced my own needs for clean sheets and continued to do my own laundry. Dad was still drinking and I stayed out as much as possible.

So I went to a letting agency and moved into a large pre-war house in Plaistow. A narrow path led to the arched brick porch, and to the left of the partly glazed red front door, there was a bay window. It was a nice square ground floor room to the left of the passage, and overlooking the rear garden. An older woman lived in a room farther down, to the right. Upstairs, the black and white chequered tiles dominated the spotlessly clean bathroom. We all shared the bathroom, except for the lady right at the back who had her own.

The older woman was very nice to me, and we got on well, although I didn't know what she did for a living. She had a beehive hairstyle, tight short skirts, a short leather jacket and four-inch high heels.

Everything about my room was better than I had at home. It was light and bright. A gold patterned table lamp sat on a small wooden bookcase. The brown fitted carpet and gold velvet curtains complemented the yellow decorative wallpaper. A single bed was dressed with a gold bedspread and scatter cushions. Most of all, it was clean, and to have a lampshade was sheer bliss.

It was so lovely and cosy. I even managed to save up and buy a portable reel-to-reel tape recorder. It was great because now I could record songs from the radio rather than buy them.

Joyce suddenly turned up. She had gone round to my mum's and she told her that I had moved out and gave her my address. Joyce seemed a little shocked that I actually had the balls to move out and get my own place.

She saw this as an opportunity for us to live together. So when one of the double rooms came up at the front of the house, she asked if she could share with me. I knew the rent would be more expensive, but we would split the costs. I would hold the rent book, and she would pay me her half each week.

Well, I loved Joyce as a friend, and so I moved to the double room at the front, and a new girl, Chris, moved into my old room. Joyce, of course, didn't have a job. The next morning I had a word with my manager at my firm, and he agreed to see about arranging an interview for Joyce.

She soon started at the company, but it wasn't long before she started to become unreliable. First, she didn't arrive for work, or would be late. She let me down and embarrassed me. I felt responsible because I had recommended her in the first place. But they said it wasn't my fault and that I shouldn't worry about it. This continued and in the end they sacked her.

One day I overheard the guys at the insurance company discussing a backpacking holiday together. The idea was to take time off and work our passage through Europe. I thought it was a great idea, a great adventure for me. After all, the guys were a reliable bunch.

Back at the house, I told Joyce all about the trip they were planning. She was well up for the idea straight from the start, and although we would have a problem funding it, she said she had an idea to raise the extra money. I wasn't sure, but the guys at work seemed quite happy to include her, and so I went along with the deal.

Joyce got a temp job, going from business to business. Then on her way home she saw an advert in the local Fish and Chip restaurant in Green Street. We both went down there and chatted for about ten minutes to the manager—Pete, I think his name was. After a bit of chatting up she managed to get us both an evening job. The plan was that she would work one day, and I would work the next, and so forth, like a kind of job share.

One evening I was working in the shop when Joyce brought in two guys. She was going out with Kevin, I think; they were both friends working together at Plessey in Ilford.

"This is Kevin, my boyfriend, and this is his mate Terry."

"Right," I said.

"I'm going back to the house with Kevin and Terry. We'll see you later, all right?"

I wanted to say something before she went. I didn't want to meet any potential boyfriends smelling of fish!

When I got back to the flat I cleaned myself up, and walked into the room. Kevin and Joyce were sitting on the sofa, and Terry sat with the girl, Chris, from my old room. We chatted and played records and had a little party with drinks. The time slipped by and we were all having a great time. I was talking with Terry while Kevin and Joyce were getting closer on the sofa.

I didn't remember what Chris was doing other than moaning about her room and the landlord, until it got so late that the boys weren't going to be able to get home. Joyce noticed the top flat was unlocked, empty, and still furnished. So we gave them something to sleep on and they both settled down for the night up there.

The next morning Terry's mum knocked on the door. Apparently she was furious at him because he was supposed to be going off on a caravanning holiday to Yarmouth. His Mum thought I was a fallen woman because he had stayed at my house all night, and she gave me a bit of a funny look when we met for the first time. I didn't know why Terry was round at our place when he was supposed to be going on holiday. But Terry seemed to do things in his own time. Perhaps it was a sign of defiance, or independence, I wasn't sure which. However, he was reliable, well dressed and I found him attractive, and so we started dating, and we made a foursome with Joyce and Kevin.

Joyce came home one day, dressed up with nice new clothes and this large blonde wig.

"Where did all this come from?"

"Well, I was in the office during lunch and my boss had left the safe open."

"So what did you do?" I waited for the answer, my eyes wide with expectation.

"I just helped myself to this wad of money." She held out a big bundle of fivers.

"What?" I didn't know what to say. My jaw dropped, and I stood there like a gulping fish.

"It's all right; I'm not going back." Well, that threw me into complete panic.

"What do you mean, it's all right? All right for whom?"

"Well..."

"Well!" I shouted, "It might be all right for you—it's not all right for me! It's not all right Joyce, it's a bloody mess!" I lowered my voice: "You will have to get rid of it. We can't have it here."

"So where are we going to put it?" She held it out to me.

"Give it here."

I took it and counted it out. There were twenty crisp five-pound notes in two bundles tied with a paper strap. I put it under the corner of the carpet for safekeeping until I could think of something better. Later Joyce found an old tin and we hid it in there, and buried it in the garden.

During that night we continually sneaked a look out of the curtains, until we saw the police arrive and quietly park outside.

"They're not watching us, are they?" Joyce asked.

"Don't know."

We turned the lights off and sat peeking through the windows. They were coming up the path. Joyce ducked down behind the sofa whilst I continued to peek through the gap in the curtains. Someone answered the front door, I didn't see who. We braced ourselves ready for the knock on our door.

I hid behind the chair, pretending I wasn't there. It was silly really, because the landlord had a key to the door and could have opened it at any time. This was it. We waited, holding our breath. Nothing.

They walked down the hallway, and then stopped halfway. They were outside our door. The voices weren't formal voices. It wasn't "Excuse me Mrs Plumb," or anything. It was more like, "Hello love, everything all right then?"

"Where are they going then?" Joyce asked.

"Can't tell." I felt my heart pounding.

"What's the time?" I flicked my cigarette lighter and glanced at my watch.

"Ten o'clock."

"Ole right." Joyce sat down.

I wondered why they hadn't come for us. Surely they would have been here by now.

We sat silently in the dark, listening. The copper left, got in his car and drove away.

I checked the time.

"Eleven," I said.

A car pulled up outside. It was another police car. This was it! I heard footsteps on the path, which I assumed was him, then the door closed with the faintest hint of a flicking latch.

Struggling to hold the mirror still, I peeked through the gap under the door. I saw high heels—black patent leather, I think they were. Sweat was trickling down my face onto the mirror. I couldn't see properly. I had to know—it was driving me crazy.

I cracked open the door and watched them walk down the hallway. She was wearing fishnet stockings and he followed in his black heavy boots. I couldn't work it out.

"Where they going, Mary?"

"Seems to be to the lady in the back room."

"What, Chris?"

"What? No, no, the lady," I said. "You know. The one with the big beehive hairdo and tight skirt."

"Ole, right."

Joyce and I spent most of the night watching the procession of coppers arriving and leaving at all hours.

"You don't think she's on the game, do you?" Joyce asked.

"What do you mean, prostitute?"

"She has a red light on the table by the window."

"What difference does that make?" I didn't understand, but Joyce just burst out laughing.

We still worried that the police might be looking for Joyce. Joyce had never returned to work after taking the money. I thought they must have guessed who took it; after all, they had her address.

In a state of panic and worry, we went to Petticoat Lane Market the next day and spent all the money on clothes and other things.

Joyce refused to get another job because she didn't have a reference, or so she said. The rent due, which now fell on me, was twice as much—because we had a double room. Without the money from Joyce I was unable to keep paying the rent.

Eventually I had to sell my precious tape recorder. I was gutted to have to part with it. Then Joyce and I had a huge row.

"Joyce," I said, "come on, you need to get a job."

"I can't Mary, I don't have a reference."

"We can't carry on like this! You have to start paying me something."

"We'll manage. Tell the landlord he will have to wait."

"I can't do that Joyce, he'll sling us out—and besides, it wasn't my idea to go stealing the money from my boss's safe while he was at lunch. That was a choice you made. You didn't ask me, and now I'm paying the price for your bloody mistake."

"So...?"

"Well, get a bloody job!" Had I been a man I would have belted her one.

"I can't, so there it is." Joyce just sat there, calmly ignoring my rant.

"The trouble is Joyce, I always pay the price for your lousy ideas. Look at the trip to Scotland with your mate Tony. I still haven't forgotten that."

"Well, if you hadn't insisted on spending it all, just because you panicked, then we would be able to pay the rent, wouldn't we?"

"That's not fair!" I turned on her and spat out the words: "You brought it back here! It's my room, and I'm the one who would have been caught by the police. Tell me what was I supposed to do?"

She didn't say anything further. I stormed off out of the house and went for a walk to calm down.

The following morning I left for work. When I came home she had kicked all my clothes out of the room. I didn't know why, perhaps because she had split up with Kevin. I didn't understand what her problem was.

I went back to live at Mum's. I invited my friend Chris, the girl who took my room to come with me, and suggested that we could both pay Mum for our keep. Jane was quite happy, and Mum seemed pleased to take the extra money. I didn't know about Dad—I didn't see much of him at that time.

Joyce started dating Pete, the manager of the Fish and Chip shop. Chris and I both stayed at Mum's for some time until one day I came back with Terry.

He was chatting away to me, when I noticed that Chris had moved out with all her things. I didn't know what Mum had said to her, but she didn't say anything to me. Chris had completely vanished and I never saw her again, not ever, not a phone call, nothing.

Terry and I had a bit of an argument over money. I found that it was difficult for me to save. He wanted to know what the problem was. I told him I had to give over half of my earnings to Mum, and then on top of that, I had to pay for all the other things. If I wanted a bath because I was going out, then I had to put money in the meter. If I wanted the lights on I had to settle the electric bill, and so it was costing me all my wages just staying at home. Terry suggested it would be much better if I went over to stay at his mum's house, and then we could both save.

Mum hit the roof, started screaming and shouting about how I didn't care about her, and didn't love her, and how she had scrimped and saved all these years to bring me up, and now look what I was doing!

I didn't understand what all the fuss was about. After all, I had moved out to my own little room before, and she didn't row like this. I suspected she was getting so much money from me that she was living quite well, and not having to work so much. Then suddenly Dad called me out to the hallway, and he said to me that if I wanted to go it was all right and he would sort Mum out for me.

I really felt his love when he did that for me. I didn't understand why I felt that way; after all, he had been totally irresponsible about bringing in the money and supporting the family all these years. He was the main cause of all our hardship, with his drinking and gambling, and he was a complete bum. Still, I felt the warmth of genuine concern from him.

I moved out after that and went to live with Terry and his parents. They had a beautifully furnished, comfortable home that I fell in love with. He had a large, close family, who all took to me and I to them. I felt happy.

I slept in his room and Terry slept on the sofa-bed in the living room. At the weekends, Terry and I would go with his mum and dad to California Caravan Site at Yarmouth. All his uncles and aunts would be there, and it would be a great family gathering.

Kevin would come round from time to time, and Joyce was still going out with Pete from the fish and chip shop. I got to know Terry's wider family at Christmas time, when a large group met for a party.

25

Married Life

THE TELEPHONE RANG early one morning.
"Hello Mum."
"Hello Mare."
Why couldn't she simply use my name?
"It's Mary, Mum."
"Ahm, right, yeah. Well, I just rang to tell you that I'm getting a divorce."
"That's good news then, Mum." At last, I thought, she was doing something.
After all the time I had been nagging, now at last something had changed. She was full of excitement as she read out an article in the paper.
"The Divorce Reform Act was passed, allowing couples to divorce without proof of guilt."
Newspaper rustled on the table.
"So I can get divorced now," she said.
"Mum, I haven't got much time—I'm going to be late for work. So what do you want me to do then?" I was impatient with her.
"Well, ah," she said, "I want you to come up to County Court with me."
"All right, I'll speak with you later, bye."

It was a few months later when I was standing at the Court that I felt the mixed up emotion spring out at me. I found it very awkward with Dad there, because I still had feelings for them both. He had his hangdog look on his face, as if to say, all right, do your worst. Mum was always spiteful and bitter, but Dad, he always had a kind word, except when he talked about all the do-gooders.

Once the Court had made the decision to grant the application, my brother Les drove to the house in Langhedge Lane. Dad sat in the chair and said he wasn't leaving. Les's moment had arrived. He grabbed hold of Dad by his jacket and hoisted him out through the front door. He must have waited fourteen years to be able to get his own back on Dad, for all the beatings he said that he had as a child. He looked as if his birthday and Christmas had both come in one day.

Dad went back to live at his mother's house in Argyle Road, or so I was told, but I didn't know, and to be honest I didn't really care at that time.

The change in the family dynamics was so immediate, that I was stunned by the speed of it.

Jane, my sister, replaced my father as the dominant force within the family, and Mother simply continued to play the victim, but now under the direction of my sister, now fifteen years old.

I felt so shocked. After all those years of living with Dad, Mum had insisted that she wanted her independence and freedom. I had thought that she might have taken responsibility. But none of that seemed to happen, and her daily routine continued from where it had left off; the only difference was that now my sister Jane called the shots.

Mum ironed Jane's clothes for work every morning, and accompanied her everywhere: to the doctors, job interviews, and dentist, just about everywhere. Jane even sat in Dad's chair every morning and evening when she got home from work, smoking and calling out for her dinner in her lap. It was exactly as our father had done before her, and it seemed to me that nothing fundamentally had changed.

I found it nauseating. I realised that all Mum's moaning was just a game she played. She enjoyed being bitter.

Meanwhile Joyce was living with Pete and soon she was expecting a baby; she gave birth to a son, also named Peter, who was born in September of 1970.

I loved Terry, and I was so excited when he proposed to me. It completed me, and I longed for a family of my own.

I married Terry in 1970 at the Havering Registry Office earlier in the year. It was a lovely big wedding, with all Terry's aunts and uncles. The reception was held at Auntie Sylvie's place at Gidea Park. I didn't invite Dad—I didn't think it was wise; instead my brother Les gave me away. Terry's family really took me into their bosom. It was my dream come true, and I was part of this wonderful caring family.

Terry and I moved out of his parents' house, and we were lucky enough to find a studio flat in Ilford, Essex. It was just two rooms and a bathroom, but it was heaven to us. Not long after that Terry's parents bought their own home a few miles away, and moved out of the council house. We moved back into their home, continued to pay the rent on their council house, pretending to be them. Florrie, Terry's mum, left some furniture for us and we settled there reasonably comfortably for some time.

For the moment things were going well, except that I had a burst appendix soon after the honeymoon, and was rushed to hospital. Terry got a job at Rayovac batteries as a sales representative, and then three months later, I found myself pregnant. It was unexpected, but I was looking forward to having a complete family.

Life settled down as I happily watched my bump grow, and I continued with my temp work, until I was nearly seven months pregnant. I busied myself at home, preparing for the baby, when I got a telephone call from Jack, Terry's dad. I was now nearly full term with the baby.

"Hello Mary," he said. "Have you seen Terry?"

I looked at the clock. It was getting late and I would have expected him to have been home. It made me worry.

"No, I haven't—not yet—why?"

"Do you know where he is?" He sounded concerned. It was 10 p.m.

"No," I said, "I haven't seen him. He hasn't come home yet, and I haven't heard anything."

If Jack knew something, he never let on, but I got the impression something was wrong.

Terry came home at 2 a.m. I didn't know where he had been.

A couple of days later the telephone rang. Terry had just walked in after work.

"I'll get it." He took the call.

"Your dinner's on the table!" I shouted.

"Okay Mary, thanks." Terry put the phone to his ear.

"Hello, it's Terry... oh, hello dad."

I heard raised voices. Jack was shouting so loud I could overhear the conversation from the kitchen, only a few feet away.

"Mary could have her baby at any time, poor girl." Jack seemed upset.

"She's fine," Terry said, "there's no problem."

"She's not bloody fine. Where were you the other night?"

"Just doing business, that's all."

"Doing business! She could have been in trouble while you were out."

"She's fine." His dad wasn't listening.

"God knows where. You should be at home with Mary, not gallivanting around all over the place."

"I wasn't gallivanting anywhere. It was just a bit of business dad, that's all."

"Up to no good, I wouldn't be surprised."

The doctors were concerned that I was overdue by two weeks. I thought that I would be all right without them interfering, but they persuaded me to go into hospital early where they induced my labour. I was at Harold Wood Hospital for a week having my baby son Colin. He was whisked away almost as soon as he was born. Then I was told he was jaundiced and I couldn't have him with me for a few days. It was a time of mixed emotions. I was pleased I had given birth to a lovely little boy, but I yearned to hold him in my arms. It was heartbreaking. I loved my baby, but it was two or three days before I could see him. When I finally had him next to my bed, I found I could tell his cry from all those around, no matter where I was in the ward.

When I came home Terry told me he had lost his job. Furious, I felt so let down. My emotions washed around my mind. Joy, disappointment, downright frustration and anger—I had them all. I felt myself start to get upset, but I carried on.

Florrie told me she thought Terry was nicking batteries, and selling them. I didn't know anything, but he seemed to have been a worry to his mum. He was probably buying them at staff discount and selling them on at a profit.

I had to admire his attempts to make more money, but he wasn't good at it. He was like a little boy lost, he couldn't seem to see the disaster waiting to happen. I thought it was about time he grew up—he was a father now.

Whatever the truth of it, he lost his job, and seemed to be reluctant to get another.

His mum came round a few times to encourage him to get a job. When that didn't work she sent Pete (Terry's sister's boyfriend) round to coax him. Pete was a big man, and that seemed to have the desired effect. He got a job at Maplin Furniture as a sales rep.

We still lived at Terry's parents' council house. The rent book was in their name and so we had to pretend that we were Jack and Florrie. It was all a deception and I found it difficult to continue because if the Council found out, they would evict us. I wanted to be the same as everyone else and have a home in my own name.

Terry and I put our name on the waiting list for a local authority home. It was difficult to get allocated a council house to rent at that time, and so we saved for a deposit for a mortgage, just in case. We were determined to get somewhere to live, either way.

We made enquiries about buying a house on a second phase of a development at Canvey Island, Essex. It was an unbelievably lovely spot, fresh air, near the sea, and only a short commute to Terry's work. No sooner had we started dreaming about owning our own home, when the Council offered us a rented flat at Minehead House, Hilldene Avenue. Really we preferred to buy our own home like Jack and Florrie, but it was a stroke of luck we couldn't turn down.

Terry was ambitious and wanted to prove to his family he could climb the social ladder, and house ownership was the first step on that rung. We received a letter from the developers at Canvey Island. The building project had been cancelled, and suddenly we didn't have a choice to make.

Bitterly disappointed, I slung the letter down on the table and cried. The only thing we could do was to take the offer of the flat at Minehead House, and wait for a year or two for the next phase at Canvey Island to restart.

We ambled on for a little while. Joyce came to visit with her little boy, Peter. She loved him so much you could see the pride on her face. We chatted all afternoon, comparing our babies and all the things young mothers do.

A few months later I unexpectedly got a visit from the police. I wondered what on earth was going on. They asked for Terry. Apparently, an undercover policeman, pretending to be a Maplin customer, had purchased kitchen taps from Terry. They were investigating because there had been a string of complaints from customers. The Flying Squad came into my home searching all the rooms. I knew that Terry had stuffed some taps behind the armchair in the corner of the living room, and so I started to change the baby's nappy on the carpet there.

The big policeman burst into the living room.

"Do you mind!" I shouted. "I'm in the middle of changing my baby!"

"Sorry." He gave a quick glance around the room and left it at that.

I was relieved that I had diverted the policeman, but then I watched out of the window as Terry was marched out of the house, and driven off to the station. It was to help them with their enquiries, or so I was told. The police didn't find anything at the house.

When I asked Terry what was going on, he told me he had gone to Maplin suppliers and done a deal to buy kitchens direct. He then sold Maplin kitchens to Maplin customers, cheaper than Maplin could. The taps he bought from Maplin at the staff discount and sold them at Maplin prices.

I guess that Maplin didn't like the idea. Although legal, it was a bit of sharp business practice. Terry lost his job again and was banned from all Maplin stores. This was the second job Terry had lost, and I began to see a pattern that worried me. It sounded just like my father. I felt myself start to get upset, but I carried on.

Despite the problems, things were picking up for Joyce and I. Terry got some commission only work whilst he continued to search for a full time job. Joyce got married in Redbridge in

October 1972 when their son Peter was two years old. My son Colin was eighteen months, and for a moment, Joyce and I seemed to be making our way in life, both socialising together with our husbands in a foursome and creating regular happy families.

26

The Good Life

LIFE CARRIED ON AS NORMAL for a while and we continued saving in the hope that we could find a new house somewhere. Then we heard that the Greater London Council (GLC) were giving 100% mortgages for people moving to places like Thetford, or Kettering, some sixty miles away from London. The only criteria was to have a job in the area.

We decided that Terry would apply for jobs in Suffolk and see if we could qualify for a GLC Mortgage. In the meantime I would stay at the flat with Colin.

Eventually Terry managed to get a job with Pedigree Pet Foods in East Anglia in November 1972, and started to work for them as a sales rep, travelling the country. He had to work for six months before he could get his own committed round in Suffolk. That would mean he would be travelling all over the place, only coming home at the weekends.

This would put a strain on any marriage and ours was no exception. However, we realised it would only be for a short period of time, and we were both looking forward to the day we could get a home of our own.

Terry managed to find a bungalow on a large corner plot on a modern estate at 47 The Paddocks, Brandon, Suffolk, not far from Lakenheath US Air Force base. It was in a lovely town, and the bungalow was for sale at £9250. I thought it ideal, all new, clean, and far enough away from London for me to make a fresh start. I was very proud of Terry because he had picked a beautiful bungalow; now there was only one thing stopping us realising our dream—the Mortgage!

We applied to the GLC straight away. But they said we both had to have a job near Brandon before they would allow us to have a Mortgage. It came as a shock to realise I would have to have a job there as well.

Terry, his head in his hands, was upset that we couldn't get the loan. I felt for him. He tried so hard. He could see that he would be away from home all the time; he could see the house and the dream slipping away; and I could see that he couldn't bear the shame of it. There was a period of frantic phone calls, of rushing around to find a way round the problem, when suddenly we got an idea.

Uncle Len had a double-glazing office up in Cromer, Norfolk. We decided to ask if he could write to the GLC to say that I had a job there. Cromer wasn't anywhere near to Brandon, of course, but it was our only chance.

Whilst Terry was dashing all over the country with his job, I was working full time for Leslie and Godwyn Insurance, Fenchurch Street, London. Joyce and I would meet up lunchtimes and exchange all the gossip. She was going through difficult times with her marriage, and I gave her a lot of support and advice.

Dropping Colin off at the nursery in Ilford, I would travel to work, then return by train to pick him up at night.

I phoned Uncle Len and told him we had a problem getting a Mortgage. He listened to me carefully. He said he would be happy to write a letter for us outlining a job offer for me. I was over the moon! For the first time in my life it was all coming together, and there was hope. Would the Council check the location of Cromer and realise that it was miles away from Brandon?

Fortunately for us, no! The Council didn't check to see where Cromer was, otherwise perhaps they wouldn't have given us the Mortgage. Instead, to my surprise and delight, they accepted the letter as proof of a job offer and gave us the mortgage at 7%. The bonus was that this interest rate was lower than the bank rate of the time at 8.5%.

Then came the bombshell—they would only lend us £9000 and we would have to find the other £250 plus all the expenses and legal fees, which came to about £1200.

Still, we managed to scrape together all the funds. Terry sold some taps, and we borrowed on the credit card, just in time to secure the home, and we moved in during September 1973. Colin was enrolled in the Nursery School and later the Glade Primary School, and I soon got a job with Target Life as a secretary.

Unexpectedly we had landed on our feet, with new jobs, a new home and a fresh start in life. Things couldn't have been better for us, and I remember feeling so happy for once in my life. I had escaped and now tasted freedom.

Colin, our son, soon made friends with a little girl called Julie, although I had my doubts about her influence on him. Julie was loveable, but headstrong. Julie's mum used to give us a lift to school. One day Julie had a bag of cakes. She told me that she had got them out of her mummy's freezer, and although I remember thinking it a bit strange, I didn't question it.

She had taken them from her mother's freezer, without asking, and started to give them to all the children at school. Colin obviously thought this was a good idea, so he took my purse from the kitchen table and together with Julie, he gave all my money away.

Life seemed to lurch from one disaster to another with Colin, and I didn't realise how much effort looking after a child took. He fell over in the street and broke his collarbone, which left him strapped up for about six weeks. Not content with breaking his collarbone once, he then fell off the shed, and broke it again!

On the whole it was happy times, swimming in the river on hot summer days, and generally enjoying the good life. Terry and I joined the Parent Teachers Association (PTA), and raised money for a swimming pool. We ran fashion shows getting 'D minor', the kids clothes designers, down to the school to put on a show. We got the kids from the school to model the clothes.

Hosting cheese and wine suppers raised a lot of money for the school. We held Bazaars selling clothes from Terry's Aunt Sylvie, putting them on the racks with the nearly new and brand new clothes. We hosted all sorts of stalls and events, raising so much money. Not only did we have fun doing it, but we were so good at it.

Colin was still a bundle of fun! I held a party for his fifth birthday and made all the Jellies and no sooner had my back turned, when he had gone down the hall plastering the melted Jelly all over the walls with his fingers. He said he was making paintings. Colin was always a challenge.

He made friends with some of the children of the US airmen, who worked at the nearby Lakenheath airbase. Rhonda was his favourite. We used to fill up a small swimming pool on the patio, and let all the children play.

Rhonda's parents became good friends, and they used to invite us to the Rod and Gun Club dances—although we were under strict instructions not to talk, especially at the guardhouse. If they realised we were British, then we wouldn't get onto the base. It was great fun to go to the dances and the movies, and at long last we had arrived!

Terry continued to have problems. He was an excellent salesman, but paperwork wasn't his strength. Selling was his strength, but the sheer number of orders overwhelmed his ability to complete the paperwork. Terry was so focused on the sale, however, that he would get awards and win competitions for meeting sales targets, even winning a week's cruise to the Greek Islands.

Whenever his paperwork was behind, he would blame it on some event. I swear that he faked a car crash when his boss began to suspect he hadn't kept up with the administration. I felt he was lying not only to his manager, but to me as well. I couldn't pin him down. He was like a ferret. The stories went on and on, without end, always plausible. I was his wife, and I had to stand up for him.

Another time I suspected he had faked appendicitis, and even went as far as having an operation, such was his determination to outfox his manager. Eventually the relationship with Pedigree Pet Foods reached an end, and Terry lost his job again.

I wondered when Terry was going to grow up and keep a job long enough for us to get on top of things. Each time he lost his job it took us two months to recover the financial loss.

I felt myself start to get upset, but I carried on.

27

The Bacon Factory

TERRY WAS WORKING FOR DC MARKETING selling life insurance policies, working in Bury St Edmonds. He was doing so well that he was promoted to Branch Manager. He trained all the reps to go out and sell insurance policies and it was going really well, until a television programme went on air.

Esther Rantzen, a presenter for a Consumer Watchdog television programme, showed some instances where insurance brokers had misled customers.

The company responded in good faith, and refunded a few of the customers who had been affected by this mis-selling. This triggered a run as customers saw the opportunity to exploit the situation, claiming that they too were mis-sold polices. The company was soon forced into liquidation. Terry lost his job, again.

It was November 1977, about the time all the firemen were on strike. I remember thinking how lucky we were because Terry had been paid, and I could do the shopping. But it wasn't long before the liquidators clawed it back and we were left with nothing.

I was used to being without money, and ran a tight budget saving as much as I could.

I got a knock on the door. The mortgage hadn't been paid. They had sent out warning letters, but I never got to see any.

When I found out that the mortgage hadn't been paid for several months, I went ballistic.

He never told me we were in so much trouble. It never occurred to me that the mortgage hadn't been paid, and the thought of losing the house now started to become a reality. After all the work and struggle to get the house in the first place, I was determined it wouldn't be lost without a fight. The very next day I went out and got a job in the bacon factory, DanePak at Thetford, Norfolk.

At first I was humping great sides of pork from the cold room, into the factory. I was a dainty girl, size twelve, struggling to carry large cuts of pork, and then trying to hoist them up onto the large hook of the assembly line; not a pretty sight! Later, because of my dainty hands, or perhaps more realistically because of the ridiculous struggle which I had lifting the bacon, I was given a dexterity test—picking up match-sticks with both hands and putting them into the two rows of holes on a Cribbage Board. I had been a typist, and I guess I was used to using both hands, had good coordination and agility, and so they gave me the job of packing the rashers of bacon into packets.

I was on the bus at 7 a.m. with all the other female workers. Inspectors continually checked our hygiene hats, and I would have to stop work to tuck my hair in. The other women on the production line would complain.

It was oppressive, and I felt like a battery chicken in the hen house. There was a core of production workers, who perpetuated a culture of bitchy hate. At times I thought the other girls would turn and peck me to death.

The swearing and bitching was constant, and I found myself uncomfortable with it. Some would have assumed that being brought up on a council estate in London, I would be used to swearing and coarse language. I was used to the 'fucking' this and that, from my father when he was drunk, but he didn't use that language when he was sober. Yes, some Londoners could be a little rough in their tongue, no 'airs and graces', so to speak, but it was rare to hear vulgar language. Let's face it, we all like to be nosey about our neighbours, but in the factory it was destructive—almost corrosive.

I sensed that the factory was divided almost along tribal lines. They started as soon as they got on the bus to the factory.

"Look at so-an'-so in her new coat—thinks she's the fucking Queen, does she?" one shouted loudly.

"You're only packing bacon love!" someone shouted from the back.

"Does hubby know you're seeing someone?"

It was all about undermining, screwing up and destroying those around them, and I couldn't wait to get out of there.

Soon I found a job at Travenol Laboratories as a secretary. I worked on the diagnostics side of the business. I absolutely loved working there; people were nice, and the job was fabulous. I was secretary to someone who looked a dead ringer for Kojak's sidekick, Crocker, played by Kevin Dobson in the TV series.

Joyce rang, and we had a chat about things. I said everything was fine—I didn't want to tell her my troubles. She told me she had separated from her husband; he had run off with another woman and she was filing for divorce. I spoke to her a number of times, listening to her and trying to help with suggestions, but Joyce was Joyce, and I couldn't always persuade her to make the right decisions.

I thought things were getting better because I was now bringing in a decent wage, but it wasn't enough. I watched the finances slip further into decline, until eventually we realised we were drowning in a sea of debt. The breaking point came when the insurance company reclaimed Terry's company car, leaving him stranded.

Terry travelled to London by train and got commission-only work. But that didn't help us much as it only covered the train cost, and on top of that, he was coming home late.

It was approaching Christmas and he realised he wouldn't be able to keep the family tradition and buy all the family presents. He phoned me up, and told me that he was at the river Thet, at Thetford, and that he felt like killing himself because it was all closing in on him.

I told him to just come home, I would make a cup of tea, and it would be okay. We would find a way.

I put it all on the credit card for Christmas, and that action bought us some time.

28

Coming back from Brandon

AFTER CHRISTMAS 1977, Terry and I sat down and discussed what to do. He hadn't been able to get a job in Brandon, and without work, it was impossible to continue living there. We decided to rent out the house and go back to Brentwood, Essex.

A lot of people were in negative equity and were losing their houses. But I was determined not to be one of them; after all, we had equity in our house and I didn't see why we couldn't pay off the arrears. All I needed was for Terry to get another job. But it was the time of strikes and three-day weeks of the Labour government and he wasn't having much luck. Finally the interest rates went up to a point when it was clear we couldn't keep up the payments on the mortgage any more.

As luck would have it, we managed to rent out our home to an airman from Lakenheath. The income didn't cover the entire mortgage, but it was close enough to manage.

I stayed in Brandon for a few months before the tenant moved in, while Terry went down to Hornchurch, where his parents lived, to organise a house and school for Colin, who was nearly seven years old.

Our tenant made an offer to buy the bungalow for £13,150, and we accepted the offer. We had bought it at £9,250 in 1973 so that meant that if we sold it, we could clear both the backlog of mortgage arrears, and credit card loans. Unemployed, we had limped on from November 1977 through to March 1978, and now, much to my relief, Terry obtained a full time job.

We heard that the Brentwood Housing Association was building a new estate of flats in Brentwood, Essex, and thought that we might have a chance of getting one of those. We still had £1,500 left over to put down on an Association house.

Housing Associations had a strict procedure for the vetting of residents before they were allowed to get a house on the estate, and our application was no exception. I was still stuck up in Brandon with young Colin, and so I had to rely on Terry to organise things.

I didn't find this out at the time, so I have to rely on Terry's account of the events. Terry was apparently full of his usual optimism and confidence as he went for the application interview before the panel. After all, it was to be fairly straightforward because he had a regular job with a large company. He had been working for them for six months, and they had given him a glowing reference. Terry always scrubbed up well, and looked every bit the upstanding pillar of the community. He appeared to be the ideal candidate. So what could possibly go wrong?

On arrival he met with the panel from the Association. The interview appeared to go reasonably well at first; after all, Terry was a very experienced salesman, always confident with people and could sell them anything. They asked why he wanted a house on the estate, and then questioned him about his family and so forth, until they came to the employment section. When they asked Terry the name of his employer, he naturally told them he worked for Webley & Scott.

Looking at each other, all members of the panel seemed to have an epiphany—they looked horrified, went into a little huddle and starting muttering. They thanked him for his application and then proceeded to tell him that unfortunately he had been unsuccessful, and that he would be unable to have a home on the Association development.

I didn't remember him telling me at the time; perhaps he didn't want to disappoint me, I didn't know. But later he told me that they apparently thought that because he worked as a salesman for Webley and Scott, he must therefore be some sort of dubious Gun Dealer. They simply refused point blank to let him have an Association house and that was it. He was absolutely furious that they could be so blinkered. But there was nothing else he could do. We couldn't afford to buy a house on the open market, so we were completely stuffed!

I moved from Brandon with my son Colin with nowhere to live. The personal disappointment I suffered was devastating. One minute a proud owner of my own home, a well furnished, large new bungalow, in rural Suffolk, and now, God knows what.

I had escaped poverty for a better life. The clean air and low crime of village life was my dream. But now I was back in Brentwood—a failure. I hadn't escaped. Not really. Snatched back on elastic, as if that's where I belonged.

Angry? I'll say I was angry! That churning anger crushed my very soul. Did I blame Terry for the loss of his job, and with it, the failure of all my dreams? Yes.

If only he had kept his job, or at the very least if he hadn't accepted half pay we could have made it. When the first letter from the bank dropped on the mat, I sprung into action. I started humping sides of bacon in the Danepak factory. I thought we could make it, that between us, we could save the dream, but it was like bailing the Titanic.

Going back to Brentwood was hard and if I could have got a Housing Association house I could have retained some sort of self-respect, some sort of pride; at least I could have mitigated my loss. But it was not to be, and even my dignity was snatched away from me at the last minute because of Terry and his job.

I had just returned from Brandon, Suffolk. We had sold the house and finally I had come back to Hornchurch in Essex with my son Colin, who was now eight years old. A friend of the family, Richard, owned a furniture shop at Ardleigh Green Road, Hornchurch. He agreed to let us rent his dingy, one bedroom flat above the shop. It was a complete dump, mainly because it had only been used for storage and that made it difficult, but it was all we could get at the time.

Terry was supposed to arrange a school for Colin, but when I got to Hornchurch I found out that he hadn't done it; he simply left it all to me! Angry? I was furious at him. Again.

Despite the misery of it all, and our best efforts to do better, we still ended up staying there for a full three months. It was so small Colin slept on a bed in the kitchen.

Luckily Terry had a friend called Ron, who sat on the Brentwood Housing Association Committee and helped us get a spacious flat. Colin started school, in Brentwood, and life settled down to the normal roller-coaster ride that we were going through.

I suspected that Terry was cheating on me for some time. My suspicions were confirmed when I found a photograph of him lying on a beach, with a woman feeding him grapes, when he was supposed to be working.

Terry was having difficulty with work again, and wanted to start his own business, but he was like some sort of grasshopper jumping from one project to another. He set up a franchise selling soft toys, and when that failed, he went on to a number of get rich quick schemes. I didn't think he could hold it together.

It was Thursday, 26th October 1978, and I was putting away the vacuum cleaner when the telephone rang. I lifted the receiver, my ears still ringing from the noise of the cleaner.

"Hello Mary." It sounded like Joyce.

"Hello, is that *you*, Joyce?"

"How are you?" I didn't answer; for a moment I found her voice comforting, as if I had slipped on an old pair of slippers.

"How are *you*?" I asked.

"Oh, yea know how it is, fun and games. I've just given my son Peter back to my ex."

Something wasn't right. I couldn't put my finger on it, but I didn't think that she was happy about giving her son away.

"What's the matter, love? I can come over, and spend some time together?"

"Can yea?"

"Of course I can—for you, anything. Would Saturday do? Then I could ask Terry to baby-sit Colin."

"Sounds grand, Mary. Aye, will yea come to my belated birthday party on Sunday night?"

"Love to. Just need to get Colin babysat. We'll talk about it Saturday, about 5 p.m. if that's all right."

"Saturday afternoon," she said. "I'll show you my new flat."

"Where's that then?"

"Hornchurch, Woodlands Avenue, Emerson Park."

"Never! It's not far from here."

"I know. Afterwards we can go for a drink at the Chequers Inn."

"Okay, sounds good, see you about 5:30 at the flat."

"Bye." I hung up the phone.

She was devoted to her son Peter in every way. She loved him so much and I remember seeing the two of them, cuddling all the time. There was nothing wrong with Joyce as a mother. She lavished love on her little boy; he was everything to her.

Yes, she sounded her bubbly old self, but it was an act she couldn't hide from me. Underneath I detected a tinge of sadness. I was worried about her. I thought we would find a moment to talk.

When we met, we ran toward each other like lovers in the park. We held each other, gripped in a deep hug, both mourning the loss of our closeness. It felt so good, yet I was anxious for her.

Joyce took me back to her flat in Emerson Park, Hornchurch. She had put on a bit of weight, perhaps from partying. She introduced me to her flatmate, a blonde fluffy dressy girl. She showed off her wardrobe full of clothes, then we sat on her smart sofa reminiscing over the events that mirrored, echoed and shaped our lives—the birth of Colin just six months after Joyce had Peter, and those moments when we told people that we were sisters. I wished we could have been. Our birthdays were only days apart.

As Joyce and I went to the pub, I wanted to talk to her privately about her son. But as we arrived, she purposely drowned herself in a crowd of friends, flirting, and cracking rude jokes. More butch and slightly vulgar, for a woman. I felt uncomfortable, as if something had changed with her.

We had kept phone contact, and tried to meet, but with one thing and another things always got in the way. I invited her to Brandon a few times, but she never came, and I never went to Essex. I thought I knew her, but with the distance between us, it appeared, really, that I didn't.

Later that evening, after a few drinks we sat down and had a moment alone.

"What are you doing back in Brentwood?" She seemed desperate to find out.

"We've lost the house," I said. "Terry lost his job, and then..." I just blurted it all out: "I found a picture of Terry fooling around with another woman."

"Oh, Mary..." She put her arms around me. I felt myself start to get upset, but I carried on. "As soon as I saw it—this girl on the beach with him—that was it, I stormed out of the house. The next thing I knew was when he roared up in the car, threw Colin out onto the street, and left me standing with him at the side of the road."

I didn't want to dump it on her, but she was the first person I had spoken to about it.

Joyce didn't say anything—she sat quietly holding me.

"Enough about me, what's happening to you?" I was concerned for her.

"I'm all right." She looked up.

"You don't seem the same, Joyce?"

"I am, I am, what do you mean?"

"You can't hide it—it's me you're talking to." I grabbed her hand, forcing her to look up at me.

"How are things really, Joyce?"

"Yeah, well at least I have Mannie, but I have always loved Pete. He's still with this woman with money and a big house."

"Who's Mannie?"

"I'm seeing him at the moment—I quite like him." She looked coy.

"Do you?"

"I'm not sure." She looked up over my shoulder.

"Hello you two," her flatmate interrupted.

"Drinks are on the bar. Coming over?" The flatmate strolled back to the rest of the group. Joyce and I followed.

"Joyce, we need to talk more." As we walked, I stopped and turned to face her.

"After the party," Joyce said, "come round and we'll talk about things. Yes?"

She hesitated, glancing at her flatmate, who was waving to her from the bar.

I felt there was something more she wanted to tell.

"All right, I'll come round then, Monday," I said. "It's my birthday, and I'll pop in then."

"Can you come?"

"Yes, I'll definitely come, I've got the day off—lunch?" I pulled her hand; I wanted to make sure she was paying attention to me.

"Great, come round 12:30. My flatmate will be at work."

"All right." I walked back to the bar with her.

She gave me the address of the birthday party on Sunday: Straight Road, not far from Gallows Corner.

I arrived at the party the next day, with Terry. I didn't want to acknowledge that my own marriage was in trouble, and I put on a brave face, hoping we could sort it out. I still loved Terry.

Joyce was on top form. The music was at full volume, and couples were already writhing in the living room. Drinks were flowing freely at the little bar in the corner of the room. I didn't think much about our worries, because we had started talking about them, and besides, I thought that we would have more time.

As Terry and I were leaving in the early hours of Monday morning, she shouted in my ear: "Happy birthday—see you soon."

29

The Shooting

NOTHING PREPARES YOU FOR IT. You never know what form it will take, this challenge that comes to you in life. You just have to bear it, stand firm and do what a friend does—be there and do whatever it takes.

The telephone rang at 3 a.m. Terry took the call. Joyce had shot herself in the chest, and she was asking for me. It was my birthday—I was thirty. Terry and I dropped Colin off at Florrie's, and then drove to Harold Wood hospital. I was half asleep and wondering if it was all a dream.

Terry and I burst through the big double doors. They slammed behind me. I didn't ask where she was—I just followed the screams.

A nurse came over. I let her know who we were. We were told to sit and wait, and no—we couldn't see Joyce!

Terry and I were taken to the large square waiting room. Joyce struggled in the trauma area next door. I listened.

"Joyce, Joyce. Look at me, Joyce!"

Scream!... "Agh! Aaaagh!.. No, Ner, Ner, Nooooo!"

"Hold still for me Joyce!—Joyce, hold still love—I'm going to turn...."

Scream.

"Move it nurse... move it, quickly now... that's it."

"We're going to look at your back."

"No, no, don't fight me!"

"Lift her leg will you nurse?.. that's right… move it… move it."

"Aaaah!... Aaaah!"

"Right!.. okay!.. Oh!... right nurse… hold the drip."

Swish, open, swish, clip, clop of shoes on the polished floor.

A man's voice, commanded, short and sharp: "X-Ray—CHEST, FRONT and SIDE—Now… urgent—Go!"

A high-speed trolley rattled past and the room fell silent, save for the distant echo of crashing doors.

She'd asked for me—I don't know why she didn't ask for her Mum. I never did find out. Was I her surrogate mother? We were almost the same age.

Foolishly, I never realised that she looked up to me; she was the outgoing bubbly one with all the ideas!

Vividly, as if yesterday, the tragic sound of her screams were painfully etched upon my very soul. Never in my life have I heard such distressing sounds as the cries I listened to that night—so stomach churning, gut wrenching, searing bloodcurdling screams, on and on. Echoing around the waiting room, in one relentless torrent of writhing agony, it bored deep into my helpless and impotent self. Each scream tore into me, so piercing it felt like a red hot poker burning deep into my mind. It was like a spear ripping into my own flesh, being twisted, and opening up, filling me up with such sorrow and grief, until I felt the unreserved burden of friendship, that was the bond between us, bearing down until I thought I could take no more.

I put my head in my hands as if to shut out the noise, and in doing so I hoped I could stop the pain for Joyce, but really I was saving myself.

They wouldn't let me in. I couldn't see her. I was trapped outside, tortured and tormented. I could hear every whimper, every howling groan, and although I could not see her face, I could sense the look of terror in her eyes. Like a mother watching her dying child, I was fettered in my frustration, not being there to comfort her, or whisper a kind word, or to hold her. I so wanted to let her know I was there.

My mind became a frenzy. I couldn't take it anymore! Dizzy, I put my head between my legs, hoping that when I looked up, it would all have gone away.

I couldn't bear to hear her, yet I felt that I had a duty to suffer and stay with her. It was my burden too and I shared in her pain.

None can know what that night was like for me. Joyce suffered. Yet my mind had been branded by a hot iron, as if it were my life-long punishment that I would carry, to hold the mental torrent of guilt and shame. I shouldn't have told her that my marriage was in trouble.

Oh, how I regret telling her. How could I believe she would do this? How could I have missed the signs? Why didn't she tell me before she did it? I was sure I could have stopped her, and yet all the questions that haunt me now, are still locked in my heart.

I sat there listening to Joyce, who was my shadow-self. We were like two little soldiers, and now she lay dying, a casualty of our struggle. I cry for her today as much as I did then. It is my wooden leg. It shall forever be there. I cannot escape from it but I can share it with those who knew Joyce, and loved her as I did.

I continued to wait outside. Terry sat silently beside me, lost in his own thoughts. He did what he could to comfort me, but there was nothing he could do. They wouldn't let me see her. They were going to operate. I had to go home and come back later in the day.

When I managed to get to her ward she was in Intensive Care, lying in the bed. I sat there and just held her hand. I kept asking myself why she did it, over and over again. I wouldn't let myself cry in case she heard me. But inside I hurt, inside my sorrow filled me up, and yet I had to give her hope.

After a few days Joyce started to improve. She was conscious.

She told me that one night they nearly lost her. They wanted her to pass a stool, but she couldn't go. She enjoyed the drama of it; as if soaking up all the attention she was getting. Some of the staff didn't like her because she had attempted suicide. I felt upset that they found it necessary; after all, she wasn't out of danger yet, despite appearances. The police were unsympathetic and said they would prosecute for illegal possession of a firearm. I didn't understand why they had to do that, as if to punish her a second time. Hadn't she punished herself enough?

After that I wanted to cheer her up. I had been given a lovely pyjama outfit as a wedding gift. I hadn't worn it, and so I gave it to her, and she looked so pretty in the bright orange pyjamas.

I asked her where she got the gun.

"At the party," she said.

"What, at the party we were all at?"

"Yeah, the guy who owned the house had a collection of guns in a cabinet—he showed me." She looked down and fiddled with her fingers. "He was a member of a gun club, and had a license and everything."

"So how…" I couldn't understand how she had managed it on her own.

"I stole the rifle out of the cabinet as everyone was leaving. No one saw me; they were busy getting their coats and shouting out to each other."

"But how did you get the ammunition? Surely it was somewhere else."

"No, there was a little box of bullets at the back."

For a moment I didn't know what to say. "But how did you get the rifle out of the house?"

She started to get upset. "Hid it in the sleeve of my coat," sniff, "and managed to sneak it out hiding in the crowd."

I felt myself getting upset at the thought of it. I still didn't fully understand how she could have planned it all.

"So did you go to the party knowing this was what you were going to do?"

"Mary, I don't want to talk about it anymore. It doesn't matter now."

That shut me up. "Okay, don't worry," I said, and we went on to talk about other things. Nevertheless, I found the whole conversation rather disturbing.

She wasn't giving me the right answers. I didn't understand how she could point a rifle at herself, and still be able to pull the trigger. I had done some shooting with Terry at Brandon, and I knew how long a rifle barrel could be. It was difficult to believe she could have shot herself in the way she said, and it left me wondering. What had become of the flatmate I saw when we first met? There were no reports of a witness in the Romford Recorder for 3rd November. It simply said she was found lying on the living room floor at 3 a.m. with a gunshot wound in her chest. A single-shot bolt-action rifle lay at her side. I had no proof and my thoughts were my own, but knowing how wild Joyce could be, it did occur to me she might not have pulled the trigger herself. It left only one other possibility. Was there someone else at the flat, a boyfriend, her flatmate, or someone who came back with her from the party? The flatmate never came to the hospital as far as I knew, and Joyce didn't mention her. Was the wound self-inflicted? It left a whole lot of questions. The police never interviewed me, and I began to wonder if someone had helped Joyce to do it?

A few weeks had passed since she shot herself, and she had been taken into a side ward. I arrived quietly, and I didn't think that she had noticed me. She was staring straight ahead, as if in a distant daydream. I sat down and stared into her big lifeless eyes.

"What did you want to tell me the other night?"

"I gave little Peter back to Pete." She looked down at her hands.

I sat silently, listening.

"I thought that I could get Pete back. Now he is saying that I am a bad mother, and he is stopping me seeing my little boy." She looked so sad.

"You loved Peter more than anything. It's terrible for you."

She glanced up at me.

"Joyce," I held her hand, "is that why you did it?" Fireworks crackled through the open window. It was bonfire night.

She struggled to sit up for a moment, but failing, she fell back and I could tell that there was something important she wanted to say. I propped up the pillows behind her and made her comfortable.

"You..." she cleared her throat "...did everything right Mary." She spoke slowly.

I gave her a puzzled glance. It wasn't what I expected.

"You got engaged, then got married, then had a child, and I..." She paused for a moment.

I helped her take a sip of water.

"I thought that if your marriage didn't work," she started to cry, "what bloody hope was there for me!"

I looked at her, stunned. I handed her a tissue from her bedside cabinet, and she wiped her eyes.

"But Joyce..." I said. She interrupted.

"You got married and then had a child, don't you see?" She paused to regain her composure. "Don't you see? You did it properly."

I handed her another tissue.

"I foolishly had a child first and thought it would make it all right to get married."

"But Joyce..."

"It didn't work. Don't you see? I did it wrong." She spoke between her tears.

I didn't interrupt. I thought it best to just let her say what she wanted to say.

"You got married and because you loved each other, you had a child. That's how it is supposed to work. But now look what's happening to you…"

She lovingly reached out to me, and put her hand on my arm, as if to comfort me.

"Mary," she patted my arm, "if it didn't work for you, then what chance do I have?"

"Oh, Joyce, this isn't like you." I lent forward and took a tissue for myself and wiped away a tear. "Joyce, we were two little soldiers and we still are. It will come right, you will see, we will do it together."

"Can we?" She looked up, wiping a tear.

"I am down in Brentwood now, we can meet up." I held her hand.

She smiled at me and her face lit up.

"We will sort each other's paths out. We will come through, we always do."

"You were the vivacious one, the one who attracted all the fun!" She looked up at me swallowing. I wanted to give her hope. I reached out and held her hand.

"Look," I said, "what about a holiday, just us girls, to Majorca or something? Let's plan it and I'll bring some brochures in tomorrow, something to look forward to."

"What about Colin?"

"Florrie will look after Colin, that's not a problem."

She looked encouraged and struck a smile, and I saw a glimmer of hope in her eyes.

"We will do it then." I raised my eyes and glanced up at her.

As she turned back at me I saw a small flicker as those deep brown eyes sparkled once more.

The next day was Sunday. Terry said I was spending too much time at the hospital with Joyce. He thought I should be at home cooking the dinner for him and caring for Colin. To be fair I had been visiting every night for nearly three weeks and I suppose Terry thought that as she was getting better, maybe she would be out of the hospital soon.

I remember thinking, 'What does he care?' This argument made me twenty minutes late for the hospital.

30

The Samaritans

IT WAS 19th NOVEMBER 1978 and as I rushed into Joyce's room, I glanced at her bed. They must have moved her; or she was up and walking round the ward. The Ward Sister came over to me as I looked through the window at Joyce's bed. It was all freshly made up. I couldn't understand why the bed was made at that time of night. Something wasn't right.

The Sister asked who I was. I told her I was Joyce's best friend. Then she told me, compassionately, that Joyce had died just ten minutes before I'd arrived.

My hand flew up to my mouth and I bit my lip. I couldn't breathe. My nose stung and then my eyes began to water.

"Oh, oh, nooo! No, no. Oh, no!" I cried. "She was getting better—how could she die?"

The Sister just stood there for a moment and held my hand. Then she turned to continue with clearing up the rest of Joyce's things.

I stood there in disbelief. I was sure Joyce could not be dead. I searched the faces, yet I failed to spot her amongst all the others patients. Joyce *had* to be there, she couldn't have gone. Not without me seeing her. I hadn't said goodbye.

Les had left without saying goodbye, and now it was happening again. I felt my legs weaken and buckle beneath me and suddenly I felt dizzy. I wanted to cry but the tears didn't come. I couldn't speak, my mind screaming inside with the pain. Oh, how the sorrow filled me.

I was stunned, devastated. My whole world collapsed in ten minutes. I stood there, struck down as if by some dreadful stroke. Shaking, speechless, and then a numbness descended; my emotions shut down and my world went into a haze. I didn't feel anything anymore.

I staggered, half stumbling out into the still night air, and wandered over to the car. Terry appeared to see the shock etched on my face and he must have known she had gone. We drove home in silence. Did I feel angry that he made me late? I didn't know. I didn't see any point in blaming him—she was dead.

I felt utterly alone, abandoned and destitute as if back down in Langhedge Lane, only this time I didn't have the fight for it; all the stuffing had been taken out of me. I was exhausted.

If I could go back and change the world, wind back the clock just a few hours, if I could be given the chance to talk to her... I would have given anything for that. I would have done that for Joyce. Not one person understood the strength of the unspoken bond we had between us. That silent understanding, as much as if we had been of one flesh and of one mind.

I returned home and had to face the split up of my marriage. I didn't know how long I spent just sitting and looking out of the window wondering what to do. Nothing prepared me for it, there was no rehearsal, it just knocked me off my feet and I knew I had to carry on. But I couldn't.

I didn't go to work. I remember thinking that divorce would never happen to me. I thought that marriage was for life. Divorce was unknown in Terry's family, until Terry felt he needed someone else. We would be the first.

He suggested we live separately, come back in later years, and tell the family we had decided to split. It was a lie and I wasn't having any of it! Terry and I had a good family and I was part of it. I was always committed to my principles, and I told him so. Yet there was part of me that just wanted to let it all drift. Joyce was dead, and what did I care what he wanted to do?

I phoned my bother Les, and he suggested I go and see a solicitor; that's all he said.

I trudged through the snow and saw a lady solicitor. I told her that Terry had left me and gone to live with his lady friend, and I was left alone with Colin. I couldn't afford to run the flat, and I didn't have any money to pay her.

She told me to take my son and go, and not to worry about Terry, or about paying her anything.

Stunned at her kindness, I thanked her and walked back home.

Speaking to my mother-in-law Florrie, she advised me to go abroad for six months, and leave Colin with her in the hope Terry would somehow see sense. It seemed a stupid idea. If Terry didn't want me now, why would he want me later?

I left Colin with Florrie, and went to the flat to pick up some things. Terry was there, and we started talking. I loved him. I didn't want to end the marriage, and so I ended up staying the night and we made love. In the morning I put a hand across to him to make love again, and he clearly didn't want to. He had just done it as a favour for me, to save his own feelings.

He got straight up to leave for work. I told him I would be gone before he got back.

I said goodbye to all the rooms. I didn't know why—it was silly; perhaps I was saying goodbye to my marriage. I gently closed the front door and was walking down the flight of stairs to the exit door, when I spotted Terry. He was walking back to the flat with Lin, or perhaps it was Teresa, I didn't know. We stopped as we passed on the ramp. I said "Hello". That was the last I saw of him until the divorce.

I wandered onto the street, knowing my marriage was over.

What was left for me?

I had lost my marriage, my home, my best friend and soulmate. Most people, when they lose their marriage, at the very least, have their best friend to turn to. I had lost everything. If ever I needed Joyce, it was now.

The strength that sustained me through childhood had gone? I had nothing, no one, no money, no home, and no hope.

I walked to a phone box and phoned the Samaritans.

"Samaritans—hello, my name is Anne," she said.

"I have," I sobbed uncontrollably, sniff, sob, "I have..." It was like a cork floating in a bottle of words. Each time I went to pour, the cork jammed in my throat.

Sob, silence.

"It's all right, you take as much time as you want." She heard me, yet I said nothing.

I just cried and sobbed into the telephone. I had so much to say, but the hurt wouldn't let me. It was impossible; my mind deserted me in my desperate struggle for help. I choked and cried. My words were my tears, and each tear, my pain, dripping into the phone like blood from an open wound, as surely as if I had just slashed my wrists and let all the blood pour out.

"It's okay," she whispered gently, "I'm still here."

Despite all my efforts, I could not speak. I wanted to—God how I wanted to tell her. My tears, my inner screams of agony, twisted and all churned up, as if a hurricane had slammed into me, and now the aftermath. I was looking at my shattered self, broken, and completely destroyed.

Language did not have enough for me.

Silence, sob, sob, sniff, swallow. I wiped the tears.

She said nothing, but I knew she was there, holding me close. I heard her swallow and I knew she felt for me, this lady I did not know.

"I'm still here," she said. "It's okay to take your time."

"My friend... my best friend..." I couldn't finish anything.

Sob, sob, sniff, sniff. I wiped away the tears and blew my nose. I caught a glimpse of my face in the mirror, my panda eyes, all red and blotchy.

"I am here still, it's all right, take your time."

People passed by the phone box on the street. They must have heard my cries and sobs. Yet they scurried past.

I did not believe that anyone could feel so alone, so utterly, so desperately alone. I felt in a wilderness so vast that time itself was absent, save the gossamer thread of hope that dangled at the end of that phone line.

I tried to say something again. Nothing came and I clutched the phone like a drowning man. If only I could have told her—I had to tell someone. But still I was struck dumb and no matter how hard I tried, the words did not flow.

"She's, she's err… and I am all alone," I stuttered into my soaking hanky.

"I am still here for you," she said. "It's all right."

I was spiralling down some black hole—I had no more to give.

I dropped the phone and walked out of the box back onto the street, empty.

31

Leaving the Marriage with Colin

TERRY SUGGESTED I LIVE IN THE FLAT but I couldn't face it. The flat had held all the memories of my marriage, and the death of Joyce. I picked up the *Romford Recorder* from 24th November. There was still no mention of a witness, and nothing was said to question the shooting. It seemed the case was closed, but was it murder after all? A shudder ran down my spine. I couldn't think about Joyce any more. Things were just too painful for me, and I was in shock. I ached for Terry and the utter loneliness that I lived on coffee, and watched my weight plummet to a size ten. It was Terry who left the marriage for another woman. He told me that Colin and I were holding him back in his ambition to make money, and to be rich.

I made a telephone call to Mum and she said, "Come home, John will pick up your things." It was such a relief to have somewhere to go, and I was grateful to Mum for having me home. Mum's friend John lived in the maisonette above my mum's house. He came and picked Colin and I up in his van.

I phoned Terry and told him I didn't want to live in the flat. We agreed that I could take the dining table and chairs, and he would buy a new bed and a chair for me. He let out the two bedrooms at the flat to Kevin's brother, and another guy I never met.

Terry was mini-cabbing and I believe living with some waitress who worked in a cafe. He was also seeing another girl,

Theresa at the time, although I couldn't be sure—and honestly, I didn't really care; for Terry and me, it was over! Secretly, I thought, he didn't waste much time, did he? I wished my feelings would fade, but the truth of it was I still loved him.

I just seemed to give up and let it all happen without a fight. I became a victim, like my mother in those troubled times—I had lost all my self-esteem and let everything go. Like a puppet, I agreed to whatever Terry wanted. The stuffing had been knocked out of me, and when I left Terry I had just a pound in my pocket.

At Mum's house, I set about placing Colin into my old Junior School. It was a big change for him. Changing from the leafy village to a concrete city school was to be difficult for him. I was determined and anticipated the problems. I shaved another layer from my credit card, and bought him a new school uniform. I knew it would help him blend in.

Mum and Jane were pleased to see a carpet in the living room, the smart dining suite, and the use of a refrigerator in the kitchen. I even managed to cut and fit some carpet tiles, laying them throughout the living room and along the full length of the hallway.

Colin and I shared my bedroom, and I thought that things would settle down.

With the extra things I brought to the house, I imagined it would ease the tensions, and it did for a little while. Jane, now twenty-two years old, was firmly positioned as head of the household. She called Colin a 'little brat' because he ran around the house making a noise, but Colin was a seven-year-old boy—what did she expect?

I started to have doubts about my decision to return home. Everything was costing more than I imagined. I was getting into more debt and unable to pay off the credit card. There was only one thing I could do—sell my table and chairs. Mother didn't have a dining table and chairs, and she clearly expected me to leave it there for her to use. But I had no choice. They wanted me to give it to them for nothing. They had no understanding what it was like for me. Every time I had to look at the dining set it broke my heart. All the emotional memories of happy family meal times, with Terry, Colin and myself, together each night. I couldn't bear it, and so, for that reason alone, it had to go. I sold it through the local newspaper, and paid off my debts.

Domestic life worked for a little while. Mum routinely picked up Colin from school and Terry would see him at the weekends. I was working at Mappin & Webb in Regents Street as secretary to the financial director. It left me constantly juggling the demands of work and home. It was difficult to cook food for Colin and I in Mum's kitchen. Jane smoked constantly; she occupied the living room and I had to listen to all the television programmes of a twenty-two year-old. Mother had no say in anything. It became impossible.

Having no car, I had to walk everywhere. It was exhausting, arriving home on the train after working late into the evening, and then shopping. I was providing everything that was needed to run a whole house, the washing powder, cleaning fluids and even toilet rolls. It was as if I was a landlord in some dingy boarding house, except that Colin and I had only one room; I even had to pay the entire telephone bill, regardless of what calls Mother or Jane made. If I wanted any hot water, I had to put money in the meter. Nothing was free.

Lugging the shopping through streets in the rain was starting to take its toll on my health, and more often than not, I would come home drenched to the skin in my flimsy coat, and sit, without energy, shivering by the old gas stove in the kitchen. I couldn't afford to get ill like my mother did; what would happen to my son—would he end up like I did, starving? I needed a new coat. I bought two, a long woollen one for work, and a short cheap sheepskin to keep out the cold, when Mother dropped the bombshell!

Colin would have to leave—she couldn't have him at the house. Jane complained that Colin was too noisy.

I was shell-shocked. We hadn't been there more than a few weeks! Colin had a new school uniform, was settled and he was putting down roots. I had started to get my life back together.

Angry? I could have killed her! After all the help I had given her over the years, what was I to do now? Who could I turn to now?

My brother Les didn't help me, yet he, of all people, knew the hardship of my youth and understood the life that I endured so well. He had to beg for food before I did all those years ago.

I thought that Jane, my sister, might be more sympathetic; she might have remembered our desperate struggle through hunger together as a little girl, and I thought that she at least would have had some sort of moral obligation, but not a bit of it! Quite the opposite: if I was looking for support from her, then I was to be very much disappointed.

I phoned Florrie, my mother-in-law. She offered to bring Colin up for me. But there was no way I was going to give up Colin. I wouldn't do that. I brought him into the world and I was determined I would keep him. Joyce gave up her son Peter, and I saw how it destroyed her. It wasn't an option for me.

Terry offered to have Colin for a few months whilst I sorted out something better. It seemed the best option at the time, and so I stayed with Mother and Colin went to live with his father.

I spoke to Colin on the telephone every day. At the weekend Terry would bring Colin to stay with me.

Taking Colin up to the Wimpy Bar on a Saturday morning felt strange for me.

I started to have sympathy for all those separated fathers, who, like me, loved and missed their children, yet were only able to catch a fleeting glimpse of their passing life. Everything crammed into one impossible speedy weekend, as if caught in some time bubble for the day.

Terry would return to the house to pick up Colin each Sunday, and Mother would cook him a full roast dinner. Why she did this remained a mystery, for she had never done it for me. It was almost as if she was trying to impress and flirt with him.

It became increasingly frustrating for me trying to maintain the relationship with Colin, separated as I was, and in the end I decided it would be best for me to move out. I wanted somewhere to live with Colin, but I couldn't afford to rent a flat, or house; all I could afford was a room. He would have to live with his father and I would continue see him at the weekend.

I found lodgings in a house in Bowes Park, and changed jobs, joining a firm of accountants in Commercial Road, where I met Andrea. Living on my own gave me some relief from the day-to-day hassle of living with Mum and Jane. At least I could think clearly and get my finances back on track. After all, it was cheaper to lodge with a stranger than at my mum's.

I didn't fit anymore. I was single, yet I felt married. I had a child, but I wasn't a mum. What was I? I felt like a wife and mother, but excluded from both. I had arrived in the world of a single mum.

Andrea suggested that I do something completely out of the box. I took her advice and soon I found a job as the Manager of the Gift Shop with Pontins Holidays at Barton Hall, Devon. It was on the south coast of England. It was a long way from home, and I didn't want to leave Colin with Terry.

I arrived, feeling scared and wondering if I had done the right thing. Dropping off my bags I was shown to a room in the main hotel part of the complex. It was bare, stark and suffered the noise and steam from the kitchens below, but in a strange way it was much better than living in one room near home. I had space to think, without the worry of my mother and sister watching my every move, and I had company if I wanted or needed it.

I managed the gift shop, and I found it a refreshing change to be in charge. Maybe that's what I really needed. To take charge of my life and the shop was symbolic of that. I started to feel better about myself, and the downtrodden feelings I had slipped into I put in the past.

I would talk to my son Colin on the telephone in the evenings, sending him little notes, postcards and letters several times a week. I so loved my little boy, yet somehow I didn't feel I was ready to go back into that world. Constantly I reassured him that I would be coming back to find us a home together, although often I got the impression he was enjoying himself at his dad's flat, quite happily without me.

After a few weeks I persuaded Terry to bring him down and he stayed for a long weekend. We had a fantastic time in the holiday camp, playing with all the amusements, and touring parts of Devon. It was the first real holiday that I, or Colin had ever had, and I hugged and cuddled him as if every possible moment would be my last. I was reluctant to part with him, but I knew he had to return to his life with Terry.

As manager of the gift shop at Pontins, I was required to sit at holidaymakers' tables for the evening meal. There I met a man called Tom, a contractor, with a team of kitchen fitters. He wasn't a holidaymaker—he was there to build a kitchen for Barton Hall.

Tom was tall, charismatic, and wealthy. With his soft Irish brogue he charmed me, so he did, into leaving Pontins and becoming a partner in the business he ran.

For a time I was able to forget my troubles, and although I worried about Colin and telephoned him daily, I was pleased he was happy with his dad. Tom's offer appeared to give me the space I needed to decide my future. I speculated that it might provide the money I needed to get a home of my own, Colin and me. It was the new dream I was heading towards.

Tom made me feel attractive with his compliments, holding out the hope and promise of big rewards. He could see the potential for me to market his company, although it didn't take long for him to pester me to sleep with him. No, I couldn't. It was too soon for me to leap into another relationship; my mind just wasn't ready, and I rejected his advances time and time again.

Not only did the work come easy to me, but the accommodation and expensive lifestyle was free. I enjoyed staying in hotels, being waited on, and having Tom buy me anything I wanted. He appeared to be a walking bank, carrying wads of money; every deal was done in cash.

But like all good things that appear too good, I found myself increasingly doubting that I would ever get paid. Tom was full of words and grand promises; he paid for everything, the accommodation, the meals, the transport and everything I needed—except my wages.

It wasn't long before Tom took me to his grand home in Bury St Edmonds where he had an office. I wondered if he was going to try something on with me. He gave me a quick tour of the house and said that I could stay in the guest room that night; he promised to book me into a hotel the following day.

I wandered back downstairs with Tom. He walked into the office and picked up his messages from his answer phone. They were routine business enquiries, nothing special. The ringing phone startled me at first, although Tom seemed to expect it. He put the handset to his ear.

"Hello, it's Tom."

I didn't hear the caller. Tom scratched his head. I had the impression it was a woman.

"I need to take this call," he said, and started to close the office door. "You unpack your suitcase upstairs—I'll not be long."

The door closed firmly behind me.

I took my suitcase upstairs to the guest room. Poking around, I noticed an open bedside drawer. In it was an unopened sanitary towel and belt. It was almost as if it had been placed there on purpose. I was curious. Tom had always maintained that he was on his own. I walked back downstairs through to the laundry room. There, in the laundry basket, I spotted a pile of unwashed children's clothing, hidden beneath a towel.

His wife, a clever girl, I thought, had made her presence known. I made my way back to the hallway. It had been a sunny morning and light streamed through the windows, yet the hallway was now in shadow.

Bang, bang.

"Answer the door, will you Mary!" Tom shouted from the office.

Two men in dark pinstriped suits stood motionless in the porch way. One looked as if he could crack walnuts with his bare hands.

"We'll be wanting a word with Tom, if you wouldn't mind." His Irish voice was soft.

As I turned to Tom in the office, he was already aware of the men. He nudged me aside, sending me out of the way.

"Mr O'Shane would like his money."

The Gorilla reached forward with both hands, gripping Tom's jacket so forcefully that I could see the muscles ripple like melons swelling in the sun. He pulled Tom over the doorstep, like a helpless puppet.

"I will have the money..."

The Gorilla pulled Tom's face close to his and spat the words at him: "Time for excuses has run out. Mr O'Shane sends a message."

The colour drained from Tom's sweaty face.

"You have until 2 o'clock tomorrow. Do you understand?"

He nodded several times.

The Gorilla pushed him back inside the hallway. Tom fell backwards in a crumpled heap.

They turned, and calmly walked back down the path to the waiting car, as Tom got to his feet and quickly closed the door. He was still shaking as the men pulled away in their dark Mercedes.

It was the first time I had seen Tom visibly shaken. I worried that something nasty was about to happen. Tom hadn't paid me any wages, and I began to wonder if he was in financial trouble with what looked like republican IRA thugs.

I didn't have a good feeling about this situation. It was time I got out before I got myself caught up in something really bad. The IRA had been blowing people up and shooting kneecaps for almost ten years, and I imagined they were quite capable of doing something to me. If anything happened to Tom, then I would have been a witness.

I waited for Tom to calm down, and made a cup of tea for us. I sat at the kitchen table.

"Tom, I haven't seen my son Colin for some time. I wonder if it would be a good time for me to travel home by train, and have couple of days with him?"

"Yes, sure." He seemed preoccupied with his troubles. "When will you be coming back?"

"In two or three days, if that's all right with you."

"Yes, I guess that'll be okay," he nodded. "I'm sure it will," he spoke kindly.

I think at that moment he would have agreed to anything. He seemed happy to have me out of the way.

"Just phone me when you're ready and I'll pick you up from the station."

"Thanks Tom," I said, "that would be great. I'll leave now if that's all right."

"Sure, I have to go out for a bit..." He didn't finish his sentence. He just stood there as if thinking of something else. I went upstairs to fetch my suitcase as he dashed out, racing off in his car.

I rummaged around in the office, looking through his files, frantic to discover if he was married, but I found nothing. As I peered in the wastepaper basket, there amongst other demands, was a current gas bill in joint names. There it was—Mr & Mrs Fisher. I was certain that he was married. Tom was a complete mystery—I never knew where I was with him. I was glad I didn't fall for him.

Glancing out of the window as I was collecting my things, I noticed Tom coming up the path with this woman holding his hand. I was frightened that it might have been his wife, and so I sprang into the nearby understairs cupboard and hid, just in time to hear the heavy front door swing open, and then, fortunately for me, I heard their footsteps continue on through to the kitchen at the back of the house. Why had he brought another woman back? I couldn't work it out.

For a moment I relaxed, drawing my suitcase close to me like a comfort blanket. I didn't know whether to make a bolt for it, or stay silently listening in the dark. But whichever I chose, there was the constant worry that I might get caught.

Listening intently, I couldn't catch everything they said. He was using the telephone in the kitchen and she was making a cup of tea, the kettle drowning out some of the words. He dialled a number, very fast—clearly, he must have known it by heart.

It was like a radio call, breaking up; all I could do was to make out the odd sentence. 'Brook Advisory Centre'—and then something I didn't hear, sounded like an address or name, and then again I heard him say something like 'pay for a caution'.

I heard a scuffle as they burst out of the kitchen. I jumped back and pulled the door closed and held my breath. They hurried down the hall and slammed the door, screeching off down the road in his big Cherokee car.

I phoned Mum and asked if I could stay for a few days. She said it would be all right, as long as I didn't bring Colin.

I didn't wait for them to return. Instead, I hastily left some clothes in the drawer where the sanitary towel was, and hid some other clothes in a bag deep in the back of his wife's wardrobe. I figured I wasn't going to get paid without a fight, so I had a plan.

As soon as I got to the station, I checked the telephone book for the Brook Advisory Centre. I didn't know what he meant by the words, 'pay for a caution', until I wrote it down on the page in front of me. It wasn't pay for a caution—it was pay for an abortion, and the Brook Advisory Centre was a family planning clinic.

When I got to Mum's it was late evening. I phoned Tom.

"Hello Tom," I said quietly.

"You bitch! You left some clothes at the side of the bed deliberately so you did!"

Through the anger I heard the faint sound of children playing in the background.

I needed to play him for the money; after all, he had been playing with me all this time, trying it on just to get into bed with me on this pretence of a job. I wondered if that was what he told the other girl who got herself pregnant. I could see why his wife sent the signals, and I wondered if she was the wealthy one.

"Well Tom, there are more clothes hidden in a bag at the back of the wardrobe that you haven't found yet. I want them all brought back to me together with the money that you owe me."

"Where are the clothes then—which wardrobe?" He was calm, matter of fact.

"Are you going to bring my money? Or do I tell your wife about the other girl and the Brook Advisory Centre?"

"How the fuck do you know about that?!" His cocky confidence was swiped away.

Got him! I was never sure, but now I had him. It was an abortion clinic after all.

"Never you mind—I just want the money you owe me!"

"How much do you want then?"

"That's better, now. I want all that you owe me for the six weeks work; no more than you promised me. I gave up my job for you and you haven't paid me a damn thing, and now I want it all, otherwise I will have to have a conversation with your wife."

The phone went silent for a moment and I was sure he was thinking about how he could wheedle his way out of it.

"How much?" he asked, as if biting his lip as he spoke.

"Nine hundred pounds would be about right."

He swallowed.

"Now, where are the clothes?"

"I put them in your wife's wardrobe, right at the back hidden in a Harrods bag. I'm sure you will find it."

"All right, I'll come down in the van tomorrow night, your mum's place, 7 o'clock."

"I'll be waiting. Now make sure you bring my clothes and the money you owe me," I said, hanging up the phone.

But I had a nagging doubt—he seemed to agree far too quickly and I wasn't at all sure he was going to pay me; I needed to do something else. I explained to my Mother what I planned to do.

She was horrified and started to argue with me not to do it, but she didn't fully understand my desperate need for a home of my own with my little boy. I needed the hard earned money that Tom had promised. After all, his business had benefited from my marketing, and as a consequence the sales had risen by more than ten percent; I had seen the figures and I knew. I wanted what was mine and I wasn't going to be fobbed off by some lame excuse, and so that very afternoon I rushed down to the local electrical shop, Mosses.

Turning up in his old Ford Transit van about 7:30 p.m. at my mother's house, he knocked on the door. We walked back to the van, I got in and we sat outside in Langhedge Lane.

"Tom, have you got my money?" I said. "I gave up my job to come and work for you and you haven't paid me a penny."

"Well then, I'll have to send you a cheque, sure, I don't have it with me."

"I'm not sure about that. Have you brought my clothes?"

"Sure I've got all your clothes here in the bag, and the stuff you left in the wardrobe. You bugger, caused me a lot of trouble with the misses, so yer did. You didn't have to do all that you know. Ole, I would have paid you anyway, it's just that I was a bit short at the moment and besides, how'd you find out about the Brook Centre? I'm sure I didn't tell you!"

"I heard you talking to her about paying for the abortion whilst I was hiding in the understairs cupboard. So if you don't pay me my money I shall have to go to the police."

"I'm not paying you here and that is final."

I sensed the anger, now deep within him and I could hear the hackles rising in his voice. Inside, I was frightened about what he might do; after all, I was a lone woman in a dark van at night; anything could have happened.

Preparing for the worst I moved my hand and grabbed hold of the inner handle of the van door. He glanced sideways at me, wondering what I was about to do as he fidgeted in his seat, clearly uncomfortable. I made ready to make a quick exit if I needed to, then delivered the final line that I hoped would persuade him to part with his money and pay me what he owed.

"That's a shame," I said, "because I have a tape recorder in my handbag on the floor here and it's been taping this conversation, and before you ask, I also recorded the conversation that we had on the phone. So unless you want a problem in your social life I suggest that you hand over the money now. I need that money for my son Colin. We need a home together and that's my goal."

I could see him almost explode, his hand gripping the steering wheel hard, his fist clenched and his face screwed up as his eyes narrowed in the darkness. I was scared, but at the same time I felt an intense anger come from within me.

Perhaps it was the anger I still felt for Joyce and I was reminded of the way that men treated her. I didn't know, but if I needed that anger to get my money, then it had served me well.

"Well now, okay, I get the message. I only have eight hundred and fifty on me though."

"That will do." I snatched the money from his hand, picked up my handbag, and sprang out of the van with my parcel of clothes.

I didn't look back and I had no intention of hanging around. I ran back into my mum's house thankful that I had eventually been paid.

32

Boat People

WITH THE MONEY FROM TOM, I was now looking for a home for my eight-year-old son Colin who was still living in his Dad's flat in Brentwood, along with two other strange lodgers; it was far from ideal. I found it heartbreaking to be separated from Colin, always wondering what was happening to him, and I so desperately wanted him to be with me.

I applied for Local Authority Housing immediately after leaving the flat, and since I hadn't heard anything about my application, I decided to visit the council offices in Silver Street, Enfield. They told me to go to Redlingtons, a once proud building that stood alone in Baker Street. Humbled, and black with soot from the chimneys nearby, it served as the Housing Department.

I walked up to reception. They told me to wait. The lady's brown hair had a fringe, flickup's and butterfly glasses. She called me into a stuffy little office. Dressed in a twin set with pearls, and high heels, she sat down behind her smart modern wooden desk. I judged her shoes more expensive than my entire wardrobe. I didn't have a good feeling about this meeting. She was young, and inexperienced; and then she spoke.

"My name is Felicity Ursula Carlin-Kent."

"Hello, can you tell me what's happening to my application please?" I gave her my name.

"Well, you are far down the list, I'm afraid." She spoke as if sitting on her horse. "If only you had more points it would help you a great deal."

It wasn't a surprise to me. As soon as she opened her plumy mouth something told me this was going to be about as helpful as a pickaxe in a china shop. In fact, I couldn't think what town she might have come from, but it certainly wasn't anywhere near Edmonton!

"So how do I get more points?"

"We have to give priority to thousands of homeless people first, you know. The Vietnamese Boat People are coming over to the country, and they have a much greater housing need. Did you know they have fled their country in fishing boats with nothing but the clothes they were standing up in?"

"Very commendable, but how does that affect me?"

"Well, there is a war on in the East, you know. Vietnam has attacked Cambodia, China has attacked Vietnam, and now thousands of refugees are fleeing their country, some drowning and others sold as slaves. A British Oil Tanker has picked up fifty-three from the open sea. It's very dreadful, you know, and we have a duty to house anyone who is homeless. Mr Callaghan, the Prime Minister, has agreed to take over twenty thousand, and of course they will be homeless; you at least have somewhere to live."

She spoke as if I didn't know who the Prime Minister was. I looked at the ceiling and sighed.

I didn't know what to say to that. I felt humiliated. I didn't understand how my social deprivation and the psychological hardship that I suffered separated from my son, was somehow insignificant, or, worse, unimportant. Didn't I pay my rates and taxes like everyone else? Hadn't I earned my right to some sort of support when the chips were down?

"So what do you suggest I do then, go to Vietnam and throw myself into a boat, tossing my son in the water for good measure?"

"There's no need to be sarcastic!" She looked down her nose at me. "It is a humanitarian need of vast proportions and I think we all need to do our bit for the world's people, don't you?"

No, I didn't think so. I had known enough hardship in my own country and I certainly wasn't too happy about the response I was getting.

"How do I get more points and increase my chances of getting housed?" I asked again. "I am lodging in one room, my eight-year-old son is living in the flat with his father, and two other strange men. He lives miles away over in Brentwood, and my son Colin is picking up all sorts of ideas and language that I don't approve of."

"Well, you need to have more babies," she trotted out bluntly.

"More babies?" I screamed. "Oh, that's a great idea, that is! I have just got divorced!"

She looked surprised at my onslaught.

"Do you know what that is like?" I continued. "My best friend has just died and I am living in one grotty room as a lodger, desperately trying to keep myself alive. I am in no position to start having more children. What do you want me to do?" I said, "Go on the streets, pick up someone like a common prostitute, get myself pregnant and live in a tent down the Blackwall Tunnel, just so as I can get more points on your bloody housing list!"

She stiffened. "Well, if that's the way you want to look at it, then I'm afraid I cannot help you!" She got up from her chair and pointed to the door.

"Well, you haven't been very helpful, have you?" I turned on my heels, held my head high, and made a brisk exit from the office.

I walked out past the reception, through the swing doors into the bright sunshine, but I couldn't hold back the tears. They burst onto my cheeks as I reached the steps. I stopped and searched for a hanky.

Walking into a phone box at the end of the road I spoke to a friend of Andrea's, a girl called Janet, who lived nearby. I needed to take shelter in her house and have a cup of coffee, and I hoped she might be able to help me.

I was crying when I knocked on her door.

"Hello Janet," I said.

"Mary, look love, I don't have time at the moment for coffee, but just tell me what's happened." She invited me in and we sat on her sofa.

I explained what had happened at the Housing Department.

"Right," she said, "here is a direct line for Mrs Amy Emsden. She used to be the Mayor of Enfield; she is the Chair of the Housing Committee now." She scribbled on an old envelope. "Phone her now, mention my name, explain what happened at the Council Housing Office."

I looked up at her, hesitant. She thrust the note in my hand.

"Do it now," she insisted. "Phone them straight away and see if she might be able to help."

She got up to leave.

"Thank you, you have been such a help. I'll do it as soon as I get home." I left it at that.

I rang Mrs Emsden as soon as I got home. I managed to speak to her over the phone, as Janet had told me. I blurted out exactly what had happened at the Housing Department. She asked some questions about where I was living and what access I had to Colin. I told her I was living at my mum's, only seeing my son at the weekend.

She said that it sounded like I was overcrowded. I asked her if she knew what it was like to be living like a single woman, only seeing your son for the weekend. She told me she fully understood the pain of it and the difficulties I was suffering. She was due to attend a Housing Committee Meeting shortly after and promised to raise the matter on my behalf. In the meantime, someone would be sent to talk to me and get some details.

A lady called a few days later. I gave all the details, and then it all went quiet and I didn't hear any more.

Mum telephoned me at work to tell me there was a letter for me. She had opened it and told me that it offered me a place at Dendridge Close, in Enfield.

"It's lovely, Mary." She sounded excited.

I caught my breath for a moment.

"How do you know?"

"I've got the keys, and me and Jane had a look. It is so clean Mary, bright and lovely. Just decorated. You will love it."

"What do you mean, you have been round there and had a look? Before me?"

"Yer, me and Jane got the keys."

"You should have waited until I got there, Mum."

I was a bit upset that Mum had gone round there without me, nosing, before I had really had a chance to see it myself, but at the same time I was so elated that I had managed to get a home; because it was now only Colin and I, and the long wait to get back to a family was over.

I dashed round there on the bus and let myself in. It was a little two-bedroom end of terrace maisonette in a quiet cul-de-sac just off Turkey Street, Enfield. I ran up and down the stairs, thinking how bright and airy it was, and the wallpaper so tastefully decorated, with pastel colours—perfect, just perfect. There was a train station just five minutes' walk away, direct to London. A little green for Colin to play. It was my little piece of heaven.

I phoned Janet and Andrea and asked them to meet me at Janet's house on Saturday. I went to the baker's on my way and bought some fresh cream cakes. It was my way of thanking them both for all the help they had given me. I was overjoyed.

I ordered a new single bed for Colin, a double for myself, a new chocolate brown carpet for the hallway and stairs, and a rich deep piled claret carpet for the living room. Now the cash from Tom had made it all worthwhile. I rang Terry straight away, and arranged for him to bring Colin over at the weekend to see his new home.

It was the first sign of my independence. I felt so good! I was ready to start building a life for myself. I found a reliable babysitter for Colin nearby, and he enjoyed playing with their children. It all worked out very well, for both Colin and myself.

I took driving lessons and passed my driving test, although I couldn't afford a car.

Despite all the joy of having my own home at last, one problem seemed to dominate my life; I was still terrified of the dark. It had been there since losing Les in 1957, left over from my childhood, and now it all came flooding back to me. The way the electric would cut off when you least expected it, and then crawling round the walls, searching for the cupboard, fiddling with a coin to put in the meter. The trauma of it was tattooed on my mind. It was all there.

I hadn't been able to shake it off no matter how hard I had tried. I just couldn't get to sleep at nights. I would sit up with the light on, drinking endless cups of tea, and checking all the windows and doors. It became an obsession.

Andrea called me and we met up with another friend, Vaz, a tall, slim, elegant Greek woman. We went to Martha's Wine Bar, in Cricklewood to celebrate my new home. The three of us were chatting away in the bar while a musician, Billy his name was, sat playing his guitar and singing. He was Scottish, and his accent reminded me of Joyce. He could be found singing his quiet casual songs in the wine bar most nights, and when he wasn't singing his songs, he would be found up against the bar chatting to the manager and his wife about tales at university and life in Edinburgh.

Billy was pleasant and easy going enough. He seemed to enjoy chatting with our little group between songs, buying us drinks and joining in on our jokes, with saucy comments. It seemed that we were all having a great time. The wine bar became a regular haunt, meeting with the girls and enjoying their company. It was such a relief to be able to get out and put all my troubles behind me.

Now that I had a stable house and friends to share my worries, my mood lifted. I saw hope in my life once more.

The last thing I was looking for was a relationship, though. I just wasn't ready. But soon Billy started to single me out from the rest of the group, talking to me more frequently whilst we waited for the others to arrive.

33

Beating Up

BILLY WAS TWENTY-SIX and I was thirty-one, when we met. A Scotsman, over six feet tall, dark, slim and good looking. Intelligent, or so I thought. He had won a scholarship and came top of the class at school; he carried his grades in his back pocket. Studied Civil Engineering and Astro Physics at university. Dropped out twice. Why didn't I pick up on that?

At least he had been to university, something I or my friends never managed to achieve.

Martha's wine bar was a frequent outing and I used to stay and play charades with the owners on a regular basis. On many occasions Billy would join us, playing his guitar, and singing. Soon we were left alone to talk at the bar.

"Would you like to come out next Saturday?" Billy asked

"No, I'm having a house warming party."

"Aye, right," he sounded disappointed.

"Would you like to come?"

For some reason my mouth just blubbed it out, like some flustered schoolgirl on her first date.

"I'll bring a bottle!" It didn't take him long to answer.

"Oh..." Something made me feel I wished I hadn't offered, but it was too late.

He brought some of his friends with him, and some gate crashed. I felt uneasy with six of them in the house. It didn't feel right, and I wasn't used to this. I told myself it would be all right.

289

I put it down to first date nerves. Billy was such a kind, generous person, I was sure he would keep everything under control.

Yet this anxious butterfly feeling persisted in making me tense.

Everyone had a great time, but I started to have doubts about some of Billy's friends, who left two cigarette burn marks in my brand new carpet, right by the doorstep.

Billy came round the next day to help me clear up. I showed him the burn marks, but he didn't take too much notice and seemed unconcerned. Whenever I opened the front door, they stared at me, like devil's eyes. It gnawed away at me until I could stand it no more. I cut some remnants of carpet to hide the marks, but it was never the same after that.

In the months to come, Billy became a regular visitor and I was flattered by the attention. The memories of burn marks slipped away, lost in dreams of a family, Billy, Colin and me.

Was I being selfish with my own needs for a partner?

I worried that my young son, now nine years old, might not approve. It was his home too.

Mother asked why I needed a man. "They're all no good," she would say. "Always after only one thing."

She was always so bitter, and blamed Dad for everything, even after he had left.

I didn't listen. She enjoyed being bitter, and I wasn't going to be the same. What was the point of having my own thoughts, if I took notice of everyone else? Right or wrong, it would be my decision. Struggling alone, could I give Colin the best without a father? A strong feeling of unity was important for me.

It wasn't about me anymore, it was about bringing Colin up in a safe and loving family. To experience all I never had. I couldn't let him suffer as I had done. It wasn't fair on him. He had seen his own father walk out the door. He didn't talk about it, but I knew he must have felt it. Loss—I felt it at his age. I didn't so much lose it, as have my childhood surgically removed as the victim of some awful experiment. It wasn't going to happen to my son. Not now, not ever!

I wondered if this was my opportunity to make everything right for him, to show him a family could be happy with a father, albeit a stepfather. Not only did I have to feel secure, Colin had to share those feelings. I so desperately wanted to do the right thing that my mind flip-flopped faster than a politician on polling night.

A thought flashed in my mind, as if in a passing mirror—did I mistakenly reflect myself as the child? In truth, did I want to rescue myself after all these years? Suddenly the notion was lost almost as fast as it had appeared, and I was preoccupied with Billy and Colin once more.

Billy would make a fuss of Colin, bringing him little presents, and lark about with him. Much to my relief they got on very well, and for a moment I put all doubts behind me.

I had found everything. I had my home, and now a new father for Colin, and things were looking up. It wasn't long before Billy and I were setting a date, in spring 1980, to get married.

It was a beautiful day for the wedding. I wore a pale pink suit and a floppy hat. Billy wore a cream jacket and pale blue shirt. We married at Enfield Registry Office. Jack and Florrie, my mother-in-law from my marriage to Terry, prepared all the sandwiches and food for the reception. She was lovely.

Jane, now twenty-four, made a cake, which was a nice surprise. Mother didn't contribute anything. Well, she came and watched.

Florrie phoned the following morning.

"Mary, I don't know how to say this, but there's £100 missing from my handbag."

"No!" I sat on the end of the bed, "I can't believe it."

"Yes Mary, I had a hundred pounds in my purse when I went to the wedding."

"Oh, Florrie," I said, "I don't know what to say."

"I checked this morning because Jack wanted some cash..." she started to get upset "...and it's all gone."

"I'm sorry, where did you leave your bag, Florrie?"

"I left it with the coats in the bedroom," I heard her cry.

I was lost for words. She had been such a help with the wedding, and I never wanted to see her hurt in this way.

Suddenly I felt ashamed, and let down. I looked down at the burn marks in the carpet. I didn't know anyone who would do that sort of thing. I understood her frustration. I wanted to try and help her.

"Do you want me to call the police?"

"No, no, don't do that," she said. "I don't want to make a fuss."

I suspected she didn't want to tell Jack, her husband, she had brought so much cash with her to the wedding.

"Are you sure, love?"

"No, please don't. I just wondered if you'd found anything?"

"No Florrie, I haven't. I'm sorry love, if I do find it I'll ring you straight away."

"All right, thank you Mary."

I did recall seeing Billy's friend, George, coming out of the bedroom. He flew down the stairs right past me, and I thought it a little strange at the time, because he didn't have a coat. There was little I could do, and the guests were long gone.

I told Billy exactly how disappointed I was, let down by him and his dubious friends.

He shuffled uncomfortably, and so I wandered upstairs for a shower. I Just wanted it all to go away.

I emerged on the landing after about thirty minutes, when Billy took a call in the hallway. I didn't think he realised I was listening, but I wanted to know if he was going to do something helpful—raise the issue with his friend, possibly help Florrie out by offering to replace the money. It was one of his friends—'cronies', my mother would have called them—congratulating him on his marriage, or so I gathered from the end of the conversation that I could hear.

"I'm very lucky," he cupped his hand to the phone, "I have a good package. The house, all the furniture and everything ready made."

Suddenly I was reminded of the struggle I had made to get everything. Had I woken up to the realisation that I had, in an instant, given it all away? I felt as if I had been taken for a fool, and wondered if I had made a horrible mistake in marrying Billy. He didn't have a regular job, paying tax and National Insurance like everyone else. His entire working life seemed to have revolved around his income from busking. In my mind things were starting to add up and I found myself resenting his lifestyle.

A few weeks after the wedding the electricity bill dropped through the door. I thought it was time I spoke to Billy about how we would manage the finances. I was no longer a single parent, I was married with a child to support, and I felt it reasonable that we share the cost of running the home, but other events seemed to overtake me before I was able to raise this issue.

George started to drop in on a regular basis. He would stay for lunch, and by dinnertime I was still feeding him.

I went upstairs and spoke quietly to Billy in the bedroom.

"Billy," I said, "your mate George comes here for lunch, then stays for dinner. I can't keep paying for all this food."

"Aye. Well, he's my mate, that's what mates do. So what should I do?"

Sling him out, I thought, but didn't say.

"So how are we going to pay for it then?"

"We'll manage, and besides, he's nay got anywhere else to live."

"Don't you think that as we are married you ought to pay towards the running of the house?"

"I give you what I have, I doon'na have anything more to give."

"But don't you think you need to get a proper job, instead of busking all the time?"

"I give yer £30, is that nay enough?"

"No Billy, it isn't. I earn £200 per week, you earn £30."

"Well, I only eat £30 worth of food, so what's tha problem?"

"I need you to share the cost." I could see this was going to be difficult.

He said that he couldn't get a regular job because he hadn't declared any income tax for five years. I didn't believe him. All he wanted to do was sing and play his guitar in a bar.

I suggested he telephone the tax office, and be honest. They would probably wipe the slate clean and let him start again, but he wouldn't hear of it. Officials made him stutter, and in his frustration he would simply hang up. I spoke to the tax office for him, and they confirmed he could start all clear. It removed the last obstacle for Billy to make a new career for himself. I gave him a copy of the local paper to look for a job, but then he pointed out he didn't have a driving licence.

Undaunted, I got in contact with the local Driving School, organised and paid for a dozen driving lessons, and set a date for the test. He passed first time, appeared confident and now all the obstacles to employment had been removed. To celebrate, I bought a used green Renault 5 on credit, confident his earnings would pay off the debt.

Looking through the local paper he spotted a job for a milkman. I practised interview technique with him, and was delighted when he was offered the job. It wasn't a great salary, but it was a start.

As a milkman he would have to get up at five in the morning, and I didn't think he had given that any serious thought! He wasn't good at getting out of bed. I did everything to get him up, but nothing seemed to work. I tried to pull all the covers off him and make his breakfast and coffee, but still he would not stir. It became so embarrassing the company would send down drivers to knock on the door at 5 a.m., but he wouldn't open the door. I told him to sleep in his car outside the depot, so they would have to come out, and wake him up: nothing.

On the rare occasions when he did manage to get there on time, he still couldn't finish the round. Winter brought with it the rain and ice, and more whinging from Billy. He just couldn't cope with it.

Coming back from a music gig, late at night, he decided to set off for his milk round. But when he came home he said that he was scared of the dark, and refused to go back to work. They fired him. It was a relief.

Colin was away at his father's for the weekend and Billy was playing at a gig. After the gig I drove Billy home in our little green Renault 5 in the early hours of Sunday morning. As I approached Dendridge Close, the exhaust pipe collapsed and the engine roared like some gigantic machine gun on bonfire night. He couldn't bear the noise. Nursing the car gently, now only yards from our home, I cautiously drove into the close. I tried to minimise the sound of the exhaust, but still it was too loud for him.

"Stop the car! Stop the car now!" Billy exploded from the passenger seat, lashing out in frenzy, flaying punches hard into the side of my face. Again and again, his clenched fist ripped into me, leaving my face feeling like a lump of meat.

"What the..."

I fumbled for the door handle, but missed it. I tried again. The door flung open, but my seat belt was still locked. I reached back to release it. Another hail of blows landed; one caught me full on the side of my left ear, violently jerking my head to the side. I turned my face away from him, pulling frantically at the car handle with all my might.

The door gave. I fell out sideways, and then half tumbling, half spilling, I toppled backwards out onto the hard concrete. Grabbing my handbag, I scrambled to my feet and ran off down the road as best I could in my high heels. Finally, I reached the relative safety of the Plough Inn, on the corner of Turkey Street and Cambridge Road. It was closed. I sat on the little wall that surrounded the car park and rested before wandering home in a daze, my face stinging.

Silently I put the key in the lock and slipped into the kitchen. It felt strange. I sensed the heat from the kettle. I wandered into the living room. There was an awful stench of rubbish. Curiously I switched on the light.

"Oh. Fuck!" I didn't normally swear, but there in front of me lay the entire contents of the large kitchen waste bin, tipped up, emptied and then scattered all over my beautiful wine coloured carpet.

Forgetting the pain of my face for a moment, I collapsed in a crumpled heap. I was crushed, unable to speak. I cried at the sight of it. How much I had fought for everything, and in one selfish act, Billy had done this to me! I felt something snap inside me. I rose from the floor. Angry? I'd say I was! I was furious.

"You fucking bastard, where are you?" I mouthed the words.

Walking up the stairs, I slowly searched in the darkness of the landing, but saw nothing. I opened the landing cupboard. There he was, spread-eagled against the back wall. I walked away and down the stairs and straight into the living room, where he followed me in.

"You had better leave," I said quietly.

"I'll patch things up."

I raised my voice, and pointed at the door.

"Pack your things and Get Out." I got louder, forcefully sweeping my arm and stabbing my pointed fingers in the direction of the door.

"I'll clear it up."

We both looked at the mess on the floor.

"How could you do that?" I squared up to him. He stood there like some naughty child caught with his pants down.

"I'll clear it up," he said

"How *could* you, after everything I have done for you? Go on!" I shouted. "Fuck off."

He just stood there.

"I'll clear it up," he said, "I'll clear it up," over and over again. But I couldn't hear him because it made no sense to me.

I stood there in a daze. I just felt so puzzled as to why he had done it. It was his home as much as mine. Did he think that he was doing something to hurt me? I didn't understand how this person I loved could hit me so hard. It was not like it was just a slap around the face, like some men might have done— this was full on, fists clenched with the bare knuckles of a mugger.

I felt I had been raped.

I simply left him and wandered up to the bathroom. This was new to me. Terry never hit me, not once, no matter what we rowed about.

I looked at my face in the mirror, all swollen on the left-hand side as if I had hit a wall. Colin was staying at his father's house, so I went up to my son Colin's room, and went to sleep.

34

Living with Billy

MY LIFE LURCHED ALONG with Billy, but like some antique bus, it kept breaking down. Things would be patched up for a while and he would say sorry. In the aftermath of these episodes of violence he couldn't have been more helpful. I told him I wasn't going to put up with the violence anymore. He promised to deal with his temper, and get another job.

After a few weeks of searching he managed to get work in the sales office at Polyliner. For a few months we were getting on fine, or so I thought. He used to tell me about problems at work—how the manager kept holding reviews with him.

"The managers at work held another performance review with me on Friday."

"What did they do?"

He lowered his head, then looked out the window.

"The manager called me in the office after lunch ..." He cleared his throat. "...and, er, he asked me how things were going with the work."

"What did they want to know?"

"They wanted to know, er," cough, "how was I coping?" He kept wringing his hands.

"So what did you say?" I waited patiently.

He was sweating. I wondered what he was hiding.

"Oh, I'm getting on fine like," sniff, "enjoying the job an' that. Yer know, the usual thing."

"But it's not fine, is it Billy?" I took the bull by the horns.

"Yeah, it's fine, I doona know what they're on about." He avoided my eye and started picking the skin on his fingers.

"Can't you see your managers are trying to find a solution to some problem here?"

I worried if there might have been complaints about him, and I didn't want him to lose his job. I wondered if he was expecting to get the sack, and trying to prepare me for it, like a student before an exam.

"You know nothing about what's going on at work. How can you know what they're on about when you're nay there?"

I just let him rant.

"I'm tha' one with the top grades in 'A' Levels. No' you! So doon'na keep telling me what they're doin'—yer know nothing aboot it." His Scottish accent got thicker as his fuse got shorter.

"I'm just trying to help you Billy," I backed off.

To me it was obvious what they were doing, but I didn't understand why Billy didn't see it.

A few weeks later I joined Billy as he performed a gig at The Woolpack pub. It wasn't far from the house, so we walked there. It was late at night when we both strolled back. We hadn't got more than one hundred yards when, without warning, he lashed out with his right arm, caught me a sideways blow to the stomach that lifted my feet from under me, and left me sprawling on the ground.

He just walked off and said, "Fuck you!"

I lay there: shocked. Writhing in agony, I clutched my stomach struggling for breath. I lay there gulping air like a drowning fish, floundering as the pain locked my mind. I only thought about breathing and my handbag—there was no room for rationalisation or anger. Boy, did that hurt! My ribs felt as if the splinters were piercing my lungs with every gasp.

After some time I raised myself from the cold damp paving stones, clung to the railings by the stream, and rested. Was I bleeding? I didn't see any blood, but then it was dark. I wandered over to a nearby street lamp.

I was all right, only a grazed knee when I fell. I slid my hand to my ribs, feeling like a blind man. They seemed to be still there. "Ouch." I kept my thoughts like my breathing; shallow and calm.

This was new. There was no argument, no run up to the spluttering smouldering discontent; instead, it was the emotional explosion of a suicide bomber! One moment strolling along after a successful evening, the next, I was on the floor. Why did he do it? I never found out why. I was simply left to accept it was part of life with Billy.

What was I to do—accept it as part of life with Billy? No, no, no! What was I saying?

If he thought he could do this to me and just walk away without a fight, then he had picked the wrong woman. I wasn't a doormat, and he was not going to wipe his boots on me.

The following morning I felt ill. I started vomiting. I worried about all the bruising around my stomach and ribs. I felt myself panic, flushing over my face and chest. I wondered if he had done some serious damage.

I rang the doctors and made an appointment straight away. I saw Dr King. She arranged a blood and urine test. The following week I went back to see the doctor. She told me I was expecting a baby, and I was nearly two months pregnant.

I telephoned Billy to tell him. He was overjoyed, said he had this vision of five children around a big kitchen table, playing happy families with the chatter of little voices, dolls houses and footballs; although I had my private thoughts. But for now I shared his dream about the little girl I had always wanted.

I was eight months pregnant when the next incident occurred.

Billy was performing at a gig, playing his guitar with another guy who lived nearby. Roz had been married to Jimmy as sweethearts since they were at school. She always thought he was a dead ringer for Elvis Presley, and I have to say there was a resemblance.

Billy and Jimmy shared an ambition to make it as singers, and became good friends. Roz was nice—she didn't live far from my house, and we would often be seen at the gigs as a foursome.

On one such night, as the gig came to a close, and as I wandered over to a table at the side of the stage, Jimmy found some chairs for us whilst Billy was clearing away his sound gear. Jimmy paid me a lot of attention, doing more fussing than a wasp on a jam jar. I didn't think anymore about it, especially since I was so pregnant, and I was huge!

I bade Roz and Jimmy goodnight, and Billy and I strolled to the house. Turning the key in the front door, I stepped into a heavy fist that caught me, tearing into my arm like I had just been shot. It was so sudden I fell backwards in shock.

"You will be put in prison if you hit me whilst I am pregnant!" I screamed.

For a moment I thought that was the end of the matter, but as we stumbled into the house, he resumed hitting me, and then, unexpectedly he stopped and it went quiet.

I ran up the stairs to the bedroom. He followed me.

"I'll show you!" he shouted above the sound of splintering timber. I watched in disbelief as the last of the shelves were ripped from the walls and thrown into a heap on the bedroom floor.

I didn't know what to say anymore. I went into Colin's bedroom, but he followed me in.

"I'm going to call the police."

He started laughing, then smacking me round the face and punching my body. I curled up to protect myself until he staggered off and went to sleep. I was left to nurse my wounds.

The next morning I saw an enormous bruise on the upper part of my right arm. I covered it with a bandage to hide it. It was part of my baggage, to keep the secret life from the outside world. I was frightened of Billy and I didn't know what would happen if others found out.

I wandered out to the front step to bring in the milk. I forgot the bandage still wrapped on my arm. My neighbour caught my attention.

"Mary?" she said, "The noise last night." She probed: "I was worried about you. Did he hit you?"

"No," I said, "we were having a bit of a discussion and I lost my footing and fell down, hitting my arm on a balustrade on the stairs."

"You sure you are all right?"

"Yes, don't worry, I'm fine." I covered up my bruises. Then turning awkwardly I shuffled back inside.

Billy was so charming and kind most of the time, I didn't understand what I had done wrong.

When he came home from work the next day he was full of apologies, and said he was sorry. I simply glared at him and gave him a wide berth; there was nothing I felt I could say to him. I didn't understand any of it. I was numb.

I didn't dwell on it anymore. I switched into a form of coping strategy and tried to do what I could to survive; my childhood had taught me that!

Billy burst in on the scene with a new dishwasher and a plumber ready to install it there and then. He kept saying he was sorry and that it was a present for me, and it wouldn't happen again; but I still never got an answer as to why he had done it in the first place; that bugged me more than anything else.

I was being told, by some of his friends at work, that he was having loud arguments with his colleagues, apparently over quite trivial things. I understood he would raise his voice and start shouting at them. They would apparently absent themselves from the workplace, to leave him with his animated rant and no doubt worrying about their own safety.

In the end, the company had to sack him and soon he was searching for another job.

I thought that perhaps it was the stress at work, which had been responsible for the violence, and although I was used to arguments in my childhood, I was starting to seriously consider what was going on in my life. I sat in the bedroom and rang a policeman friend.

Barry was an old trusted friend from way back. He said it wouldn't get better. He told me that once they cross that line, they don't go back. I sunk down on the bed. I knew inside he was right.

I thanked him for his advice and I promised to stay in touch.

I searched for a type of job for Billy, which would get him out of the office. Like my previous husband Terry, I thought that he might be better equipped for a job as a sales representative, and on the road on his own.

Within weeks I had discovered a job in the local paper working for Thorn Lighting as a sales electrical lighting engineer, in Cambridge Road. I did as last time, prepared him for the interview, and he got the job.

Soon Lindsay, my daughter was born at Chase Farm Hospital, Enfield—the little girl I always wanted. She was everything I wished for—a healthy eight pounds, with dark hair, brown eyes and a smooth tanned complexion.

Now I hoped that things would improve between Billy and myself. I hoped that a new baby would glue us together.

My son Colin was now twelve and this triggered a rule in the social housing legislation. It was designed to prevent the sharing of different sex children, where there was more than a twelve-year age difference. I had a daughter, and suddenly I qualified for a three-bedroom home.

It was a new start. We had everything going for us, and I hoped that things would change, as if somehow the old house had been responsible for all our troubles.

Things settled down to routine. Lindsay was growing fast, Colin was getting on well at school, and Billy was doing okay at Thorn Lighting enjoying the use of the company car, and then I felt a lump in my breast.

The Doctor examined me and confirmed that I had a lump. He told me that these things happened after just having a baby and he wanted it removed. I waited in the surgery and listened to a flurry of telephone calls. I was told I had to have X-rays to check, and then I would probably need a small operation at the Chase Farm Hospital to remove the lump.

I didn't understand how he could tell me that these things happen after childbirth, as if it were to be expected, then frantically phone the hospital to book me in for an operation.

I went into hospital for the operation on the day that we were due to move to our new home.

35

New Home, New Baby

ARRIVING FROM THE HOSPITAL into my new home, I sat helplessly like some broken butterfly. Luckily the lump was benign, although it signalled changes in my breast tissue. I held myself and curled up on my bed, surrounded by the musty boxes of cardboard that littered the house.

Lindsay was at my mum's, so I didn't have to worry about where she was at least.

The living room was full; the hall was full; the kitchen was full; the baby's bedroom was full; my bedroom was full; Colin's bedroom was full; even the bathroom was full. With my arm all strapped up, the house piled high, there was nothing I could do except sit on the boxes and look at it all. Billy hadn't done anything.

I sat down and cried. My heart sank at the enormity of the task ahead.

Turning to the church, I hoped they would influence Billy to bring some discipline to my chaotic lifestyle and curb the violence within him. I called upon my church friends to help me. They collected Lindsay and then bought some basic shopping.

They were brilliant! They unpacked and got rid of all the boxes for me. I was able to start to clear the mess and make sense of my new home. At least the bathroom and kitchen were in a functional order, both the dishwasher and washing machine plumbed in, and the kitchen shelves stocked with food. They cleared the worktop, tabletops, chairs and the sofa so that by the time Colin had bounced in from school, the house was starting to appear more like something normal.

Naively I thought that Billy would be pleased to see the house all cleared when he got home. Not a bit of it! All he wanted was his dinner on the table, and when that wasn't available, he simply sloped off down the pub at the end of the road, like I had seen my father do many times before. Colin and I were left to get on with it.

Billy appeared back some hours later with a kebab, which he sat and ate in the kitchen before disappearing upstairs to bed without saying a word.

Pressing redial, Billy questioned me about the phone calls I had made. He wanted to know my movements during the day, as if he didn't trust me anymore. I started to feel oppressed in my own home and I felt uneasy about him; it didn't feel right to me.

Terry, my former husband, was never like this. I kept wondering what I was doing wrong

I walked to the train station to the phone box where I spoke to 'Refuge', a London charity for women founded in 1979.

"Hello," the woman said, "My name is Joan. How can I help you?"

"Hello," I nervously bit my lip.

"What's your name?"

"M... Mary." I wasn't sure I wanted to be identified.

"Well hello, Mary. Where are you phoning from?"

"A call box by the station."

"Are you safe calling from there?"

"Yes, my husband is at work." The truth was I didn't know where he was.

"Would you like to tell me how I can help you today?"

"I'm just making enquiries. I think I need some advice."

My life tumbled out and I told her about the first year of bliss, when Billy was so gentle and kind. I didn't understand why now? Why had the violence only started after a year? I wanted to know what was wrong with me.

"Mary, love. You're not doing anything wrong—it's a pattern they all go through," she said. "A husband and wife should never hit each other—it is wrong. Tell me, Mary, does he give you anything after he hits you?"

"Yes, he buys a present."

"Quite a big one—say a washing machine or something like that?"

"Yes—a dishwasher—he bought me a dishwasher."

"Does he get upset that he has spent so much money that he can't afford?"

"Yes he does—complains that I made him do it."

"Then falling over himself to be helpful until things settle back to being normal? Until you think that things are all right?"

"Yes, that's exactly right."

"Does he tell you it's all your fault?"

"Yes, but sometimes I think that it must be my fault because he says that I provoke him."

"He must not hit you, regardless of how angry he gets. Now listen to me carefully, dear. This is what you must do. Each time he attacks you, go to the doctors and get him to record your injuries. You will find that there will be a cycle of attacks, perhaps every week, or six weeks, or months or so."

"No, no. It's not like that. No, you don't understand, he doesn't hit me every week! I'm not a battered wife—I am not abused or anything. I only rang for advice."

"Yes, you *are* abused."

"I'm not." I closed my eyes and put my hand to my face. "You don't understand." I couldn't stop the sobbing, "I don't want my marriage to end, I don't want to!" The tears washed away my words.

"Mary, now listen to me dear. Mary, are you there? Mary, do you hear me?"

"Yes," I sniffed. "I'm still here." I wiped my nose.

"Mary, love, stay with me, I know it's hard for you to accept, and I can hear you getting upset. Are you hearing me, Mary?"

"Yes, I hear what you are saying."

"It varies from person to person, and the attacks may be more or less frequent, but there will be a pattern. Believe me Mary, I'm sorry love, but it *will* happen again."

"What do I do?" For a moment I couldn't take in the immensity of what she was saying. It didn't fit in with my thinking.

"You need to start keeping a diary, love. There will be a pattern."

"But how will I know?"

"Check the time between incidents recorded in the diary. That will help you to come to terms with it and make a decision for yourself." She was firm with me.

The phone clattered as I put it down. I stood still in the relative silence of the phone box for a moment, overwhelmed. I recognised the pattern that she had so vividly described. Sense was springing from chaos.

I opened the door of the telephone box and let sounds of the trains drift back into my thoughts, like flotsam on the tide. I sat on the steps of the railway crossing nearby, and pondered the catalogue of events with Billy. The rows, his friends. The way he and his cronies treated my home, the violence and my conversation with the charity Refuge.

Through my tears I felt my anger shine. I was going to stop this. I felt myself getting upset, but I had to carry on. I phoned my doctor's surgery for an appointment. I didn't want anymore children and I didn't share Billy's vision of five children around a table. It was all clear now—I didn't see another child as being helpful; quite the opposite, I now was convinced in my own mind that it was time to plan my exit strategy. A sterilisation was the first step along that path. It had been a productive day and I was delighted to achieve so much.

Within a few days I was in the doctor's surgery. I told the doctor I wanted a sterilisation, about my worry for the future, and this violent relationship with Billy. He told me straight that in his opinion I had many more babies in me yet. This didn't seem to be the answer I was seeking, and so I made an appointment with another doctor for the very next day.

Again, I stressed my relationship anxieties, and about my conversation with the Refuge charity, their advice and my fears and expectations. He gave me one answer—yes okay, but you will need to have counselling.

"Agreed." I went off to make an appointment with the counsellor.

I told Billy that I had to go to the hospital for a check up, but had a sterilisation instead. I phoned Billy from the hospital and told him I couldn't have any more babies. He was furious, but I was determined to take control of my life. I was in hospital for a few days, and arranged for Mum to check up on Lindsay each day.

Despite the discomfort of having the operation, it was worthwhile. I would not be controlled—it was my body and I didn't feel that I wanted any more children.

Billy was doing a gig with Jimmy at 2 p.m. on Sunday afternoon. Roz and I arrived later to a big marquee set up, with stalls, events, boot sales and everything that field events have. Everywhere was the smell of canvas and wooden trestles in muddy little tents, which lined the edge of the field. A makeshift stage was erected, with balloons hanging from the bunting strung across the marquee, like some old 1940's street party. Loudspeakers, mixers and microphones were festooned with wires. It was set up and ready to blast out to the assembled crowd.

Lindsay sat in her pushchair, watching everyone milling around, when Jimmy first came up to me.

"Where's Billy?"

"Don't know—thought he was with you?"

"No, he's not with me," I shook my head, "haven't seen him.. Hasn't done a runner, has he?"

"I don't know."

I wandered around the site and searched all the tents.

"He doesn't seem to be here, Jimmy."

"Oh, no." He rolled his eyes upward.

"I'll leave Lindsay with Roz, and drive home."

"Yeah, that would be good. If you find him—get him back here pronto! Wanker! We're pushed for time now."

"Okay." I drove back to the house.

When I got there, I found Billy in bed, hiding under the covers, frightened and paranoid, saying he couldn't do the gig. I left him, went back and told Jimmy and Roz.

"He's crying and refusing to come back to the gig. You'll have to do it on your own!"

"Fuck it! I bet he's taken some stupid drugs or something—fucking bastard. Now what do I do?"

"You'll have to do it alone, Jimmy. But look on the up side, you won't have to share the take!" I chirped up. But it didn't make him any happier.

"Fucking bastard—I'm sorry Mary, but Billy is becoming a complete waste of my fucking time. Did he tell you that we have a manager interested in us doing a recording?"

"No. Didn't say anything to me."

"Yeah, all set up to go to Austria for an audition, right? Billy is all over the place like a fart in a trance. He fluffs his frets, has so much drink before he goes on that he can't remember the lyrics, then he stumbles on the stage and falls over! I've fucking had enough of him and, to be honest, the manager guy—well, he wasn't best pleased with him either.

"This is fucking it with Billy! I'm sorry Mary, but Billy has pissed me about so much that this is the last straw. I am going to have to go it alone from now on. I tried to keep him in on it; the guy wasn't that interested in Billy anyway, but at least he would have been in the backing group, but now! I just don't know."

"Okay Jimmy—don't worry."

He turned to go, walked a few paces, and then spun round and spoke tenderly.

"If there's anything I can do for you Mary, just let me know."

"Thanks Jimmy, I'll be okay." I gestured with a little wave, then left to go back home.

I was sickened with the prospect that Billy was now taking drugs, on top of everything else. I was furious. I didn't know he was screwing up his stage performances; this was news to me.

Billy left for work on Monday morning. He said he had thirty-five grievances with the company, and was going up to their head office, in Leicester, to complain about the management. I said good luck, but inside I was very sceptical about what the company would do about it.

He came home some time later, exhausted, having had to travel down from Leicester by train. He told me they took his car keys from him there and then, gave him his cards, and he was out of a job again.

It was some months later that we decided to go away for a caravan holiday break at Hastings. He ended up jumping on the bed, banging his fists on the wall, breaking all their cups, and it ended in disaster again. I left him there and walked down to the beach with Colin and Lindsay. Then when I got back to the caravan I simply packed up and we came home.

The hunt was on for another job. He managed to get two job offers, one with less money and one with slightly more money than he had been getting at Thorn Lighting. He wanted to take the job with the lower salary so that they wouldn't expect so much of him, and he got quite stressed when I told him we couldn't live on it. I managed to persuade him to take the job with the higher money, although even that wasn't great.

It seemed to stress him out and he started hitting me again, landing the first blow on my upper arm. He spun round on his heels, strutted into the kitchen, and opened the first kitchen cupboard.

"Don't tell me what to do!" he shouted. "I'll teach you!"

I watched in disbelief. He pulled it open with such force that the cabinet tore away from the wall. Plates and cups all tumbled and crashed onto the floor, exploding, shards of broken pottery bursting in every direction.

Holding my head in my hands, I listened to the deafening onslaught as the torrent of it all fell around me. The words of the lady at Refuge echoed in my ears as loudly as a church bell. "He *will* do this again," she had warned.

My hopes, like my kitchen, lay shattered as I was reduced to a quivering wreck.

Each cupboard in turn was pulled from the wall, glass shattering, spinning and spitting around the kitchen, until it all lay in a jumbled heap on the floor. I felt like an earthquake victim, stumbling through the rubble, for that was what it was.

Lindsay, sucking her dummy, walked through the chaos of white flour, eggs, and shattered glass. I leaped into action, snatched her up in my arms, and ran upstairs to the bedroom. Wiping her feet over the Mickey Mouse waste bin, I cuddled her and bathed her with my sobbing tears. I slept in her room that night. Restless thoughts chased round in my mind. In the morning I rose early. My decision was made. I kept my powder dry.

Rallying help from friends at the local church, I was able to rebuild the kitchen as best I could, limping on with what crockery I had left, but none asked the question about what was going on in my life.

Soon Billy started to complain about the cost of the dishwasher, and how we couldn't afford it—blaming me for making him buy it. He didn't know what was coming next. War had been declared.

36

The Final Blow

SITTING IN THE SOLICITORS' OFFICE I had time to think about what I wanted. A short elderly man sat in front of me, and had clearly been practising law for many years, seemingly intelligent, although I began to sense an unwillingness to take on the full confrontation with Billy. I started to tell him about the violence. He shrank down in the chair. I could see that he didn't want to take the case, and I listened to my inner feelings; I got up and left.

On my way home I passed another solicitor's office in Waltham Cross and just walked in. I was annoyed enough to demand some action. The rooms were covered with so many documents—scattered on desks, tables, chairs, in fact, just about anywhere where there might be a horizontal surface on which to keep them above the ground. It didn't bode well. I was one for organisation and tidiness, and this was far from the organisational skills I was looking for. Still, I had come, and so I approached a small gentleman, his grey balding hair suddenly appearing from the chaos, as if risen up in some sort of dumb waiter from behind another pile of documents.

"I'm sorry about the chaos," he said, "our receptionist is off sick at the moment." He cleared a space. "Can I help you?"

"Yes, I am looking for a solicitor to take on a domestic violence case. I want a divorce!"

"Oh, well, er, I can't take you on, I'm afraid." He walked backwards, then, turning, he gestured for me to follow him.

"But you might want to talk to Mr Williams here." He pointed into another dingy office. I peered carefully into the room, wondering if I was about to fall into some black hole.

A hand appeared and was thrust towards me. He led the way to his office. "Hello, my name is Peter Williams. Can I help?"

He was a young man, probably around twenty-five, clean looking, glasses, neatly set wavy hair, smartly dressed, very well spoken. I had my doubts: was he too young? Yet I felt comforted by his sharp approach.

"Hello, my name is Mary. I will get straight to the point. I have a violent relationship and I want a divorce. Now I warn you that my husband is a big man; he will come round to your office and may attempt to intimidate you. He has beaten me up on a number of occasions and…"

He put his hand up as if to stop the traffic.

I stopped; he stopped leaning backward; I turned; he turned, swinging his chair to face me. He put his hands down and clasped them before speaking.

"It's okay. Get the gist." He frowned, then nodded.

"Will you take it on?"

"Yes of course I will, no problem."

"What about the violence? He may come round, pace up and down outside, come in and threaten you. I have had one solicitor tell me that he thought that Billy was 'a red rag to a bull', and said that he didn't want to do anything that might upset him. Now can you deal with that?" I stood in front of his desk, ready to leave.

"Mary, I might be young but I do not take fright. We have a police force, and that is what they do. I have the law and that is what I do. I want to make a name for myself and in order to do that, I need a cause to champion, and yours sounds good to me."

"Right," I said.

"Please do not concern yourself on my account. I have a very experienced assistant who will pick you up and take you to court if necessary. You just leave that to me. I simply call the police if we have any problems."

"Aren't you afraid of the violence—he's a big man?"

"I will deal with that, it's not your worry. He will not have any effect on me and I can assure you that he will not intimidate me. My assistant, Andrew, will make sure that no harm will come to you, and rest assured, nothing will prevent you from getting your case heard."

"All right. You give me confidence that we can work together—let's do it."

"Now will you sit down, and I will take some details."

"Thank you." I smiled at him. "I look forward to working with you."

I shook his hand. It was like his manner—firm, dry and straight. I sat down.

Shortly after the meeting I moved out of the main bedroom and slept in Lindsay's room. Billy received a letter telling him that his wife had petitioned for divorce on the grounds of his unreasonable behaviour.

He didn't say anything, just grunted, then he went out, and I went to bed.

Billy was towering over my bed in the middle of the night, swaying from side to side and the light blinding me. He was spitting his words and slurring his speech, trying to say something, but I found it difficult to understand what, exactly, and it took a few minutes to adjust my focus. Lindsay didn't wake, so I quietly got up. Colin continued to sleep in the other room, undisturbed as far as I knew.

"I've taken thirty-five paracetamol tablets, with five cans of lager and I cannot do this anymore."

"So what do you want me to do about it?" I rested on my elbows thinking what a pathetic prat, wondering how on earth I had married this excuse for a man.

"I would rather kill Lindsay than let you have her," he said, now lurching down the stairs. "I'm gonna take her back to Scotland wi' me, then when I come back—you've heard of the Hungerford Massacre!"

In 1987, a man walked down the high street of a little town in Berkshire, called Hungerford. He shot sixteen people in his path, including his own mother, before finally killing himself.

I felt a mixture of anger and pity for him, and it reminded me how I had felt about my father. My childhood amounted to full blown coping strategy, and that's exactly how I dealt with him. I got up and quickly got dressed and went downstairs, chasing after him as he lurched out of the front door.

"So what have you taken?"

"Thirty-five paracetamol and cans of lager."

I believed the cans of lager, but wasn't sure about all the paracetamol that he had taken. He always said thirty-five whenever he couldn't think of a good number; still, I couldn't take a chance and as he stumbled out of the house, he fell face down in the snow. I went back in, and dialled 999.

Five minutes later, arriving in a cacophony of flashing lights, the medics were dragging Billy off in the early hours of the morning amongst the hoard of twitching net curtains; however, he wouldn't go with the ambulance crew and came back into the kitchen. He moaned about the Divorce petition to the policeman.

"She's taking my little girl away and I won't be able to see her," he muttered amongst his drunken tears. "I would rather kill her than let her have her!"

"Have you taken any tablets?" the ambulance man asked.

"Yes—Paracetamol."

"How many?"

Billy nodded.

"Thirty five," I volunteered. "Washed them down with beer, though I don't believe that he took that many."

"Okay, thank you madam."

The policeman pulled Billy to one side and spoke to him. He listened patiently, and although resistant, Billy was eventually persuaded to go to hospital.

In the meantime my attention was distracted by the sight of my three-year-old. Lindsay. Woken by the shouting, she stood in her little pink pyjamas, looking on, puzzled and helpless, amidst the chaos. Colin wandered down the stairs and stood next to Lindsay.

For a brief moment I saw another image, that of myself standing there as a child; an onlooker, as if the images were so close in my imagination, that somehow my brain had selected the wrong one. I was horrified.

Covering my face, I felt this sudden deep gut-wrenching sadness grab me by the throat. The trauma of my childhood; my wooden leg was upon me. Was I creating a repeat of my own childhood destiny, I wondered?

Wandering back into the kitchen, the young officer started to speak to me. He told Colin to take Lindsay upstairs out of the way and then turned to me. I spoke first. I was worried that he would tell me off.

"I'm sorry—I will have to stop the divorce action! I can't risk it—you don't know what Billy is like when he's all fired up. I can't have him harming my little girl."

"You mustn't be upsetting yourself." He spoke softly, seeking out my eyes. "You must keep in mind that you meant to go through with a divorce when you handed him the letter." He waited for me.

I nodded.

"Now this is emotional blackmail and I've seen many cases. Don't you take it to heart, love. If you want a divorce, you just carry on with it. Go on—don't let this stop you. Have the strength to go through with it; don't listen to emotional manipulation."

"You think I should carry on with the divorce?"

"I do," he said. "If you don't do it for yourself, do it for the kids." He was very precise.

"Thanks—that's really helpful. I feel better about it already."

He strengthened my resolve to end this nightmare, for myself, Colin and Lindsay.

Billy remained in hospital for three days whilst they pumped his stomach. If he had taken thirty-five paracetamol as he claimed, then he would have been dead, and the fact that he wasn't gave me a much greater strength to see this situation through. He was due to see a psychiatrist, but he discharged himself before the appointment and came home.

He started to do things differently and claimed the main bedroom as his, using it like a lodger, staying in there all day and night, only leaving to pick up more cans of lager. I slept in Lindsay's room and she slept on a little red single foam bed. She didn't mind and thought that it was quite nice to have me sleeping with her.

We all chugged along for a week or two. When I say chugged, I mean on tenterhooks, wondering what he was going to do next. Billy started a new game.

Colin earned twenty pounds a week from his part time jobs. He had his own bedroom at the front of the house. He tried to keep himself out of the arguments and tensions, trying to stay in his own world to some extent. He paid me a little for his housekeeping, the rest of the money he kept for himself, and in return, I let him do pretty much what he wanted most of the time. With the small income from Colin and my child benefit, which I saved for emergencies, I could manage.

As Colin came home from work, Billy stood at the door and demanded Colin's wages. Then he rang Social Security and tried to stop me from getting my child allowance. He wasn't giving me any money himself, and now, I guess, he thought that he could starve me out.

Right, I thought, if there was one thing I was equipped to deal with, it was hunger. I had done it before and I could do it again. If he thought he could starve me out, then he had picked the wrong person. I was more than capable of living on bread and jam.

I started to get very much stronger. I raised myself up and on this day, I made a decision. There was no turning back and no matter what Billy did, I would be there, stronger and smarter, until I had finally got rid of this man. I had declared outright war.

He started to record my voice. He would play with Lindsay at bedtime, or bath nights and stop her from cooperating, until I would get fed up with it and shout at her. Suddenly he would start recording my shouting at Lindsay hoping he could prove I was a bad mother, and so obtain custody.

I would wake up in the night, and hear my voice booming out over the house. He was playing tapes of the conversations I had during the day. When all this didn't work he came home drunk, muttering about taking Lindsay, and threatening me with all sorts of rants about what he was going to do to me. I worried about it, but thought it was all words, until one night it wasn't.

The bedroom door exploded, scattering splinters of wood over the floor. He burst in, stood over me, swaying from side to side like a sailor in a storm as I lay cowering beneath him in my bed. For a split second I was so frightened that I couldn't move, as if my body had suffered a seizure. He was shouting.

"You'll never have her! I would rather take Lindsay back to Scotland wi' me and kill 'er, than give her up to you!"

He pushed me down with his clenched fist, clawing at my throat, his rough hands locked in a pincer grip around my windpipe. Burrowing deep with his fingers, my muffled scream dulled into a rasping choke that shot into my paralysed jaw.

I lay there, prostrate, stunned and utterly defenceless.

Lindsay had woken and got out of bed. She sat there in her nightdress, bewildered, her little face flung amongst the chaos of it all. She was rubbing her wide eyes, trying to make sense of what was happening. I tried for a breath, but none came. I watched her anxiously; my last dying memory, hoping that it wasn't, but what could I do?

"I'll kill you—you bitch." His bulging glazed eyes shone out as he squeezed harder and harder, ripping into my throat like a lion ending the kill.

Gurgle.

Unable to speak, I looked across to Colin for help, pleading with my eyes for action, but none came.

He didn't do anything. He didn't rescue me, he stood there and watched. Suddenly I knew I was done for.

Was this the way my life would end? I felt the world drifting from me.

My vision was the first to go, flashing in and out with a black redness, like dark cherries in the black soup, and suddenly I was blind, but aware of sounds and feelings. Then my hearing started to fail; sounds got softer, fainter, as if I were getting further away, drifting, floating; my body tingled until there was emptiness and numbness.

Someone had turned up the volume control: my vision snapped back in a buzz of vibrant speckled colour; my body tingled once more. I lashed out and fought for my life in a frenzy, but it was no use; his weight was far too much for me. I snatched a breath of sweaty air as I felt his grip slacken. Colin grabbed Billy's hand and made a vain attempt to pull him from me. It wasn't enough and once again he held me down and grabbed my throat with a renewed grip, more tightly than before.

"You bitch—die, you bitch! You're not 'aving her!"

"Leave her alone!"

Was that Colin's voice?

Shaking me like a rag doll, Billy cold-bloodily squeezed the lifeblood out of my body. Again and again I tried to fight back, flailing him with my arms and trying to kick him in the crotch, but nothing worked, and soon the world returned to black and white.

High-pitched screams pierced through my mind. It was Lindsay.

"Mummy, mummy, don't hurt my mummy!"

Her voice triggered something in me. Mothers will know what I mean. Adrenaline coursed through my body and fuelled the oxygen of my escape. I felt the sinews rip from my shoulders as I clawed at his face, tearing at him with my bare hands, and gouging out his eyes with my fingernails.

I wasn't going down without a fight. I punched, kicked with everything I had; I felt no pain, despite my knuckles, now raw with blood. Colin pulled his arm, I grabbed his little finger; I loosened his grip enough for me to tear myself away from his grasp. I spun round like a crocodile as he clambered to my body once more, but I was too quick for him and rolled out of the way.

Staggering and wheezing, I rolled over to Lindsay, holding her close to me. Then scooping her up in my arms I made a dash for it before my energy expired. I ran downstairs, half stumbling for all I was worth, screaming for Colin to call the police, but he didn't seem to move. I kept running into the night in my bare feet. Exhausted, I slumped down on the pavement in the darkness.

I was still struggling to breathe when the police arrived. Lindsay was crying, and sobbing. I was trying to comfort her as best I could.

The blue lights flashed outside. The police radio crackled in the background as they took Billy back into the house, keeping him well away from the rest of us. They wanted the story from each of us, although it was clear to see the red fingermarks that decorated my neck like a speckled band.

I would not stay in the house. As far as I was concerned, Billy would have killed me there and then, and from now on there was to be no way back. I phoned my mum, taking Colin and Lindsay in a mini-cab and staying overnight.

I understood that the police suggested that Billy find somewhere else to live, but I didn't know if he had.

At the Solicitor's the following morning I saw Peter Williams.

"He tried to kill me last night. I called the police and he threatened to kill Lindsay, my three-year-old daughter, and he tried to strangle me. Fortunately my son was able to help pull him off."

"All right, this is what we need to do. We need to apply for an injunction. When we have that, your husband will have to find somewhere else to live, and will be prevented from approaching within a certain distance of your home."

"Okay. Will I have to attend the court?"

"Yes, but don't worry, Andrew here will pick you up at the house, and take you over there in our car."

"Where will it be?"

"We won't know at the start. I'll need to check to see which court has the time free. It might be Hatfield Magistrates Court. But it doesn't matter because, as I said, my assistant will take you there. Now that's all we need at the moment, so I will give you a ring when I know the exact time and place."

"Thank you," I said, turning and leaving.

Andrew, an older man, picked me up and drove me to Hatfield, where we obtained a Non-Molestation Order. He brought me back and arranged for all the locks on the house to be changed. At last I had someone routing for me and things were starting to get me out of this mess.

Stunned, my ear glued to the phone, I listened intently as Mr Williams gave me the news.

"Billy has his name as the Lead Tenant, on the Rental Agreement for the house."

"So what difference does that make?"

"It means that it's not your house, it's Billy's." He waited for me to realise what it meant.

"I had been the only tenant of the house in Dendridge Close, and so I naturally assumed that the same would have happened at the new house in Cheshunt?"

"No, Billy is clearly the Lead Tenant."

"You are telling me that I don't rent my own home?"

"I'm sorry, but yes."

"Are you telling me that I don't even have a right to stay in my own home?"

"No, I'm sorry, but there it is."

"Can I get it changed back to my name?"

"You can, but you need to get Billy to sign the form transferring the tenancy to you, and of course, that may be tricky."

"Send me the form," I said. "I'll get it signed, you mark my words!"

When I returned home I discovered that he had broken into my house and stolen all my child benefit money that I had been saving up—all £80. I couldn't work out how he knew that I had hidden it under the carpet in the living room.

I rang Florrie, my mother-in-law from my first marriage to Terry, and she suggested I go to her place for a weekend break and get away from it all. After everything I had been through I thought it was a good idea; I needed a break so that I could make sense of what was happening.

I grabbed a suitcase, packed a few things for Colin, Lindsay, and myself, and called a cab ready to leave. It was then, at the instant I had put the phone down, that Billy turned up in his car.

I wondered what he was going to do. I opened the front door to leave, but before I had a chance to close it, he barged right past me, snatching my handbag as he shot into the hall. He grabbed me and before I understood what was going on, started jumping up and down on my feet with all his weight.

It felt as if he were trying to break all my toes and, judging by the pain I suffered after that attack, I think he succeeded. I screamed at Colin to phone the police, but he wouldn't. I never understood that.

Billy took all my money and keys out of my purse, slung the bag back at me, shoving me out of the house and slamming the door; effectively locking me out of my own home.

I didn't know where Colin was at this time and it didn't seem to matter, for he didn't help me. It was like he was a referee at a football match.

I could have spent time banging on the door and swearing at him, but I was better than that. I told the cab driver what Billy had done. He calmly got out and, walking over to Billy's car, he deflated all the tyres before driving us away to phone my solicitor. They were closed for the weekend. The taxi driver took us to Florrie's house as arranged, and she was good enough to settle the cab fare.

But I still had a nagging worry at the back of my mind. How did Billy know that I was going out at that time?

37

Bugging

IT WAS MONDAY 10th FEBRUARY 1986 when I returned from Florrie's house. The taxi dropped Colin, now fifteen years old, off at his school. I continued to the house with my three-year-old toddler, Lindsay.

It was locked. Billy had the keys.

Florrie had lent me enough money for the taxi fare, and I was left with ten pence. It wasn't enough for the locksmith, so I walked to the phone at the end of the street.

The red telephone box stank of cat's piss, and a pane of glass the size of a cat flap was missing. At least the phone worked. Propping open the door with my foot, I dialled my Solicitor's office. I pressed a ten pence coin firmly into the slot. I got through, but he wasn't in his office. They went to find him.

Bang, bang.

Lindsay kicked at her pushchair. I worried if I would ever get through to Mr Williams before my money ran out. I was irritated at the way my life was going, and this morning was a sharp reminder that things were out of control.

"Mr Williams?" I said.

"Yes Mary, how can I help?" His voice was cultured.

"I'm sorry, but I'm locked out again." I was getting upset.

"Okay." He was calm.

Lindsay was kicking the door. A bus roared past and belched out black smoke into the box.

"Billy stole my keys," cough, cough, "and my money from my purse... well, I'm down to my last ten pence!" I shouted.

"Okay, don't worry, I'll get the locks changed right away. Have you... money?" The traffic noise drowned his words.

"I'm going to the bank, thank you." It felt good to have someone on my side.

"Andrew will arrange it. Be about an hour—will that be all right?"

"Thank you." I glanced at my watch. "I'll meet the locksmith about 12 o'clock, if that's all right."

"Fine, leave it with me." He ended the call.

Mr Williams was so reliable; I couldn't have done it without him.

I tumbled out of the phone box into the relatively fresh air of Cheshunt High Street, made my way to Lloyds Bank, and drew out what little money I had. I went for a coffee in the Wimpy Bar with Lindsay, thinking about what I could do next.

I started to wonder how Billy knew where my money was hidden. It was inconceivable that he was spying on me all the time, although he appeared at times to be living rough.

It sounded ridiculous, but I really thought that I was being bugged with some electronic eavesdropping device. I didn't mention the money on the phone to anyone, so he didn't find out from me. I started to question my own sanity and thought I was going crazy.

I returned to the house with Lindsay and waited outside. Heather, a neighbour who I occasionally saw at Lindsay's playschool, spoke to me. She was curious. I told her I had locked myself out and was waiting for the locksmith.

There didn't appear to be any damage inside the house, and I assumed that Billy had left shortly after our confrontation. He wanted to unsettle me, and in that he succeeded. I couldn't get the thoughts of bugging out of my mind, and decided to phone the Solicitor again.

"Mr Williams?"

"Yes Mary." He knew my voice.

I heard the shuffling of papers and male voices murmuring in the background.

"I'm sorry to bother you again. I know you're busy, but I'm worried."

"Yes, its okay, I have a few minutes, and then I shall be out all day I'm afraid."

"Billy couldn't have known I was about to go out on Friday. Yet he arrived, at the very instant I was leaving."

"Yes."

"I think Billy has planted some listening devices in the house. How else would he have known?"

"Oh, I don't think you need to worry. Those devices aren't available in the general marketplace."

"Mummy, mummy," Lindsay said, tugging at my skirt.

"Can you hold on for a moment?"

I pulled out Lindsay's play tape and headphones from the overnight bag.

"Be quiet Lindsay!" I said. "Here's your tape recorder and headphones. Now be a good girl, sit down in the living room, and I'll get you a drink when I've finished on the phone." She sat on the sofa listening to her stories.

"Hello Mr Williams, I'm sorry about that."

"That's okay, now as I was saying, I don't think you need worry about bugging." He sounded authoritative.

"All right, thank you for your advice."

"You're welcome. I'm sorry I've run out of time."

All my instincts told me something had been going on. Billy was cunning, not stupid. Unable to settle, it was bugging me, like unfinished business.

Settling Lindsay with a drink at the dining table, I took the opportunity to phone Mum. I asked if she could arrange for John, our neighbour at Langhedge Lane, to visit to fit some locks on the internal doors. I was worried Billy might break into the house. Uneasy butterflies fluttered in my stomach.

It was Sunday afternoon when John arrived, to set about fitting the locks on the internal doors. Colin was mooning around the house not knowing what to do with himself. Whilst John was working on the doors, I told Colin my worries about being bugged. He seized upon the idea with the challenge of a treasure hunt, and soon he was looking everywhere searching for bugs, like some secret agent. He searched all over the house: under tables, chairs, behind cupboards, beds, under carpets. Nothing. Then I heard him calling.

"Mum, mum, come here!"

An excited Colin was waving frantically in the living room. Being quite tall for his age, he was able to pull the wall unit away and peer behind. Lindsay rushed over. I put my finger to my lips and signalled to whisper.

Tucked neatly, and concealed behind a shelf, Colin had discovered a device, so small that two would have fitted neatly inside a matchbox. Lindsay called it a mouse, because of its little tail. Colin ripped it off and dropped it into a fruit bowl with a clang.

"That's it, Mum!" His face beamed with the widest smile.

"I knew it," I whispered. "He's been bugging me all this time."

"He would have heard everything you were saying."

Colin broke it open and removed the battery.

"That's why he knew about the money I had saved under the carpet."

"Yes," said Colin. "I'll carry on looking for the others—there must be more."

Colin quietly emptied the shelves, placing the books neatly onto the floor of the living room.

Lindsay wandered around the house wearing a pair of her dad's big headphones. She looked so funny, with the black curly lead trailed along the floor behind her. Colin and I had to laugh.

Moments later I was in the kitchen talking to John, when Lindsay started shouting.

"Mummy, I can hear you!" She thought it was some sort of game.

I stopped talking to John. I was curious.

"What do you mean you can you hear me, Lindsay? You're not connected to anything, darling."

"I can hear you talking in the kitchen through my big ears." She pulled off the headphones. She wandered over to where John and I were standing by the cooker. I bent down to her as she clumsily fitted them to my ears. I wandered into the living room.

"Say something for me, Lindsay."

"What do you want me to say Mummy?" she squeaked.

"I can hear her! It's loud and clear. John, she's right! What's happening?"

"The headphones have acted as some sort of aerial, like an old crystal set, picking up the sound."

Colin poked his head around the living room door. "What's happening?"

"We can hear voices in the headphones."

"So does that mean we can use this to find the bugs?" he asked.

John nodded and put his finger to his lips. "Shoosh."

"Yeah, Mum, why don't you walk over to the kitchen, and see if the signal gets stronger?"

"That's a good idea."

I wandered back dangling the lead around the cooker.

"It's buzzing louder, John." I was quietly excited.

There was a three-way adaptor plugged into the cooker socket. Each time I put it close, the headphones buzzed. I switched off the cooker socket. The buzzing stopped. I walked back into the living room. Silence, the voices in the kitchen had gone!

"Got it John! It's the adaptor on the cooker! It's the adaptor!" I jumped up and down.

John unplugged it and rerouted the wires.

"Great—you're clever Lindsay, thank you—you smart little girl!"

I scooped her up in my arms and gave her a big hug and kiss, and then I sent her all over the house, sniffing out any other bugs.

"Colin, go with Lindsay and start searching with the headphones."

He was brilliant. He searched in places I would never have dreamt of until he had found five in all.

Monday morning I arrived at the Solicitors, Lindsay in the pushchair, and my bundle of bugs in my pocket.

I strutted into the office like a peacock. Mr Williams was impeccably dressed in his smart white shirt and pinstriped charcoal suit. Cleanliness, fingernails almost polished, they were so clean. Everything about him was neat, like his work, as if it was an obsession. He was sitting at his desk.

"Five we found, Mr Williams!" I dumped the bugs onto his desk in a heap and watched his reaction.

"My goodness, I didn't think these things were available," he said. His thick mop of dark hair flopped over his glasses. I stood over him as he craned his neck to look up at me.

"Here." *Thud.*

I dropped a recent copy of the *Exchange & Mart* on his desk, open at the page advertising surveillance equipment. His blue steely eyes followed like a child being fed in a high chair.

"I'll put them in the safe right away; they will provide good evidence of intimidation when we go to court. Well done. You've taught me something today."

I recounted a brief account of my discovery, and left. It was one battle I felt I had won.

Empty beer cans soon collected by the back gate. It was strange at the time, but I took no real notice until the cans were joined by footprints in the mud. I felt uneasy.

Woken by a noise, I worried that someone was breaking in. I opened my bedroom window, lent out, and shone my torch down the wall at the rear kitchen door. Caught in the flashlight, Billy was spread-eagled against the living room window, trying to be invisible, but it wasn't working.

It was as if he was trying to listen, now that his bugs had been removed. I quietly filled Lindsay's Mickey Mouse waste paper bin with water and tipped it out the window as close to the wall as I could. I returned to my bed, cosy and dry.

I phoned Mr Williams in the morning, and he applied for another Non Molestation order.

Struggling to keep things going with a limited income, I got work serving as a checkout lady at the local Tesco supermarket. It wasn't ideal, but it had to fit in with Lindsay. I had arranged for Mum to baby-sit for a few hours each day, and I fitted in the work to suit.

Billy was a continual threat. I took as many precautions as I could to prevent him screwing up my life. I always took the back alley route to the store. I tried to stick to paths, and tracks, avoiding the roads where I knew he would cruise in his car. Yet despite all my efforts, somehow, he found out that I was working.

I was serving a long queue of customers on the checkout, when he started ranting for all to hear. He screamed all sorts of profanities, innuendoes and downright lies. Personal things, even intimate things I couldn't repeat to my own mother.

The stalking, the turning up unexpectedly—I couldn't take it any more and I was reaching the end of my endurance. It was so spiteful; so hateful, it crushed me. It was all going wrong for me again. Something about Billy could reduce me to a quivering wreck, and weaken my resolve, but I wasn't going to cry.

Keeping my head high, I calmly gathered my things and walked away from the till, telling the supervisor I had to go home. If I thought I could escape, I was wrong.

Following me, kerb crawling in his car, he continued to shout and swear in one long monologue. I watched as a woman walking towards me crossed over to the other side of the road. I felt my face flush as I banished a tear. I ducked down the alley that led to the house, and suddenly I was free. I stopped and listened as his abusive swearing petered out. I wanted to know if he was going to sit and wait, or drive off and give up.

I heard him drive away, and ran home as fast as I could.

I slid indoors, sat down in the living room, as if a prisoner in my own home, and sobbed. I was drowning, clinging to sanity by a thread. I wiped my tears, downtrodden again, but I was determined to carry on. I promised myself I had to do it for Lindsay, as I had for Colin.

I phoned Mr Williams to stop Billy stalking me. He told me he would arrange an injunction, but it wasn't long before I arrived home in the afternoon to find a ladder propped up against the back wall of the house. He had broken in through the bedroom window and I found him asleep in the master bedroom, lying amongst a pile of empty beer cans.

My first reaction was to call the police, to exact revenge because he was so vulnerable lying there. Then I thought better of it. I went down to the kitchen and rummaged in the drawer for a telephone bill. I extracted the tenancy form that the Solicitor had given me from my handbag, and snatched a pen from the nearby pot in the hallway. Returning to the bedroom, I woke him. He was still drunk from the beer and difficult to rouse, but I persisted.

He grunted into consciousness, and I waved the bill in his face. I pushed the form under his nose, carefully placing it on top of the telephone bill, and placed the pen in his hand.

"Telephone bill that arrived today. It's in your name." I wanted him to hear the word bill.

"Well," he said.

"Shall I send the bill to you?"

"No."

"Then sign here." I placed the pen on the form. "Put the telephone in my name." My voice was firm.

I held my breath as he signed it. I was so frightened I almost wet myself, but I kept my nerve.

I snatched it away from him and raced down the stairs.

My heart was pounding so loudly that it felt as if it would explode in my chest. I sat on the stairs, and waited, expecting him to follow, but he fell back to sleep.

Calmly I made two phone calls. One to the police, and one to the Solicitor. I dialled 999.

"Emergency, which service do you require?"

"Police."

"What's the emergency?"

"I have a Non Molestation Order against my husband, and he has broken in."

I gave the details, and within ten minutes a police van arrived outside, and two large policemen removed Billy.

They didn't have the power to arrest him; instead, they physically removed him, took him to his dingy flat he rented at the end of the road, and spoke to him.

The important thing was to get the house transferred to my name. Until that happened, I was in danger of losing my home.

I dialled the Solicitor.

"Mr Williams, are you listening?"

"Yes Mary," he recognised my voice.

"I have the tenancy agreement signed over to my name!"

"Wow, that's very good news." He sounded so pleased for me.

"He broke into my house and was asleep on the bed, so I put the form…"

"Don't," he interrupted, "I don't want to know how you managed it." He stifled a little chuckle.

"I'll need to come and see you about the divorce."

"Yes of course Mary, tomorrow morning, about 10 o'clock, would that suit?"

"Perfect, thank you."

Before picking up Lindsay from Mum's, I needed a moment alone. I didn't feel I wanted to celebrate in the way that some might expect. It wasn't like winning a prize, it was more like the gates to my freedom were being suddenly opened. I felt like a caged bird, slightly afraid to leave, fearful of the future, yet at the same time a warm glow of satisfaction dominated. It was a small victory in a troubled path. It wasn't the end—it was more like the end of the beginning.

I was not yet safe, not until the form was in the Council Offices. I couldn't risk Billy snatching it from me; after all, there still might be an undiscovered bug in the house.

I walked to a neighbour, Heather. We hadn't spoken much, but she understood some of what had happened. I asked if I could call a taxi from her house, and while I waited, I told her the good news. She got out some cakes and we celebrated together over a cup of tea. I sensed that she had some experience of these matters, though she had never disclosed the circumstances. As I left, she held my hand. "You can live on bread and jam, you know Mary." She patted my hand. She seemed familiar with Billy's behaviour, as though it were a well-trodden path and it made me warm to her after that.

I wasted no time. I made my way to the Council offices and handed in the form. I even stood over the official to make sure the house was transferred into my name. I didn't want to take a chance.

Finally I got my divorce, and with it my freedom from Billy. It was a difficult time.

I began to realise I had this baggage. Not only from my childhood, the death of Joyce, but more importantly the devastating impact of the divorce from Terry—not to mention the crushing trauma of my life with Billy. It was a time of much reflection and personal development. Determined to find a new approach to my future, I sought help to exorcise the demons of my past.

I went in search of a counsellor. I needed therapy to understand myself so that I could put my life back on track.

38

Back on Track

RUTH, MY COUNSELLOR, had seen me for a number of weeks, and I was making progress, but the money ran out. She offered to defer the fees when I told her I was finding it difficult to afford the cost of the sessions as a single parent. Although she suggested I could pay her back later, I didn't want the debt.

She had no idea about the hardship I suffered trying to keep the house going. I had lived in debt for most of my childhood, my marriage, losing the house, and now she wanted me to build up debt again. No, no, no, not this lady.

I worked with her for a number of weeks and made clear progress. I set goals, focused on life choices, and found a new direction for myself and my family. These were all positive things, but I was stronger than she had imagined. She had become too controlling and crossed that fine line between listening, and reflecting. She told me that the choice of my next partner would be a joint decision, to be taken with her guidance.

Enough, this was too much! I had outgrown her. She was advising, not counselling, and she seemed to have lost her way. How dare she presume to pick my next partner? I could see why, and perhaps my past decisions had been clouded by my history, but it was *my* life, and it would be my choice.

Although I spoke about my life, I never spoke about Joyce, or the affect it had on me; yet to me that seemed to be the nub of the problem. Billy had a similar Scottish accent to that of

Joyce. It felt as if my mind, in its grief, had carried out some subtle sleight of hand. I wondered if I convinced myself it had brought me closer to Joyce. It appeared as if my mind, in its turmoil, could not have rejected him any more than a bee could have rejected honey.

When I met Billy, I was uncomfortable living on my own; I am ashamed to say this, but I was desperately frightened of the dark—a legacy of my childhood that I could trace back to Les leaving home.

As I began to decipher my baggage, in analysis, I began to see more clearly.

Stubbing out cigarettes on my carpet, stealing money from Florrie's purse at the wedding, and the fact that Billy never tried to redress these misdemeanours—all this told me that he was fundamentally different; we never shared a common goal. I needed to feel like two horses in harness, but what I got was an inadequate puppy on a short lead. He never completed his university education; hadn't committed to a full-time job, and he couldn't take the pressure of responsibility. If he couldn't do that for himself, it was unlikely that he could ever do it for me. The clues were there, yet I never saw them.

I was ready to choose someone myself; I would take the responsibility for the choice; I had to correct my nighttime phobia from childhood. It was time for change.

Putting locks on all the interior doors was the first step of many. I slept with a knife under my pillow.

I considered my income and how I could get off of State Benefit. I felt depressed on the benefit and I needed to raise the game. Billy wasn't paying any maintenance for Lindsay, and it looked increasingly obvious to me that he never would.

I needed to improve my standard of living and I had to do it by myself.

Lindsay had never known Christmas or holidays, other than the odd day out, and the galling truth was that it smacked of my own childhood, and I was determined I wasn't going to give her that.

As the weeks and months tumbled by, I managed to keep myself going financially, and give Lindsay a day out as a holiday. Colin was becoming restless after Billy left, and although I suggested he take a computing course at the local college, he preferred to earn more money. Despite arranging an interview, nothing would persuade Colin to gain any further qualifications, and in the end he went his own way.

In the meantime, Mother had got mugged and was in a terrible state. I spoke to the local authority about re-housing, and fought to have her transferred nearer to me. There was an empty flat across the road, and eventually I made such a nuisance of myself, that I was able to persuade the officials to give her the flat.

With all my church friends, I painted and decorated it. She bought a new carpet, I fitted it myself, and set her up with everything she needed. She couldn't have been happier, although when Jane visited to have a look, she complained about the colour scheme.

Colin was now a very tall, sixteen-year-old—very respectable, smart and impeccably spoken. He presented well at interviews, and had an easygoing and friendly nature. It was not long before he obtained a job at the Builder Group.

Soon he was enjoying a better income, and with it a subtle change in his attitude. He started to arrive home late at night, asserting his position within the family as if he had suddenly replaced Billy in the pecking order. Like Jane did to Mum when Dad left, Colin wanted to do with me. He saw himself as the head of the household. I loved Colin; he probably thought he would be very noble; be there to protect, and look after me. It wasn't his role—I was his mother, not his wife. It was my responsibility and my burden, not his, and I couldn't let him sacrifice himself in that way. It left me no choice: I couldn't let Colin control my life anymore than I could let Billy.

Nevertheless, I found myself struggling to be able to control him.

Things eventually came to a head after about six months when he gave me an ultimatum. Either I would have to change, or else he was leaving to live on his own. I told him straight. I had every confidence in him, and left him to make his free choice. He chose to leave.

Florrie had lost Jack to cancer a few years earlier and was living on her own in Hornchurch. I didn't want Colin to go off on his own because he was too young. Unfortunately Terry, now married to Theresa, was unable to have him at this time.

Although Colin didn't know, I arranged for him to move in with Florrie, his paternal grandmother. She always liked him, was glad of the extra income and the company he provided. It was the ideal relationship.

I arranged for Florrie to phone Colin, and offer him lodging for a nominal rent. He jumped at the chance. He got the freedom he wanted, and I knew that Florrie would keep an eye on him.

Colin came over by train and visited Lindsay and me from time to time, keeping in close touch. It seemed to work out very well.

Billy didn't disappear from my life, as I had hoped. He had stopped stalking me, but continually insisted on access to Lindsay. When I gave him access, he either turned up late, or not at all. Lindsay would become so distressed, one moment longing for the day with her daddy, and then the crushing disappointment. He never paid maintenance, and continually played mind games when she was in his company. She frequently arrived back home in tears.

I found her crying in the bathroom.

"What's wrong, darling?" I spoke through the door.

"I don't want to keep secrets mummy," she sobbed.

"Little girls don't have to."

"Daddy is going to take me to see his mum and dad."

"Did he say where?"

"Doncaster, I think…" sob "…he said." Sniff.

"That's a long way."

"Mummy, I'm scared." She tore off some toilet paper to wipe her nose. "I don't want to go without you."

"You don't have to. It's all right darling."

"Don't I, mummy? Daddy will be cross with me."

"It's all right darling, come out of the toilet and I will give you a cuddle."

I scooped her up in my arms and I sat for a moment, drying her eyes.

Everything was on Billy's terms, and I had a continual battle of mind games. Lindsay kept getting caught in the crossfire and it was breaking my heart. I needed to get a job and become independent.

With Lindsay getting older, now four, I returned to full-time employment as a secretary, for a local company in Waltham Cross. Mum was living so close that she frequently offered to baby-sit Lindsay for me, picking her up from school and giving her a small plate of chips for tea. The arrangement worked for a little while—until one day I came home and found Mum sitting in my house, in the dark, muttering to herself like she was back in Langhedge Lane.

"What you doing sitting in the dark?"

"Can't yer live on benefit?" she snapped.

"No Mum, I can't, I need to go to work to keep my self respect, to get on with life; and I can't just sit on my hands and do nothing."

"Why do you need a man?"

I didn't understand why she brought it up.

"I don't particularly, but it will be my choice. I want a father for Lindsay, someone to show her the way, show her that all men are not bastards like you would have us believe."

"Why can't you be like Jane? She used to be all right on her own."

"You just hate men, Mum. I've come too far, I'm in a rut, and I'm not giving up my fight and settling for this. I want to become my own woman, show my children the way, give them hope, give them the promise that they can do anything they want in life if they fight for it. Just like Joyce and I said to each other all those years ago, I've not forgotten the dream, and it feels close now. I have not too far to go."

"I don't want to be relied upon—I'm not doing it anymore," she shuffled.

"I'm sorry you feel you can't help me. Do you love me, Mum?"

She shuffled again, looked down at the floor before blurting out:

"You're the capable one! It's like you're the mother and Jane and I are the children."

I wanted to cry inside. I had been to hell and back all through my life! I thought that by doing everything for my mother, she would love me.

Experience: the hardest lesson in life and I hadn't learnt it yet.

I closed the door behind her, sat down on the sofa, and sobbed every bit as much as I did when Joyce died. It had all been for nothing. Pouring love into my mother was like catching water in a sieve—futile. She gave me no choice. I had to stop working. I was gutted. Dealing with my mum was like walking through treacle.

The next job I had was part-time. She offered to help look after Lindsay, but it wasn't long before she let me down.

Mum said she couldn't baby-sit because Jane had a cold.

Jane at this time lived in Bromsgrove and was married to Jack. He was a branch manager for Lloyds Insurance. I wouldn't have minded, but Jane was thirty-years-old, and quite capable of looking after herself.

I didn't get it. I had helped Mum sort out her new home, get her out of the dump in Edmonton, furnished it and decorated it all for her, and when I thought I could count on her, she let me down again, and again.

I felt myself get upset, but I had to carry on.

39

College: Meeting Mike

THE WORLD HAD CHANGED. It was September 1988 and Word Processing and office computers had become an important feature of modern day work. I needed to develop the skills to enable me to find a better job.

It had been eighteen months since my divorce from Billy, and I lived alone with Lindsay as a single parent. Colin was still living with his grandmother, and I was ready to start life again. I took in a lodger, Fran, an overseas student from China. She spoke excellent English, was very clean and tidy, and I found her a joy to have around the house. She got on well with Lindsay, and at the same time, it helped plug the hole in the finances until I found a job.

This time I had a checklist. Any man had to clear all the ticks on my list before he would get anywhere near me:

1. No debts or unresolved complications such as maintenance issues, ongoing loans and such;
2. He should have a nine-to-five job and come home at nights.
3. He must be intelligent enough to help me plan our future.
4. Own his own house, or at the very least his own car.
5. He would have to share a common vision of the future; and finally,
6. He had to be taller than me!

I wanted an ideal family unit; someone affectionate, to be a good father for Lindsay. Colin was now living with Florrie and fiercely protective of his independence.

Few of the men who took me out to dinner met my checklist. I told them, 'It was nice meeting you, but I have an agenda and it's not going to work.' I felt sorry for Steve, Ian, Alan, and Richard, but if I didn't hold firm, then I was only letting myself down.

It was time for part one of the plan, get my skills updated for the marketplace. I attended a Monday class for City & Guilds 726, Computers & Computing, and Wednesday for Word Processing. I couldn't afford both classes, and so I had arranged with the college that I would see which one I preferred, and then drop the other.

I arrived on the Monday evening class at room C41. A wooden bench formed a U-shape around the room. Twenty computers were all connected and switched on. Each had it's own metal framed plastic chair facing the screen.

I took a seat, the third chair from the exit door. To my left was a Czechoslovakian woman, Jadranka, a small awkward looking bookworm. With olive skin, shoulder-length dark hair, and her face framed by her spectacles, she appeared intelligent and chatty. For some reason, perhaps I was the first person she spoke to, I didn't know, but she took an interest in me right from the start.

The lecturer walked into the room, dressed in a smart three-piece pinstriped suit. With his light brown hair and neatly shaped dark beard that hid a cheeky smile, he introduced himself as Mike and proceeded to start the lesson.

Glancing down at my navy skirt, I noticed the torn lining staring back at me through the pleat; it was the only one I had.

As soon as he began leading the class, I noticed something about him. He melted the daunting 'complexity' of the course. Frightening and fearful things suddenly dissolved into the familiar and friendly. He made me feel intelligent, and then something happened so unexpectedly that it took my breath away.

Our eyes met, and in that instant I found myself staring too long. Unusually for me, I had to force myself to look away, and then I couldn't stop the feelings of blood rushing to my face. I coyly looked down to avoid his gaze.

Explaining things with humorous anecdotes, he had all the students laughing. I glanced up again, but as soon as I did so, I found myself repeatedly staring. It was as if I couldn't avert my gaze. I had already decided he was shorter than me!

At coffee break he would talk to all the students, going round the tables, before getting a coffee for himself. I sat next to Jadranka. She was inquisitive, and in my nervous excitement I talked about myself, revealing that I had a child and that I wanted to get a better job. She asked me how I managed on a very low income, caring for my five-year-old child. I told her it was a struggle: I had to watch every penny that I spent, and that sometimes I lived on bread and Jam.

He settled next to Jadranka. She always sat opposite me. The chair scraped as he moved closer. He put his coffee down and focused his attention towards me.

"What brings you to this course then?" He cupped the coffee in his hands, and smiled.

I ignored the smile. I lowered my gaze to the coffee cup in front of me, and glanced back to Jadranka.

Realising I had told Jadranka many personal things already, I worried that she might have already spoken to him. I flicked my eyes back to my coffee.

"I want to get a better job. The world has changed since I was a secretary." I looked up at him.

"Are you married?"

I lowered my eyes. Wow, that was direct. I didn't want to answer. I shot an accusing glance at Jadranka. She gave a lopsided grin.

"No, she isn't, she's divorced," Jadranka volunteered.

I glanced sideways and shifted uncomfortably. It seemed I didn't need to answer the questions—I had this Czechoslovakian parrot sitting on my table!

He moved his coffee cup closer to me, and spoke.

"So what's it like being divorced then?" His piercing eyes pricked my bubble.

I felt myself shuffle uncomfortably, but held my focus on him.

"It's too expensive—you don't want to go there," I chanted, lowering my gaze once more.

"So does that mean you're a single parent?"

A whiff of freshener on his breath caught me off guard, but it didn't matter, my parrot replied on my behalf.

"Yes, she is, she's got a five-year-old daughter."

I flashed a lopsided smile at Jadranka. She grinned back at me and I felt her game.

"So how did you get here tonight then?" he asked.

This man was persistent, and direct. Ouch!

"By taxi." My manner stiffened.

"Which way do you come, Cheshunt or Hoddesdon?"

Wow! He didn't give up. Part of me was trying to hide under the table, and yet there was something within that was refreshing about his direct approach. I had seen so many men dither, not knowing what they wanted in life, and here was someone like me. He had me flushed.

"She gets a taxi from Cheshunt; not far," my parrot answered.

My hair prickled. He glanced sideways at Jadranka.

"Thank you," he said, before turning his attention back to me.

"Now can you answer this one yourself?" He smiled, turning away to look at Jadranka.

"What's that?" I asked.

"Do you want a lift next week?"

"No," I snapped, "it's all right, I'll get a taxi." I picked up my handbag, cleared the three paper cups from the table, and dropped them in the waste bin.

Jadranka looked sideways at him, screwed up her face and gave him a toothy smile.

My parrot had done her worst, and I felt annoyed that she had told him so much about me.

At the end of the lesson my taxi didn't show up and I was left at the college in the dark. I had to walk over the road to the New River Arms, and phone for another taxi from their pay phone.

I went to the Wednesday class for Word Processing. It was taken by an Italian gentleman who stank of body odour. It wasn't fun, he never got round the class very often, unlike his smell. I never went back.

In contrast, Mike's class was lively, fun, exciting, and above all, I found myself looking forward to Monday nights.

The next week my taxi didn't turn up again, and I was half an hour late. It didn't go unnoticed and the next time he offered, I accepted his lift, and he started to pick me up in his silver Jaguar.

"Do you like my car?" he said.

"As long as it gets from A to B, it's a car to me." I wasn't impressed.

The following week as he arrived to pick me up, he chatted to Lindsay on the doorstep. My babysitter Dot was a lovely retired lady who lived nearby. She had just arrived and was sitting in the living room. Preparing to get ready, I eavesdropped on their conversation; what surprised me was how well they got on. There was something about him that was different, I didn't know what exactly, but there was something I couldn't explain. My mind was like a magnet; no matter how hard I tried to get him out of my thoughts, he would pop right back into my head.

At the end of the evening, he would drop me off at my home, and I would dash straight out of his car and into the house. I never stopped or acknowledged his gaze. I always rejected him, although the infuriating thing was that he didn't make any advances anyway! Never at any time did he attempt to touch me. Not even to hold my hand. He just held me in intelligent conversation and caressed me with his words, his humour; anticipating my thoughts most of the time.

As I walked into the house, Fran was in the kitchen washing her dinner plate, and made coffee for me. She offered me the coffee, but I put my head in my hands.

"Oh, dear, what am I going to do?" I asked.

"What's the matter with you?" She looked worried.

"Well, this lecturer taking this class has given me a lift again. He's so nice."

"Ahmm," she smiled, "so, what's wrong with that?"

"I try not to tell him anything... I don't know, I don't know!"

"Don't know what, Mary?"

"Jadranka keeps telling him things about me."

"Well, if he's nice, what's the problem?"

"I don't want to wash socks anymore!"

Fran cupped her face with her hands and shook with laughter. I wasn't sure why—I didn't see the humour.

"I really like you Mary," she was still giggling. "You're funny."

"Yes Fran, we get on, don't we?" I said. "I hope you stay a while."

In all thirteen weeks of the autumn term I never invited Mike in for a coffee; it was purely a lift and that was all. Yet I couldn't stop thinking about him. He ticked a lot of my boxes, but not all. He believed in saving up and paying for things outright; he owned his own home, his own car, and didn't have any loans apart from a mortgage. But he was still an inch shorter than me, and that bothered me. Terry, and Billy, were both over six foot tall. I was dazzled by his foresight and his positive grasp on life. Height started to become unimportant because he showed that he didn't need it.

I skipped a class. I had a bad migraine, and naturally he came to the house. Lindsay had to tell him I was in bed. He left his phone number to save wasted journeys.

The very last week of term I again had a migraine and couldn't attend class. I rang him. "Don't worry," he said, "I will drop a work book round on Wednesday afternoon, so that you can read up on what you've missed. Take the test the following term." I agreed and left it at that.

On the Wednesday I was still in bed with a migraine, although feeling a bit better when there was a knock on the door. I wasn't going to let whoever it was see me—well, not like this, so I ignored it. I didn't expect him to phone, so I picked up. It was Mike. He would be here in ten minutes. I had never got ready so fast in all my life, before or since.

He held a bottle of brandy. I thought what a nice thing to do, and for the first time I invited him in. I sat on the sofa with him, side by side. I don't remember how long we talked, but it was an effortless conversation. So easy, so free, I found myself laughing, something I hadn't done for such a long time. It was unsettling; he spoke my thoughts before even I was aware of them.

He was so clear about how to deal with things; it was as if he could see through the fog of decision making, slicing through the layers of confusion like a bacon slicer. He asked me what I wanted to do in life, as if I had all the choices in the world. The fact that I was a single parent didn't seem to make any difference to his expectation.

The thing that impressed me the most was that he opened my door to hope, yet asked nothing of me.

In that moment, it could have only been a few minutes, I was caught up on a sea of optimism. It was as if I had been lost all those years in the eternal grieving for Joyce. It was as if I had been given a Sat Nav for the first time, showing how to navigate the sea of life.

I had recovered a little from my migraine, and I needed to get out. I suggested he might take me to The Massey pub, 7 o'clock, the next day, Thursday night. I had butterflies in my stomach, like a teenager on her first date. This would be our first official date, and for some reason I trusted him. I suppose that I had seen him for so many weeks at the college, and of course, I knew where he worked. It wasn't as if we were strangers to each other.

He picked me up on time. I noticed he was always there on time, not before, but exactly on time. We arrived at the Massey, a roaring fire crackling in the middle of the room between the two bars. He ordered some drinks. I had a dry martini, he had half a bitter. Like my Dad, he liked bitter, but I noticed he only had a half pint.

He started talking about himself and his life. About the love that he had when he was eighteen years old.

"So do you want to tell me about her?" I asked.

He looked down into his beer.

"Well," he said, "her name was Maureen. We met at the Catamaran Yacht Club. I took her sailing, and we were inseparable. We were so passionate and tactile. We saw each other every weekend for six months, until she joined the

Women's Royal Army Corps, and was posted to Catterick in Yorkshire."

"She joined the Women's Army?"

"Yes," he said. "She had always wanted to join up, and I felt it wasn't my place to stop her. I thought we would still be okay, but life didn't work out that way."

"Why, what happened?"

He glanced up from his beer and took a deep breath.

"I don't really know, but she met a previous boyfriend. He was an officer." He lowered his eyes and shifted uncomfortably. I sensed it upset him, yet I could see that she had made a deep impression on his memory of love lost. He seemed to be mourning the loss of that love after all these years. He was now forty-one. I didn't want to pry, but as he described his passion, I hid my secret from him.

He was describing me. I was just as tactile and passionate, but at the same time I was afraid. I couldn't let myself be drawn in. Not now, after I had been through so much. I couldn't risk it. Already I was allowing myself to get too close.

Suddenly, I felt a draft. I shuddered. It appeared that despite my resistance, the helpless tentacles of young love were reeling me in.

Soon the regular customers were crowding us out and I couldn't hear myself talk, and so we drifted over the road to the Bull's Head. He ordered some more drinks. He had another half of bitter, and we sat in a quiet corner, admiring the low ceilings and exposed beams; looking every bit its four hundred years of age.

I wasn't shy about asking questions. I wanted to push him away and try to protect myself.

"Why haven't you got divorced?" I landed the first blow.

"Getting married because your girlfriend is pregnant isn't a good idea." He looked me straight in the eye.

"Why's that?" I asked. "You were married for eighteen years?"

"It leaves you with someone you stay with out of loyalty. It's not the right reason."

"So?"

"I stayed because I thought she would change. I hoped she would grow to love me."

"Ahmm, I've heard that one before." I raised my glass to my lips.

"No, don't get me wrong. She has always been a good wife and mother to the children. It's just that..."

He reached for his drink, and turning, looked up at me with his green eyes.

"She isn't affectionate." He cupped his hands around his glass.

"I've heard that one before as well, Mike." I raised my eyebrows.

"Well," he said, picking up his drink, "it's true. We were too young."

"Why didn't you leave her?"

"Well, the right person hasn't come along, and besides..." He let out a sigh.

"How have you stood it all these years?"

"Well, as you can imagine, it's been difficult. You have the children to bring up, you busy yourself, and besides I am very loyal. She's done nothing wrong." He looked back at me, his eyes so sad.

He could be telling the truth, but I wondered if he just wanted an affair.

He took me home and we kissed goodnight for the first time.

It was two days before we met again. We went to the Bull's Head.

Billy would never buy a house—it was too much commitment for him. I needed to find out what Mike's attitude was.

"I intend to buy my own house," I said. "What are you going to do when you're divorced?"

"Buy one with you," he said.

I choked on my martini. He turned to the barman and called out.

"Can I have a glass of water please?" He patted me on the back and walked to the bar.

"And a packet of crisps please—plain," I shouted.

What surprised me was the conversation was identical, not the words, but the wavelength; the same sense of direction and purpose; the clarity of vision; he was in my mind, reading it before I was.

Intelligent; here was a man ahead of me, and another box was ticked. The last box—common goal—was nailed firmly to the mast. He wanted everything I wanted. To buy a home together, develop my career, to build a family with Lindsay. Christmas's and holidays in the sun. But one impediment remained. He was still an inch shorter than me!

He dropped me home at about 10 p.m. that evening. I didn't sleep. My mind was in turmoil, not in sadness but in decision-making.

His approach threw me. Other men pestered me to move in, tried to kiss me, yet Mike was different. He didn't force me; he brought me along with him, as if we were standing side-by-side. I didn't so much feel as if he was in charge, yet I did what he wanted. I was so confused, and I began to wonder if I was being subtly hypnotised in some way.

Did it really matter about his height? It was far more important that he was intelligent, kind, with the innate ability to guide me through life, and make good decisions. In that he had it in spades!

Over the Christmas holiday, we met a few times. The more we met, the more certain I became. He had ticked most of the boxes on my checklist, and I had ticked all his boxes. He wanted only one thing above everything else, affection.

I worried about Lindsay; after all, he was still married and living with his wife. I was hopeful that Mike would make a good father. He had two grown-up children of his own, but would Lindsay take to him?

I began to wonder—would he really want me with the prospect of rearing another man's child?

40

Marriage No. 3

A FEW DAYS LATER I was sitting on the sofa, to Mike's right. He was talking.

"You and I know," he said, "we have something between us. Don't you?"

"Ahmm," I nodded, but didn't want to comment. His eyes twinkled.

He reached forward and pulled me round to face him. His arm brushed across my breast.

All at once, I felt embarrassment, the thrill of excitement and shock.

"You did that on purpose, didn't you?" I shot him a stern glance.

"What?"

"Brush my breast." I looked shocked, but it was nothing more than I expected.

"Mary, you know there is a magic between us." He held my hand.

"Ahmm." I wasn't helping him out.

"We have a common agenda, we get on fine, and well, you and I both know we have to check to see if the chemistry is there."

"Hmm…" I knew where he was leading.

I was forty years old, he was forty-two, and I was thinking we were no longer young lovers.

I didn't have time to mess about, and more's the point, I didn't want to pussyfoot like young lovers did. He was right. I needed to know if our relationship was going to work or it wasn't.

"So," he said, "you know it's crunch time. It's time to find out if we are going forward, or whether we call it a day."

"You mean that we can't make a decision until we sleep together?"

"Yes." He leaned forward, held the back of my head and nudged my face. He kissed me tenderly on the lips.

There was something there I couldn't explain; it was more than magnetic and I was drawn to him, as helpless as a moth to a flame. Our lips touched and I felt the warmth of his breath.

Suddenly everything about Mike consumed my waking thought.

"I have to go." He withdrew from our embrace, slowly and carefully. He continued to hold my hand, so tenderly, with such grace. It felt so natural, as if my hand were being held for the first time.

I didn't understand why I was experiencing such feelings for the first time, as if I'd never been in love before. Everything he said was an echo of my mind. It was as if we were lost twins, bonded in cognitive symmetry.

He got up from the sofa. I walked with him to the door and he held me in a farewell embrace.

"I want you to sleep on what I have said." He embraced me and kissed me on the lips. He reached forward and opened the door.

"When will I see you?" I asked.

He turned. "I'll give you a ring." He waved, and I watched as he drove out of sight.

The following Wednesday I was out in the garden when the phone rang. It was Mike. He'd finished teaching at lunchtime.

"Are you free?" he asked.

"Give me half an hour." I was free—it was the turn of my neighbour, Heather, to fetch Lindsay from school.

"I have some good news," he said excitedly. "I'll see you at twelve thirty."

"Okay."

I was still tidying the house when he knocked on the door. I let him in and made two cups of coffee. The weather was unusually crisp and bright—such a lovely day.

"Let's go out," he said. "Walk over Whitewebs, or something."

"Okay."

He brought with him a bottle of wine and put it in the fridge.

"This we can have later when we get back," he said.

"Oh, okay, do you want coffee?"

"No, let's just go out now. I want to talk to you."

He took my red coat and gloves from the peg, handed them to me and bundled me out of the house.

I can't remember how long we walked, or how long we sat in the little cafe talking about everything, and nothing. It seemed time passed so quickly that I felt a little robbed. I wanted to stay on the little bridge over the gurgling brook, as we dropped pooh sticks in the water, watching them bob up and down as they emerged on the other side. I didn't want it to end. Outside, I was cautious and calm, but inside I was a mess of emotional dialogue. He had plans, and we were excited about them. We walked back to the car, arm in arm.

As we arrived through the front door, the phone was ringing.

"Hello," I said as I picked up the phone.

"Hello Mary, it's Heather."

"What's wrong?" I glanced over to Mike.

"Nothing, it's just that Lindsay wanted to stay for tea. Would you mind if she stayed till 6 o'clock?"

"No, that's fine, do you want me to pick her up?"
"No, it's all right, I'll drop her off."
"Okay, thanks."

Mike had poured some wine, and as I turned from the phone call, I slipped into his arms. I never got to taste the wine before we drifted up the stairs, and into the bedroom. His warm hands reassured me, and as he held me close, we sank down onto the bed. I turned away from him, sliding across the covers to the other side. As I began to undress, I sneaked a glance at his bare bottom before timidly ducking under the duvet.

His tenderness caressed me with such passion that he took my breath away. I was transported into a new world, with a yearning so powerful that it filled me up, overflowed, and left me glowing in tears of joy. I felt complete for the first time ever that I could remember. Totally loved. I could have stayed entwined all afternoon, drenched in the flames of my own desire. If I had any doubts about the chemistry, they were dispelled without hesitation. I hoped it would never end. I lay still for a moment locked in my own satisfying pleasure, with the erotic memories still lingering in my mind.

The bedside alarm snatched me back to reality and my dream had to end. I ticked another box on my checklist. Lindsay would soon intrude upon my adult life, and I would become a mother again.

He was still one inch shorter than me, but now it didn't matter! He reached me in other places where height made no difference.

It was the start of a relationship that burned with a passion so bright that nothing could quench it. I wondered if I was going crazy, or if this was how true love was supposed to be.

We started to see each other on a regular basis. Every Wednesday afternoon, Mike was free. It sounded strange when he had a full time job, but because he worked one evening a week, he was entitled to an afternoon in compensation. The next time we met, he said something rather profound.

"If the pain of being apart is greater than the pleasure of being together, then we should live together."

It confused me at first, until I realised the wisdom of what Mike was saying. He was asking how I felt about him, and was that feeling enough to live together? I didn't tell him anything; perhaps I should have, but I wasn't ready and I didn't reply.

A week passed before I got an unexpected phone call. It was Mike. He seemed upset. He was playing the piano, and talking on the phone at the same time.

"The pain of being apart is too great," he said. "Can I bring... I just... I'll bring some clothes?"

He played the melody as his voice crackled with emotion

"Are you just coming for the weekend, or do you mean move in permanently?" I said.

"I'd like to move in with you, properly, but I'll bring my clothes a few at a time."

"Well yes, okay." I was confused. I wondered if I could trust him, yet at the same time, I realised he must also be placing his trust in me. I felt we were both vulnerable.

A few hours later I opened the door, and he stood there with a small overnight bag. I invited him in, and we embraced.

Rather than being excited about the prospect of living together, he appeared subdued, as if mourning the loss of his marriage. He sat on the sofa, and we talked.

"My wife and I have discussed this moment for so long," he said. "I told her I couldn't carry on living this way, with no affection. She knew she wasn't capable of giving me the love I needed, and we agreed that if I met someone who could give me love, I would leave." He kept rubbing his hands together and looking down at his shoes.

I waited patiently for him, and held his hand. I didn't know what to believe. He appeared so upset, and the tears were real enough. It must have been a difficult time for him, leaving his own family home, and moving in with me in a small terraced council house.

Over the coming weeks, events unfolded in an unexpected way. Lindsay seemed to enjoy talking to Mike, and she seemed to take to his way. Although, not unexpectedly, she jealously guarded her rights to be close to me. She would nuzzle between us and insist on holding my hand rather than Mike's. I kept pushing Mike to get close to Lindsay, but he said it would be better for her to come to him, in her own time. Perhaps I was too anxious for it to work, and kept nagging at Mike to play with Lindsay.

Eventually he sat me down and we had a long talk about the best strategy for Lindsay. I wasn't convinced his way was right, but I agreed to give it a few months, during which time Mike said he would just give her space.

Mike's mother Eva refused to speak to him anymore. It was his worst nightmare, to be cut off from his parents. His father, Charles, came to see us. He said he didn't want to be cut off from Mike, but he also told us that Eva was very upset.

Charles was a seventy-something, quiet, well-spoken man—short like Mike, well dressed, with thinning dark hair that framed his tanned balding crown. Fit for his age, he had a soft kindly face.

I asked Charles if Mike's wife, Joan, was close to Eva.

"No," he said, "quite the opposite. They never have had much in common, but Eva feels strongly that it is against her religion." He looked up at me, seemingly puzzled at his own words.

Mike said, "It was more a pride, than God." I didn't know the truth of it, but it gutted Mike because he had always been close to his parents.

"It's the price I have to pay," Mike said, "to have my freedom, and be with the one I love."

It was such a comfort to me to hear him say that to his dad. I felt it best to leave Mike and Charles alone to talk. It was the least I could have done.

Two hours later, as Charles went to leave, he warmly shook my hand. I felt he was pleased for us both.

"I'm sorry," he said, "I won't be cut off from my son, but you must understand that it is difficult for me. Eva is adamant that she won't speak to you both, and there is little I can do." He turned and left.

Mike and I watched as he drove away. I pulled Mike towards me, flung my arms around him, and we stood hugging in the hall.

I didn't understand the relationship between Mike and his wife. Perhaps it was the insecurity in me, but I wanted to find out if what he told me was true. We had a discussion about it, because Mike kept insisting on phoning his wife once a week to make sure she was all right. He was still paying all the bills for her, and I guess I was terribly insecure. Mike got upset with me.

"All right," he said," I'll invite Joan round so that she can tell you herself."

I was astounded when she came into the house, and stood in my living room. Mike asked her the question.

"Yes," she said, "I didn't think it would ever happen, and I tried to forget it. Hope that it would all blow over. We had a number of upsetting discussions. Mike said he would rather live on his own than live without love." She looked directly at me. Mike sidled over towards me and firmly held my hand. It was such a strong signal to me, and I felt the warmth of his devotion. I was standing opposite his wife, and he was holding my hand. It made me love him all the more.

Joan moved to the sofa.

"Mike was unhappy because I didn't love him as much as I should," Joan said. "It's just the way I am."

She was so sincere, bowing to the inevitable in a rational way, but at the same time I could see a sadness in her face.

"I think it would be best if we get a divorce," he said, "on the grounds of my adultery."

"I wonder Joan," I said, "if you would like me to leave you both alone to talk?"

"It's okay Mary, we've talked about this before. You can stay, really, I don't mind."

"So Joan, will you agree to a divorce?" Mike said.

"Yes... What about the custody of the children?"

"No problem," he spoke softly. "They can stay with you, and I don't want anything from the house. I'll give you three years to sort your life out before we sell it."

I was shocked. Joan smiled.

I think she was relieved he had promised to give her three years. I got the impression she had taken advice from neighbours, and friends. She told him she had changed the locks and was prepared for a bitter dispute.

Mike took the wind completely out of her sails in a single statement. Joan went away after a cup of tea, looking happy and confident, but I was left with the feeling of insecurity once more.

He ordered the divorce papers from the clerk of the court, filled them in and sent them off together with the £40 fee.

It was May, 1989, when Mike's divorce came through. Rushing up the stairs, he bounded into the bedroom. I was sitting at the dressing table at the time.

"Let's get married!"

I flashed a glance in the mirror. As he came up to me, he flung his arms around my waist and gave me an affectionate peck on the cheek. I held his hand and spun round on the stool.

"I'm not sure I'm ready," I said.

He looked crestfallen. "I have to keep introducing you as my partner, or girlfriend, and at my age it is continually awkward. I would much rather introduce you as my wife, Mary." He bent down to me and held my hand.

"I'm sorry, I know, but I still feel uncertain about the future."

I didn't know why I said that. Sometimes understanding my own feelings seemed a mystery even to me. I wanted desperately to become a family unit, but at the same time my journey through life had been so badly scorched, that I needed more time.

It was nine months after we had got together. We were having a drink in the garden of The Woodman pub. The sun was shining and it was a lovely birthday. Mike was forty-three.

"Do you think that we should get married?" I said.

"Not bothered now," he said. "I've got used to having a partner." Leaning backward, he picked up his drink.

"Oh," I felt myself swallow. It was the last thing I expected.

This wasn't in my dream, being turned down. I felt such a fool.

"It's okay now, I quite like being single!"

As his bright eyes twinkled with smugness, I felt myself get angry.

"I'm not sure I want to settle down." He took another laid-back swig of beer.

"Well," I leaned forward, and raised my voice. "Perhaps you'd like to move out then—I don't take lodgers anymore, if that's the way you feel."

He leaned forward and put down his drink as if to whisper. His cheeks widened, and he took my hand.

"We'd better get married then," he whispered.

He was teasing me after all.

When we arrived home, Mike phoned the registry office. What date would we like?

Mum, Jane and her husband Jack were going off to their time-share in Spain, and so it was the perfect time to get married. Mike chose Saturday, 11th November 1989.

We broke the news to six-year old Lindsay. She was delighted, and asked if she could have her name changed to Mike's, so that we both had the same surname after the wedding. Then she asked if she could be a bridesmaid.

"What, wear a dress?" I asked.

She never wore a dress.

"Yes," she squeaked, "pretty please."

"What, a proper dress?" I knew she never wore a dress.

"A proper bridesmaid's dress. A pink one." She looked seriously at me.

"Okay," I said, "you certainly can."

I took her out to a shop that afternoon, bought her a nice pink dress, little headdress, and a posy of flowers to hold. To finish off I found her some matching pink shoes. She looked a picture with her long golden hair curling at her shoulders. A little princess for the day!

Using the sewing machine, and a pattern, Mike made me a cobalt pinstriped blue suit. It fitted me perfectly. I phoned all our friends.

Mike took me to the jewellers in Waltham Abbey, and bought me a lovely diamond and emerald engagement ring. He said he wanted to match my eyes. We ordered two wedding bands; my one had 'Mike' engraved around the outside, and his 'Mary'. Everything was set for the date.

It was Armistice Day 1989, and the wedding was booked for 11:30 a.m. at Broxbourne Registry Office. All our friends were waiting; there were no other relatives but Colin, now eighteen, and Lindsay aged six. It was to be our day, shared with only friends.

Colin arrived in a smart grey suit and blue tie.

"What about carnations Mike?"

"I thought we'd wear poppies," he said. "It marks an end to the struggles with Billy."

"That was Mike's idea," we all laughed so much.

Our friends came to see our happiness, and we took them back to The Vine, for a buffet and drinks to celebrate the end of a lovely day and the start of a new life. This time there were no doubts, no regrets, no nagging worries. Instead, there was a degree of certainty, so complete I was sure it only came but once in a lifetime.

Decision made, checklist completed, we bought the council house I rented. Mike introduced me to a lot of things. One, was the setting up of a three-year plan, which proved to be such a guiding force in planning the future. Lindsay was part of the plan, and her getting to know and love Mike, was also part of that plan. "She will come when she is ready," Mike always used to say.

We would be in a shop, and the assistant would say, "Is that your Mum and Dad?" and she would say, "No, that's my Mum and that's the man that lives with us."

Children: so honest.

For the first year Lindsay called him Mike, then one day we were in a restaurant, owned by the parents of Paolo, one of Mike's college students. He waited on us.

"Hello Mike," he said, "is that your daughter?"

"Yes," Mike said.

Nothing was said about the incident until we returned home, when Lindsay raised the issue.

She went straight up to Mike. He was sitting on the sofa in the living room.

"Mike, you know when we were in the restaurant?" She glanced up at him.

"Yes." He turned towards her as she stood in front of him.

She looked down, fiddled with the hair band in her ponytail, and glanced over at me.

"Well, why didn't you say I was your stepdaughter?" Her eyes stared up at him wondering what he was going to say.

"Does it matter?"

"No," she said. "Would you mind if I called you Dad?"

"No," Mike said, "that would be lovely." He stretched out to her and scooped her up in his arms. They cuddled for a moment, before Mike spoke to her tenderly.

"You are my favourite daughter," he said.

Lindsay flung her arms tightly around his neck and kissed him on the cheek.

I choked up and I felt a lump in my throat, and for a moment I didn't know what to say. It was as if my dream had come true at last.

It sealed the family unit, and confirmed that Mike was right all along. By allowing Lindsay the time, she had made her own decision. From then on Lindsay called Mike Dad, although it would cause some aggravation from Billy.

Lovely as she was, and Lindsay was angelic with her thick light brown hair, dark brown eyes, and full lips, she had some issues left over from Billy that needed correcting. It's natural that children suffer during divorce, but sometimes it causes difficulties in families reformed with new partners, and ours was no exception.

It was Christmas and we went into a bookshop to pick a book for her. She was told she could pick any book. She wanted two and I said why don't we just buy both of them, but Mike wouldn't hear of it.

"She must learn to make choices," he said.

Mike gave her five pounds, knowing it would only be enough for one book. She scampered back into the shop. I stood outside with Mike, and we watched her.

I complained to Mike. I thought he was being cruel.

"No," he said, "she has learned bad habits, refusing to choose and take responsibility for her choices."

It wasn't about being mean, it was about learning.

"Watch." He was confident.

Lindsay came out beaming, after picking *Fireside Poems*, by Roald Dahl. She didn't stamp her feet or throw a tantrum, she got what she wanted, and learned to make a choice. Mike didn't say she couldn't have the books she wanted, he empowered her to make the choice.

Mike demonstrated that change for Lindsay didn't have to be confrontational.

She needed to learn how to take control and make decisions. When she threw a tantrum in the supermarket because he hadn't bought what she wanted, he simply left the trolley full of shopping in the store, and came home empty handed. He didn't scold her or complain to her, she simply learned there was a price to pay for her behaviour.

Seeing that she wasn't singled out, and that we all shared in the price to pay, made the lesson so powerful.

It wasn't all discipline. Mike organised a panto for Lindsay and we would go to the theatre.

Puss in Boots, Jack and the Beanstalk, and shows like Rolf Harris. She enjoyed singing in the choir. Billy was musical, and being a pianist himself, Mike thought she might like to learn to play the piano. He organised private piano lessons for her at the nearby school.

We set aside Sunday as a family day, so that we all had time together, away from other distractions at home. Walking in

Whitewebs Park, feeding the ducks, throwing pooh sticks in the river, we would lunch in the little cafe by the golf course.

Such an experienced, and intelligent approach just made me love him all the more.

Billy came to the house to pick up Lindsay for the weekend. He was shouting on the doorstep. Mike had left me to deal with him until now, but not any more. He strolled right up to six-foot Billy, pointed his finger at him, and told him to be quiet. Then he proceeded to tell Billy what the arrangements were going to be from now on regarding Lindsay.

I was amazed to see Billy so cowered down. Mike was in command, and much of the mind games with Billy were eliminated.

I began to learn about choice.

Mike suggested that, instead of earning my living as a secretary, why didn't I think about taking up teaching because I was so good with people?

I laughed, but he was serious, and soon he had persuaded me to start an evening class in teaching practise.

Learning I found a challenge. My childhood had left me fragmented, but Mike helped me to overcome some of the practical issues that threw me, until I was able to gain the confidence for myself. Soon I was teaching at Enfield College, twenty hours a week.

Frightening, yes—I was terrified, yet I learned so much. It wasn't until students thanked me for my skill and patience that I realised I was good at it. It was as if I had been transformed from a moth to a butterfly. Students took to me, and I found working with people enjoyable and rewarding. It appeared that giving was an important need in me.

I was enrolled for my Certificate in Education for the coming September, until, that is, I started to get pains in my groin. On examination, my doctor diagnosed cysts on the ovaries. He later confirmed this with ultrasound, and Mr Harlow booked me for a hysterectomy operation.

The surgery went fine, or so I thought. I returned home to a thirst that wasn't normal. I called my doctor. They said I was okay—I just needed time. I spoke to the surgeon at the hospital. "No," he said, "it does sound like you have a problem." My kidneys were backed up with urine caused by a blocked urethra.

Suddenly I was worried beyond belief, and the prospect of more surgery to remove a kidney put my mind in a spin.

They put a drain tube through my back directly into the kidney. The theory was that this would allow the urethra to uncoil. They checked the progress with an IVP Intravenous Pelogram, injecting a dye and then doing an X-ray that left me with blinding headaches. I hated them, but I had no choice.

Mike was building a new bathroom in the house, studying for a Masters Degree at University in the evening, working full time at the college. It couldn't have come at a worse time. Yet he was my rock.

Mike could visit the hospital any day, except Wednesday—his evening class. He asked Mum to baby-sit the one evening he couldn't visit and she agreed. Mike told me at the hospital that Mum was going to baby-sit. I told him that she would let him down, but he didn't believe me. All was fine, until Wednesday. She left him a note to say Jane had a cold and she was travelling to Redditch where she lived.

He was furious with her. Experience: the greatest teacher.

I got a phone call from Highlands Hospital: my father was suddenly taken ill with a suspected heart attack. I was still in Chase Farm Hospital at the time, and it was difficult for me to see either Lindsay or my father. Mike was looking after Lindsay, and doing all the things a mother did. It was a dreadfully distressing time for all of us.

Mike bought a dress and modified it to let the tube come out of the side, leading to a bag strapped to my thigh, with the cooperation of the nurse on the ward. The consultant, Mr Harlow, would check the X-ray each week, and if that showed some progress, then I was allowed home for the weekend. Mike took me up to Highlands Hospital to visit Dad. He was totally irresponsible as a father and I asked myself why I cared. But he had no one. I couldn't let him suffer, in spite of the way he had treated me.

When I first saw him in the ward, I was so shocked! I found it difficult to hold back the tears. It was as if I had just visited an inmate in Belson. He said he wanted to go to the toilet. I waited patiently for him to return, but it was a long time. I took the opportunity to discuss his condition with the doctors. Dad couldn't eat—they said he had a carcinoma in his liver, although I didn't fully understand what that meant. I was told his time was measured in weeks.

Thirty minutes had passed before Dad returned from the toilet, and I began to understand what suffering he might have been going through. I turned and walked back down the ward to let him know what I had discovered. But I couldn't bring myself to do it.

Mike spoke to him as kindly as he could. Dad really wanted to know what was wrong with him, and although he suspected, he wanted it confirmed. It was the hardest thing I had to do. I didn't hate my dad, and I didn't wish him dead.

It gave me the time to say goodbye—to give him a chance to make his peace with me, and at the same time I felt I could come to terms with my own thoughts and feelings about my life. I asked him about the difficult times, the food, the poverty, the hardship which I had to endure. He told me he was sorry. That was my dad; drink was his untreated illness, and it had finally done for him.

I always felt so different from Mum and Jane. He told me he knew.

"Even as a child," he said, "Jane was always jealous of you." He started coughing.

I found him a tissue and let him carry on. I just listened.

"Some people can't stand the sight of beauty," he said.

"Dad, you loved us both, didn't you?"

He looked up at me, smiled.

"Yes, of course I did, it's just that you were always so pretty." He gave me a lopsided grin.

It was his way.

"Your mum has got to Jane, moulded her to hate men, passed on her bitterness; there's nothing yer can do about it now, but I know what happens. You don't have to tell me about it, I have always known it was that way."

"Was it my fault?"

He reached out to hold my hand.

"It's nothing you do," he said, patting my wrist, "it's just the way things have turned out. I'm sorry, love—I've let you down."

"I understand," I said. "I'm arranging for a place for you with St Joseph's Hospice."

"I don't want to go there." He looked like a little child lost.

"There's a bar there, Dad," I said. "You can have your drinks."

His face brightened.

"Really? I'll go then."

That's the last time I saw him.

I contacted his social worker who said she would organise it. She rang me back the day Dad died, but before I had a chance to tell her about his death, she told me he wasn't ill enough yet. I couldn't say anything: the words stuck in my throat. I passed the phone to Mike. He asked how ill she thought someone would have to get? Then he told her he had died that morning. It was his sixty-seventh birthday.

Mother refused to help. I arranged the funeral from my hospital bed. I contacted his sister Hilda, his other siblings, Alice, and Bobby. Mike modified a handbag so the drain tube could be hidden in it. When I got to the crematorium, Hilda tried to help me and take my bag. I managed to stop her just in time; it was attached to a plastic bag strapped to my leg.

Dad was cremated at Enfield Crematorium, the same crematorium where I had been thirteen years earlier with Joyce. It didn't register at the time; perhaps so much was going on in my life. Hilda organised everything at her house—tea and sandwiches for everyone. She was a lovely woman.

Visiting the hospital each night, Mike brought me iced water and salmon sandwiches. Not once did he fail me. Studying for his Masters Degree during the evening; tiling the bathroom at night until the early hours of the morning; and cooking and cleaning the house somewhere in between. Lindsay was more than happy with Mike, and he brought her to see me, but only once because she became so frightened I was going to die.

Patients gravitated towards me, as if they found comfort in my words; young and old sought me out, yet most of the time I just listened. That's all they wanted, really—to be heard, as if someone who would listen, answered some sort of need in them.

I found watching people die most distressing, yet I was thankful I had shared their last moments. What should I do, next?

Become a Counsellor, I told myself.

I was in hospital three months in all, until finally I got the all clear and my nightmare was over. It was another three months before I felt fully back to normal

Mike sold his home, and I sold mine. We watched the house prices plummet. We banked our money, used the interest to pay the rent on a repossessed very large house in Goffs Oak, and there we weathered the housing crisis.

It was summer, and we all went straight on holiday to Cornwall, meeting Colin on the way. We spent six weeks at Trelowarren, at the Lizard, enjoying the sunshine, sand, sea and fresh air.

It was a lovely time, the four of us together as one united family. Colin returned home to Florrie's after two weeks, and Lindsay, Mike and I remained for the rest of the summer break. There was no more contact from Billy, despite keeping him up to date with our changes of address.

Many family experts argue the case for the father of the child to be in contact, but I don't think it is always for the best. In Lindsay's case, she settled down, was happy to call Mike dad, adjusted, and accepted life as normal.

41

Final Journey

WHEN WE RETURNED FROM HOLIDAY, it was a new home, new school, and for Lindsay a fresh start for the three of us. John Major, the Prime Minister, pushed the interest rates up to fifteen percent, on black Wednesday 16th September 1992. Three years later it was time to come out of hibernation and we bought our first home together—a three-bedroom house nearby, and we registered Lindsay, now twelve-years old, into St Mary's Church School.

We now had a home of our own and the first stage of the plan had come together, just as Mike had predicted.

In 1995, I graduated from the University of Hertfordshire with my Certificate in Education, and Mike his Masters Degree. It was a lovely day at St Albans Cathedral, dressed in gown and mortarboard. Mike's parents, Eva and Charles, came to make the day complete. Finally his mother was talking to him after more than six years, with no explanation or apology. Colin and Lindsay were there, and for a moment we were all together.

As we drove home in the car I said, "Mike, I want to work as a counsellor."

"Right," he said. "Better get you on a course at the university."

That's what I loved so much about him. He already knew what I was going to say.

He made enquiries and soon I was applying for the course.

The course was at Master's level, and there were entry requirements to be satisfied. The major requirement was for personality reports from two independent Counsellors. The degree standard essay Mike said would be easy. I wasn't so sure.

One counsellor reported that I "had so much to give," while the other thought I still had a lot to work through. At the final interview, I feared I would not be allowed to join the course, but to my delight, I was accepted.

The course opened my eyes, not only for myself, but I found the subject fascinating. I read book after book until I was developing theories of my own. Carl Rogers (1990), a psychologist, had so much to offer, yet I found his approach too slow for me. Winnicott (1988), a psychotherapist, I found so interesting because he dealt with good enough mothering. John Bowlby (1979), a psychiatrist at the Tavistock Clinic, gave insight into the making and breaking of affectionate bonds in children. Reading these professionals left me in heaven. It unlocked something in me so empowering, it was like finding faith. Faith in myself.

The experiential sessions were what I enjoyed the most. Students would talk about their lives, and I found myself under their skin, echoing their journey in my mind. I was very flattered when some of the other students far more qualified than me, came to ask me what I thought.

I didn't understand. They had used all the psychobabble, the long words I couldn't pronounce to litter their assignments, yet they came and listened to me. It sounded pretentious, yet inside I knew that I had something guiding me, unlocking the puzzles of their mind, like a blind man reading Braille.

In January 1997 I moved to Guernsey in the Channel Islands where Mike took a post teaching at the College of Further Education. It was a lovely little Island village, with idyllic beaches and little cafes. It was only four miles by three, with French place names everywhere. Hotels, street names, but not a signpost in sight! They were taken down in 1939 when the Germans invaded, and never replaced.

Navigating the Island tended to be a guessing game, as we tried roads here and there that pointed in the general direction that we wanted to travel. The natives had a language of their own, called a patois. It was French as spoken in the time of King John, when the Islands were part of the Kingdom of Normandy.

Mike bought a 30-foot yacht (Brehon) and moored it at Beaucette harbour. Although I wasn't a sailor I quite enjoyed the trips to Herm. It was a lovely time. We lived in Cobo, thirty yards from the beach.

I found work teaching at La Mare De Carteret School, and later at the Professional Centre for Adult Education. In 1997 I graduated as a psychodynamic and person centred counsellor, working with adults and young children.

Quite out of the blue, Lindsay, now fourteen, asked Mike to adopt her. He was delighted for two reasons. One, she was so confident in him as a father, and secondly, that she had made the decision for herself.

For Lindsay it set her free from Billy. She had reached a point in her life, when Mike was the only dad she had ever known. She loved him, every bit as much as any daughter loved her dad, because he had always been there for her. He treated her every bit as if she were his own.

We had to apply to the court, and Her Majesty's Grieffier (an officer of the Greffe, or records office) was assigned to organise our case. He contacted social workers on the mainland, who traced her natural father to gain his consent to her adoption. They prepared reports on Lindsay, Mike and I, from detailed interviews with us all.

The court then granted the adoption, and Lindsay was set free from any connection to Billy, and that dreadful episode in my life.

♣

When the Guernsey Education Authority realised I had a counselling qualification, the Pupil Advisory Service asked me to work counselling children. At first I refused, but I was told it was either sessions with me or sending the children to Jersey, or the mainland. I gave way and agreed to see them.

It was at the Pupil Advisory Centre that I enjoyed working with young children the most. It was to be there that I discovered my true talent—working with vulnerable children, and those disaffected; deprived by divorce, or abuse. It was with these children I found my calling.

I connected with them, and found I was able to reach them, in ways others found impossible. I communicated through drawings, and ideas that appealed to their minds, perhaps as I had done as a child. It was uplifting for me, to be able to turn my deprived childhood into such a positive outcome; to make the tragedy of my poverty improve the lives of the young people pushed aside, in societies' misunderstandings.

There was a child B, who didn't talk and hadn't been to school in over six months. B was eleven. I spoke to B each week, yet B said nothing. Then, one sunny day, I said something wrong. "It's not called that!" B shouted. Suddenly a dialogue opened up.

Within six weeks B had returned to school, one day a week, then two, until B had regained trust, and confidence. Some say B just needed to be heard, but I was not so sure. There was something between us, there in the silence, unspoken. B knew I had been there, where B stood, and B understood with silent words, that B was not alone.

Perhaps I was rescuing myself, I didn't know; but if I could give hope to others, by listening and understanding their plight, then it had all been worthwhile. I know I made a change to their lives, and that knowledge gave me my self worth. Inspiring children, never to give up, get upset, but to carry on. That's what little soldiers do. They carry on.

Finally I had clawed my way out of Edmonton, and through counselling, found my true vocation; helping people who wanted to break free, and saving children, and people like Joyce and myself.

I hope I have given the gift to my children, that by struggle and never giving in to all life throws at you, there will be success as your reward. When life seems black and desperate, keep looking for a way through, and it will come.

Perhaps now I can finally throw away my wooden leg.

—The End—

Lightning Source UK Ltd.
Milton Keynes UK
03 December 2010

163702UK00001B/1/P